Leo

A Hero of the Dutch Resistance

by

Lawrence Tallentire

Wartime photo of Leo Frijda

Copyright

LEO: A HERO OF THE DUTCH RESISTANCE

(revised edition)

© 2020, Lawrence Tallentire

Self-published

For further information, please write to the publisher at:

lawrence.n.tallentire@gmail.com

Preface to revised edition

This revised edition comes two years after I first self-published this biography of Leo Frijda. My aim has been to add information that contributes to the telling of the story. It also gives me the opportunity to thank Michael and Merlijn Frijda – nephews of Leo - for their encouragement in this project. I had the pleasure of meeting Michael in Amsterdam in July of this year.

I could not, and would not, have written this work without the help and encouragement of Professor Nico Frijda and Ms Jetteke Frijda, his brother and sister. They were both very kind to me. It is sad that I wasn't able to finish work on this book sooner, so that they could have read it. I hope that they would have recognised their brother in the way I portray him and that they would be satisfied that this book did justice to his rather extraordinary life.

Over many years I have also received an invaluable amount of help and advice from a huge number of people. To list them all by name would occupy many pages; to make any selection would simply be unfair. I am very grateful to them all. I would like, however, to express particular thanks to those survivors of the war and of the Dutch resistance who knew Leo and with whom I was fortunate enough to communicate by telephone, letter and e-mail, as well as to meet in person; it was a privilege to learn a little about their lives and to share their memories.

Lawrence Tallentire

Antwerp, Belgium

September 2020

Contents

Prologue

'What, then, is left for us to do?'

Quatrain

I will not toe the line,
Nor follow where they lead.
This life they choose to live,
Is not the same as mine.

Verse written by Leo Herman Frijda,

born 1 August 1923 in Amsterdam, the Netherlands; executed by Nazi firing squad as a resistance fighter in the sand dunes along the North Sea coast, 1 October 1943, aged twenty.

We tend to visualise the dehumanising experience of war as the bloody carnage of the battle field. In a different guise, however, it can also act like a poison on the humanity of us civilians on the home front, on our own streets, in our own homes, and especially so when our nation is overrun by a foreign enemy power. Faced with a brutal, alien regime; faced with loss of liberty and the freedom to express our individuality; faced with the harshest of 'justice' for refusing to toe the line, we might be prepared to put to one side, if not abjectly surrender, our principles. For the sake of a quiet life and the safeguarding of ourselves, our family and our friends we might even be prepared to block from our minds the compelling evidence of our own eyes and ears, and never speak of the pitiable injustices, the evil, committed on our doorsteps. In his memoir 'Goodbye to Berlin', Christopher Isherwood describes how quickly and easily his landlady Fraulein Schroeder, erstwhile communist, learns to speak reverentially of the new Fuhrer. A shocking about-turn. But all she is doing, Isherwood observes, is 'acclimatizing herself, in accordance with a natural law, like an animal which changes its coat for the winter'. Or, as Professor Nico Frijda, brother of rebel Leo, expresses differently: 'Mankind has an aversion to change. We want to know where we stand, and our inclination is therefore to wish for everything to remain the same... The longing for continuity is something almost impossible to overstate'. In other words, a paradox: one acclimatizes in order to remain as far as possible the same.

7

Conversely, these same pressures that claw away at our individuality – that work to dehumanize and desensitize us - can serve to focus our hearts and minds precisely on what is right and what is wrong; fuelling a righteous, rooftop-shouting rage that rejects what is so clearly wrong; and instilling in some of us a daunting conviction that what is right is not only worth fighting for, but worth dying for. In other words, in order to remain as far as possible the same – to remain true to one's core values and act accordingly - one *refuses* to acclimatize.

Applying these observations, it is tempting to picture wartime Nazi-occupied Netherlands as a society divided between those who 'toed the line' and those who did not. However, the situation is clearly more complex. Firstly, it is necessary to get a handle on the numbers. It is commonly accepted that of a Dutch population of around eight million, only thirty thousand brave souls joined the resistance, whilst an equal and opposite number of thirty thousand proudly sided with the *'moffen'* ('krauts'). As to the overwhelming majority, whilst one could plausibly take a harsh view that in not lifting a finger to trouble the ambitions of their Nazi overlords millions of Dutch civilians were *de facto* collaborators – 'enablers' one might label them – there is little doubt that if one were to put each family, indeed each member of each family, under a magnifying glass to examine in detail why each of them behaved as they did, they would elicit a broad spectrum of responses ranging from compassion and empathy to downright disgust. Secondly, having acknowledged that the number of those who did resist was tiny, it is also clear that they did not form any identifiable, homogenous group: they resisted in different ways, to different extents. Each of them consciously or unconsciously drew up an individual code of resistance known only to themselves; the limits to which they would be prepared to resist decided by an often agonising balancing act of competing moral scruples, complicated even further by the instinct for self-preservation. As for those who were willing to resist to the very limits - *to kill* for their country and for their beliefs, and to sacrifice their own lives in return – they were not always then (as they are not always now) revered as their nation's 'heroes': German reprisals were efficiently and disproportionately ruthless, and those who committed 'heroic' acts were therefore perceived by some of their fellow countrymen as the very cause of, and therefore indirectly responsible for, such brutality. Indeed, many would have questioned the very notion of heroism: 'Holland does not like heroes' as Dutch author W.F. Hermans, wryly observed. Nor did Holland necessarily even want to remember them: 'There's never any mention of erecting a statue to Hans Katan or Leo Frijda, whose courage was paid for in front of a German firing squad. No one remembers now who they were. Obviously not pious enough'.

Bert Schierbeek, a member of the same resistance group as Leo Frijda, but who operated outside its 'hard core', wrote a loosely biographical novel based on the group, its exploits and its awful demise, even as the war was raging around them. The very title of that work, published with apparent urgency so soon after the end of the war – *Terreur tegen Terreur* ('Terror fought with Terror') – conveys his belief in the necessity to fight fire with fire. 'I understood the situation: if you wanted to beat the Nazi scum, you needed to be at least as ruthless as the guys peddling their garbage'. But Schierbeek was certainly not claiming any *moral* equivalence between the 'terrorist' acts of resolute Dutch resistance fighters and the terrors inflicted on the occupied Netherlands by the Nazi regime. The purpose of Nazism was to *destroy* – to destroy the Jewish people, to destroy political opponents, to destroy religion, to destroy culture, and to destroy the very notion of individuality. The crowded cattle trucks that took Dutch Jews by rail from Camp Westerbork to Auschwitz were *not* Nazi retaliation for acts of armed resistance by Leo Frijda. They were the efficient implementation of a depraved philosophy of Aryan supremacy expressed in a policy of genocide entirely separate from – and largely immune to - the increasingly desperate and ultimately hopeless struggle of Leo and his comrades to confront this terror. In their attempts, for example, to blow up the railway lines heading east, and to thereby obstruct the production-line deportations of Jewish families – including Leo's own father and uncle - to the gas chambers and ovens of Poland's death camps. But hopeless in the face of such overwhelming odds as it would turn out to be, it was a fight that they believed needed to be fought. To the death.

Whether the 'illegal' underground press (the publication and distribution of which was itself a perilous act of resistance) – and indeed the perhaps too many, too uncoordinated cat's cradle of Dutch resistance groups - were sympathetic to the extreme resistance of Leo Frijda and his group depended to some extent on their own political or religious affiliations. Many of those with a pious protestant standpoint tended to take a literal and – given the circumstances - somewhat sanctimonious 'sixth commandment' view of taking the lives of others. Those less compelled by doctrine, but with a curiously Dutch fixation with sound paperwork, might have dispassionately audited Leo's actions like an accountant going through the company books: What was the ratio of cost to benefit? What were the bottom-line figures on the balance sheet? By contrast, there were others with a clear left-wing bias, relishing an opportunity to overthrow the old world order - given voice in underground newspapers *Het Parool* and *De Waarheid* - who were adamant that to defeat the Nazis there should be no constraints on acts of resistance:

it was all or nothing. On 15 October 1943, two weeks following the executions of nineteen young resistance fighters - including Leo – *Het Parool* gave a defiant answer to the question that agonised so many:

Is the killing of traitors morally justified?

TOTAL WAR DEMANDS TOTAL RESISTANCE

At times, our bitter fight to the death against an enemy trumpeting a gospel of violence throughout our peace-loving nation gnaws at many of our consciences. How far may we go? How far ought we to go? Should we confine our defensive action within certain boundaries?

Now is not the time to remain wavering on the sidelines, nor to shy away from holding ourselves accountable in order to save our own skins. At least, this is not our view. On the contrary: it is absolutely clear to us that the persons responsible for the series of assassinations of those from the ranks of traitorous scum are patriots of the first order; are combatants of an exceptional calibre; are Dutch citizens whose names deserve to be recorded in the golden book to be published at the time of our liberation.

Victory for the Third Reich signifies the destruction of a civilisation rooted in freedom, humanity and democracy. The victory of the West will mean the downfall of Hitler's belief in man as a vassal of the state, worthy only to be absorbed within an 'eternal' people, represented by one political party, ruled by just one man. When national socialists claim that in essence this war is a revolution, they speak nothing less than the truth.

We are outlawed, overpowered, shipped abroad and, in short, the prey of a total war against our very existence as a free and spiritually independent people.

What then is left for us to do? We must fight! Fight! Only fight.

After the war, Dr Lou de Jong, who would later pen the epic, fourteen-volume, 18,000-page standard reference work 'The Kingdom of the Netherlands during World War Two', gave a lecture to the First International Conference on the History of the Resistance Movements that was hosted in Belgium. He ended with the poignant observation: 'It is all so long ago now. And it is still so near'. He spoke those words in September 1958. Were the same words to be uttered today, they would ring no less true. Seventy-five years after the death of Leo, we might ask ourselves: What then is left for us to do?

PART I

I say unto you: One must still have chaos within oneself to be able to give birth to a dancing star.

Friedrich Nietzsche: 'Thus Spoke Zarathustra'

I

Mobilisation, and holidays interrupted by war

Spring, 1940. At the same time as the Netherlands desperately prepares to fend off the real and present danger of invasion by German forces, its citizens are encouraged to take advantage of a sustained period of wonderful weather, and to discover a silver lining to restrictions on foreign travel and limited financial resources by enjoying beach holidays along the country's own North Sea coast.

It has been nine months since the announcement of general mobilisation - a call-up of 200,000 reservists, the government appropriation of vehicles and horses, and the digging of trenches through streets in the very heart of The Hague. Bridges at strategic river crossings are blown up. Swathes of the country are now flooded along the 'Dutch Waterline', a centuries-old defence system created to protect the major cities of the Netherlands that just about submerges the maze of canals, ditches and roads beneath vast, silent lakes to create treacherous conditions for any invading force. Before World War I the Dutch Queen had replied defiantly to Kaiser Wilhelm's boast that her Dutch guards stood only shoulder high to the emperor's own 'seven-foot tall' guards: 'Quite true, Your Majesty, your guards are seven feet tall. But when we open our dikes, our water is ten feet deep'. In addition, the Dutch government, doing rather too little, too late, has desperately tried to procure weapons from Great Britain, Sweden and Switzerland, but it is able to tick only a few items off its shopping lists. It would later even go begging - in vain - to the Finnish government to buy Soviet weaponry abandoned in the snow after the Winter War between these two countries.

The German invasion of Czechoslovakia had led to a forlorn declaration of war by British Prime Minister Chamberlain; the scrap of paper symbolising 'peace in our time' that he had salvaged from a trip to Munich - undertaken, in the words of British poet laureate John Masefield, 'To ask that young men's bodies not yet dead, / Be given from the battle not yet begun' - long since ripped into shreds. France followed suit. In response, the Netherlands reiterated its historic policy of neutrality. A comparable 'scrap of paper' contained the impassioned words of King Leopold of the Belgians, spoken on behalf of the seven neutral 'Oslo States'

(Belgium, the Netherlands, Luxembourg, Norway, Sweden, Denmark and Finland): 'Let there be no mistake! The peace that we want is peace with respect for the rights of all nations. A durable peace cannot be based on force. It can only be based on a moral order.' It was a difficult diplomatic tightrope to tread - pleading neutrality and impartiality for the sake of self-preservation, whilst at the same time as firmly as possible rejecting any moral equivalence between the Franco-British and German positions. Whilst Queen Wilhelmina had been openly hostile to Great Britain due to its treatment of Dutch settlers in South Africa during the Boer Wars, arrangements had nevertheless already been put in place to offer her, her family and government a safe haven on British shores in the event of a German invasion and, whatever her close connections to Germany through birth and marriage, she would later proclaim Hitler to be 'the arch-enemy of mankind' and treat supposed appeasers within her own government with scorn.

The response to the German threat – especially after the German invasion of 'neutral' Denmark and Norway on 9 April 1940 – intensified with the imposition of a state of emergency that suspended all civilian law and imposed martial law throughout the Netherlands: the fear within the government and spread by the media that the country had been infiltrated by German spies, assisted by Dutch traitors, proved entirely justified. Around seventy German agents had registered themselves as Dutch border guards. German border violations had been a regular occurrence, most flagrantly when Gestapo agents in the Dutch town of Venlo captured and smuggled into Germany two British intelligence officers, a violent fracas that resulted in the further death of a Dutch 'liaison official'.

On 3 May 1940, national newspapers injected further gloom and deep foreboding by reporting that by cabinet decree the maximum prison term for espionage had been increased to life sentence - a supposedly firm action that merely fuelled, rather than dampened down, undercurrents of public anxiety. Neighbours began pointing accusatory fingers at each other with the now absolute conviction that the country was being overrun by fifth columnists. Less than a year into the job, Dutch Prime Minister Dirk De Geer spoke on radio to justify the new laws, informing the Dutch people with heavy heart of incontrovertible evidence that there were 'some of our fellow citizens whose beliefs and behaviour show so little respect for the neutrality of our country that they constitute a real danger...'. It was natural, of course – continued De Geer - that in wartime a citizen of a neutral country might have more sympathy for one combatant than the other: but what was unacceptable, he argued, was that in pleading the cause of one side or the other *any citizen should refuse to be pro-Dutch.*

Patriotism could not be open to question. Furthermore, the conduct of some fellow countrymen was causing questions to be asked abroad about the very integrity of the Netherlands' policy of neutrality. The next day, Anton Mussert, leader of the NSB – the Dutch Nazi party - in parliament, gave a radio interview to America's CBS network, in which he pointedly declined to confirm that in the event of a German invasion of the Netherlands members of his party would so much as lift a finger in defence of Queen and Country. Had the Prime Minister been made aware of this interview? De Geer was asked in Parliament. Yes, came his answer, further asserting, however, that there was nothing said during Mussert's interview that gave cause for the government to take any further action. Though the observation went unspoken, Mussert had merely spelled out what was blindingly obvious – the allegiance of Dutch national socialists to the Third Reich. More worrying, perhaps, was the realisation that Mussert's position had effectively put him beyond the reach of any such emergency laws. Thus, not only had 'international events' not been kept at bay - rattling at the locked gates of the country's borders - but they had already surged through the country and breached the doors of parliament and government, to stare down the Prime Minister. And the hapless government was all at sea.

***

Despite all these metaphorical dark clouds, however, the weather had defiantly refused to play its traditional and somewhat clichéd role as harbinger of doom.

The winter of '39 - '40 had been picturesquely cold: on Sunday afternoons well-wrapped skaters snaked hand-in-hand along frozen paths through the snow-muffled woods around The Hague, whilst more adventurous children tobogganed on trays down the ice-covered sea defences onto snow white beaches in the nearby resort of Scheveningen. By contrast, the month of May 1940 began as April had ended, with blue skies and unseasonably warm temperatures. The *Rotterdamsch Nieuwsblad* reported that the public holiday on Ascension Day – 2 May 1940 - 'was a sign that this season would be successful, provided that the weather played its part, especially since foreign travel has been virtually prohibited for tourism'.

Back in August 1939 the same Dutch newspaper had printed a photograph epitomising the supposed nonchalance of the British people in the face of imminent war: a jaunty message in the back window of a London cab loaded up with luggage that read *'Half a mo', Hitler, let's have our holiday first'*. Now, nine months later, this was a sentiment that many

15

Dutch families were encouraged to share by temporarily burying their anxieties beneath – and digging their determined heels into - sun-speckled golden sand.

All along the Dutch coast seaside resorts sprang to life. In Scheveningen, whilst the North Sea tides remained too stubbornly cold for more than the poke of a toe into the chilly trickles of water that sidled up to the sand, the beach itself and promenade were soon stoked with determined day-trippers and weekenders. A proud owner gave his old-world bathing hut a last-minute coat of paint. Nearby, family groups huddled excitedly within encirclements of hooded wicker beach chairs like cowboy camps on the prairie. Murmuring motor boats charted an idle course between the swimming-pool contours of a boating lake that jutted out into the North Sea, in the shadow of a pier that stole a further march into the waves and where, at its 380-metre end, the octagonal Café Variété entertained over a thousand promenaders with concerts. In front of the elegant Kurhaus, the chic hotel and concert hall complex, a small trap tugged by a ruffled-feathered ostrich, tugged in turn by a swarthy man in a fez, led excitable toddlers on a small journey along the sea front and back. There were queues at the fish stalls and queues for ice cream, and young men and old tugged at their collars and ties to admit a little more of the sea-salt air. Boys, whose long socks were separated from long shorts by scraped knees, chased after - and were chased by - dogs and balls and each other. And in a world of her own a full-framed woman in black, starched to the hilt, pinioned upright on a bench and pressing a pleat in her long skirt between steely fingers, perched a steady gaze on the almost invisible horizon between sea and sky.

There was similar enthusiasm all along the Dutch coast. Everything, noted the editorial of Zandvoort's local newspaper, 'breathed sunshine' in anticipation of the summer season. Everything would be done to give its visitors the variety of recreation and relaxation they could wish for. Holidaying at home was a serious business in times of financial hardship coupled with the severe unemployment that had continued long after the official end of the Great Depression. Over recent years a decreasing number of visitors, compounded by cut-throat competition springing from the countless – unofficial and unapproved - new bed and breakfast establishments offered by anyone with a spare bed, chair and space at a table, had caused economic hardship to 'bona fide' hotels and guest houses. This year, however - the editorial proclaimed - 'international events' promised more fruitful times and better business opportunities. Millions of guilders that might otherwise have been spent on foreign travel would now be spent at home. But it required proper organization by the tourist board: there was no place in Zandvoort, the newspaper lectured rather sternly, for 'humbug'. Things had to be done properly, and by the book. And so Zandvoort opened the doors of its Casino for the season. Zandvoort scheduled sports car races and motorcycle races and greyhound races. Zandvoort laid on beach parties for the children and cabaret for their parents. Already, rehearsals were underway for the latest cabaret revue from Herbert Nelson - a German émigré - and his troupe of chanteuses and comic actors in the exotic Baghdad Room of the Riche Pavilion: new songs and sketches were written - love songs and parodies of films and commercials – whilst 'golden oldies' of the twenties were dusted down and thrown into the mix. Politics, however, were studiously avoided: Nelson's troupe offered, according to one newspaper, 'good amusement; it does not aspire to be more'. So, everything would be fine – not just the weather – and business much better than usual, concluded the editorial, just as long as 'international events' were held back at the country's borders.

In the meantime, the sun also shone on Princess Juliana and her consort Prince Bernhard, as they rode in style in their 8-cylinder 1938 Alfa Romeo into Noordwijk, a seaside town whose rolling sand dunes separated the regiments of burnished tulip fields, for which the country had for hundreds of years been famous, from the sea. It was a town to which writer Thomas Mann had enjoyed several visits over previous years: 'It is a lovely place, the most magnificent beach I know'. It was here where Mann, describing the intense flavour of childhood memories carried on the sea breeze, gazed out to the horizon from his deck chair - just as Gustav von Aschenbach gazed out from the Venice Lido in Mann's elegaic work 'Death in Venice'. Sunshine gave iridescent intensity to the town's colourful celebration of its annual flower festival and soon the royal car itself was tied up like a parcel with flower ropes. Prince Bernhard, in military uniform, stopped to take photographs. A floral mural above the entrance to a villa – converted to a military base - read 'Mobilisation 1939 - ?', a question that otherwise went studiously avoided. The parade through the town and along the sea front included a tank totally overdressed in flower heads – even its two guns - but looking no less intimidating despite the softening of its lines with delicate petals. A garlanded gun carriage followed behind like some rather brutish military bridesmaid. The royal couple walked happily amongst well-wishers, Juliana in a fashionable turban hat that gave a nod and wink to all the blooming tulips around her. Later the same day Prince Bernhard participated in a golf tournament between military and civilian teams, where the upper crust, dressed in Wodehousian golfing chic, clubbed balls around the town's links course, through dunes and pine woods that – on warm days like this – carried the exotic scent of the Mediterranean.

***

'The days of Chamberlain's government are numbered', declaimed Dutch newspapers on 9 May 1940, gazing anxiously at the grim situation across the North Sea. There were no newspapers printed in the Netherlands the next day, nor for more than two weeks thereafter – not 'lawfully', that is.

In the early hours of 10 May 1940, Germany invaded the Netherlands, one target of its coordinated venture into the Benelux and France. Dawn skies thundered with military aircraft. Pinpricks of white in a cloudless sky opened overhead like flowers in springtime. Some who rushed out of their homes half asleep and half dressed first thought they were witnessing propaganda pamphlets being dropped by the Germans. But the falling payloads grew bigger and spread into billowing clouds of white parachute silk as German paratroopers manoeuvred their descent towards military airfields. Meanwhile, their tanks and ground troops trundled almost casually over the borders, particularly at those points where Dutch collaborators were on hand to wave them through. In his diary entry of 14 May 1940, young provincial businessman Goffe Miedema observed: '...the Dutch were stuffed to the gills with hate, but it was our own national socialists who got what they wanted, or at least H., who stood Saturday morning on the Groningen Road and clapped the German troops as they passed by. There will have been more examples of such jubilation in a country otherwise buried in mourning and misery due entirely to the lust for power of the high and mighty Germans over us Dutch people. Their mantra had become 'Who is not for us, is against us'.'

Despite three years or more of panicked investment in their armed forces, and eight months of general mobilisation, Dutch troops were ill-prepared to deal with one of the first uses of paratroopers in history to occupy crucial targets before ground troops could speed overland to relieve them. The Dutch army, which numbered around 300,000, relied on field artillery often more than 30 years old and on rifles including some of 19th-century vintage. Some ships of the naval fleet dated from 1897. Hampered by a limited manufacturing capacity, the air force counted 176 combat planes, most manufactured by Fokker. By the end of the first day of war – a war that the Germans had calculated would last between three and five days – the Dutch had already lost half their number of aircraft.

18

'The outbreak of war [...] dealt a heavy blow' recall the memoirs of music student Maurice Ferares. 'Actually, this was the surprising thing, given that everyone had witnessed Hitler preparing for war. From the time he came to power, and certainly in light of the show trials following the burning down of the Reichstag, it was clear to anyone who asked the question what might happen.'

On the fifth day of war, 14 May, brutal measures were required by the Germans to ensure that this would be their day of victory, as intended. They would turn Rotterdam into a furnace. Ultimatums were given, and clarifications sought, but threats alone were insufficient to bring about a Dutch surrender. And so, in no more than a quarter of an hour of an early afternoon on a spring day in the year in which the port city of Rotterdam commemorated its 600th anniversary, 97,000 tons of high-explosive bombs plummeted towards the historic inner city. Black smoke turned day into night. Bombs ignited vegetable oil tanks on the dockside that sent uncontrollable fires rifling through the city streets, made worse over the following days as winds grew fiercer and created a firestorm. As some witnesses observed, the appalling heat was so immense that horse chestnut trees suddenly sprouted spring leaves: flower buds shot out, blossomed and then turned black. Around one square mile of the old city was flattened. 24,000 homes were reduced to ash and rubble. 32 churches and 2 synagogues destroyed. 62 schools destroyed. All electricity, gas and water supplies, and telephone connections, were broken. An estimated 800 civilians died and 80,000 made homeless. The German high command then made plain their intention to wreak the same devastation on the city of Utrecht unless the Dutch capitulated. 'Not even the very worst pessimist', wrote George Puchinger, a young history student, 'would have dared to predict that our armed forces would be unable to withstand the Germans for as much as five full days'. But then, few would have predicted that the Germans would do to Rotterdam what they had done to Warsaw: after all, the Netherlands was no Poland.

On 12 May, Princess Juliana, first in line to the throne, drove under cover of darkness to the coast with her husband and children in a convey of armoured cars owned by the Bank of the Netherlands to board a waiting ship of the British navy. Meanwhile, the Dutch Cabinet in The Hague discussed the constitutional and practical aspects of the evacuation of the Queen and her Government, and concluded that the Dutch constitution did not require that they remain in the country to surrender themselves to an enemy state. Once it became clear that the Commander-in-Chief of the Dutch armed forces, General Henri Winkelman, could no longer guarantee the safety of the Queen, informing her that tank convoys had already reached Rotterdam and that The Hague, the seat of government, was no longer safe, the decision was taken for the Queen and the Cabinet to also sail for England aboard British Royal Navy vessels.

On 14 May 1940 at 7 p.m. the Dutch surrender was announced over the radio to the Dutch people by General Winkelman:

'This afternoon Germany bombed Rotterdam. Utrecht has similarly been threatened with destruction. To spare our civilian population and to prevent further loss of blood, I believe it right to give our troops the order to cease their fire. I have also instructed these troops to maintain order and to hold onto the weapons and ammunition needed to preserve good order until such time as the German troops arrive.'

There was indeed desperation: the desperation of those citizens of Rotterdam who in the space of a few hours witnessed their homes and their city reduced to rubble, and the desperation amongst Dutch Jews unable to escape – around 80,000 of whom lived in Amsterdam alone.

***

At number 3 Corelli Street, in Amsterdam, sixteen-year-old Leo, his younger brother Nico and sister Jetteke, and his parents Professor Herman Frijda and Dora Frijda, prepared to escape the country. They had obtained passports to cover this eventuality. They packed into cases such possessions of their now past lives as practical considerations permitted them to carry into their new lives, but choices were painful and time was short. In fact, it was the women of the family, mother and daughter, who remained calm enough to take command of the situation and take care of the packing, whilst the 'men', stricken by nerves, paced the floor, interrupted by frequent lavatory breaks, generally offering little in the way of assistance. Eventually, the car was loaded, the Frijda family squeezed into the remaining available space, and they headed in the direction of IJmuiden, the seaport of Amsterdam, to find a ship to take them to England. There they had some relations who could offer refuge, there was potential help from colleagues of Professor Frijda in British academia, and there was some money in a bank to fall back on.

The roads to IJmuiden were choked with countless such desperate evacuees huddled tightly into cars and buses. Many of these did not even complete the short journey to the sea before abandoning hope and turning home. Those that persevered left their cars behind on the surrounding streets and even on the beach to find a harbour pounded by bombs and reeking of smoke and spilled oil. Panic heightened as the last freight ships of any size set on their urgent course for England. On 14 May the *SS Bodegraven* was the last small cargo ship to leave port, with 250 refugees on board, including 80 Jewish children rescued from Germany (the 'Kindertransport'). The thousands who were left behind offered huge sums of money – ten, twenty, even thirty thousand guilders – to any captain of the lowliest trawler or cutter for a place on board. In panicked masses they attempted to storm the remaining boats: some fell back into the black water and had to be fished out, whilst German bombers circled low overhead like seagulls ready to swoop. When the 11,000-ton ship *SS Jan Peterzoon Coen*, loaded with ore, was scuppered by the Dutch forces, so as to block entry into the harbour by German warships, any last chance of escape was over.

For Leo and his family, it was too late, and the passports in their hands had lost all currency.

It was too late, too, for a young history teacher from Amsterdam, Jacques Presser, and his wife. Unable to reach IJmuiden, they turned back home, heading towards the black cloud of smoke now draped over the skyline.

Some Jewish people chose suicide rather than put their trust in things not changing much. Over two hundred took their lives in the immediate aftermath of the country's capitulation. George Puchinger described cycling past a Jewish cemetery and seeing the approach of four hearses: there was hardly anyone else there. 'I got off my bike to pay these poor Jews my last respects...I listened to the reciting of Hebrew prayers in the open air. The father of one of the dead... wept bitterly. One of the rabbis comforted him by citing words from the suffering Job.'

On 29 May 1940, the fanatical Austrian Nazi Arthur Seyss-Inquart – who had briefly served as deputy to the Governor General of occupied Poland, Hans Frank - was installed as Reichskommissar of the Netherlands at a ceremony in the Knights' Hall, the 13th century building in The Hague traditionally used for the ceremonial openings of the Dutch parliament. He had brought over the Cologne Radio Symphony Orchestra for the occasion, which played the triumphant overture to Wagner's opera 'Rienzi'. Seyss-Inquart proclaimed that the country would be incorporated into the 'New Europe' as *Westland*, but avowed that the occupying authorities would not impose their beliefs on the population. The emphasis was on 'business as usual'. The Royal Family and government were now in exile, but all other strata of government, the police and judiciary remained in place. And indeed, life appeared to change little at first. The weather stayed good, and that summer, in the majestic Kurhaus in Scheveningen, the World Jazz Festival would go ahead, with tickets sold out. There were star performances by jazz orchestra The Moochers, led by trumpeter and composer Boy Edgar. But things here, as elsewhere, were only superficially the same: the Germans allowed, for the time being American jazz, but British jazz was banned as being music of an enemy state. It wasn't looking good in the long term for a music style with Jewish and Negro influences.

Schoolboy Leo Frijda returned to complete the last couple of months of what was supposed to be his penultimate year at the Vossius Gymnasium in Amsterdam before heading to university where he hoped to study medicine. And it was to the corridors, classrooms and common rooms of this same school that Jacques Presser returned to continue his beloved career as a history teacher. It would prove to be a resumption of a strange and increasingly frightening 'normality' that would ensnare them both.

II

A new family and a modern Amsterdam

In August 1923, Herman Frijda was already thirty-six when his first son, Leo, was born; his wife just twenty-two. He, the son of the owner of a men's and women's outfitters in Amsterdam; his wife Dora, the daughter of the head surgeon of a Roman Catholic hospital in the small city of Zwolle. Less than two years before Leo's birth, Herman Frijda - awarded his doctorate from Leiden University in 1914 on 'the theory of money and the Dutch financial system' - had been appointed professor of political economics and statistics within a new Faculty of Economics of the University of Amsterdam. It was a faculty that he would build up almost single-handedly in the absence of any established teaching tradition in this social science. Early the following year he would give the inaugural lecture. He had met Dora in The Hague, where she had returned to live with her grandmother after finishing higher education - two years' study of Botany at the University of Amsterdam in 1919/1920, followed by two semesters at the University of Bern, Switzerland, and then by a year in London. Accordingly, with this new - and secure - position at the university and in society, it was an opportune time to marry and start a family. The new family first lived in the 'Old South' district of Amsterdam on a very respectable street close to the Concertgebouw concert hall and the Vondel Park, a district of late-Victorian vintage despite the designation of 'old', and much newer than the elegant canal-side houses that adorned the canals of Rembrandt's 'Golden Age' Amsterdam. The Frijda family was liberal Jewish, intellectual, and reasonably affluent. Religion played no role in their home life; they were a secular family and, apart from the circumcision of the two boys - Leo, and his younger brother Nico - there was no observance of any other Jewish ritual.

Leo appears to have had every reason to enjoy a happy childhood; he is much loved and cared for by his parents. In a scrapbook they record his early development – in weight and height – and there are some photos of a toddler with locks of loosely-curled blond hair, bright, intelligent eyes, and an engaging smile: an attractive-looking child. His parents are not particularly tall or physically imposing, and so Leo will preserve a small and slender frame, even as he works his passage through adolescence into early manhood. There is a piano at home. His mother is an accomplished pianist and a young Leo sits by her side and learns to play. He is a caring and considerate brother to his two younger siblings, Nico and Jetteke, and interacts well with them. Nico has fond memories of the three of them at home, with their mother at the piano – of a 'rosy childhood' - all three children singing along to her piano accompaniment. Nico likes to play with toy planes and cars, and has dreams of being a pilot. The children also like boats, and make up imaginary sea journeys on an imaginary ship, in which Leo takes charge as the ship's captain, equipped with a pair of binoculars to look out for land; Nico is appointed ordinary seaman/engineer, whilst Jetteke recalls, much to her annoyance, being sent below decks by the boys to work as the ship's cook and cleaner! But that, after all, is how it was with their parents: as Nico recalls, as fond as they are of their father, 'he was withdrawn behind the four-inch thick door of his study. My mother was his wife who cooked and sang with us'. But Nico's childhood games with toy planes and cars involved fighting with evil strangers – 'the preludes of political disasters to come, and the war' - and he also remembers an incident when he tells his father, in a childish flight of fancy, that he can fly. His father picks him up. Asking Nico to show him how he can fly, he releases his hold; the little boy falls straight down to the ground with a thump, and left somewhat emotionally perplexed as well as suffering a bruised knee, unable to fathom out why his father would do such a thing.

***

Not everything, therefore, is entirely 'rosy' at home. Nico describes both parents as 'highly strung'; their father usually tied up with work and somewhat distant. Jetteke agrees; she uses the word 'neurotic'. This creates a palpable tension and arguments at home, and Leo, whether through the roll of the dice, or through any additional pressures and responsibilities often said to be felt by a first-born child, absorbs and is affected by this atmosphere more than his brother and sister. He is a sensitive child and becomes preoccupied with a fear of germs and infections, and a dread of dying. He acquires an obsessive urge to repeatedly wash his hands clean. This rather compulsive behaviour is of concern to his parents and although, as Jetteke insists, Leo was not 'ill', and not 'treated' in the way one would normally understand the term, he is nevertheless sent away in school holidays to spend time at a children's holiday home in the countryside. Here, amongst open spaces, trees and water, he finds some release from the anxieties of home life, and forms a fond attachment to the lady of the house who oversees his care. These problems must have continued for some years, because at some point Leo has the creative skills to compose a verse aimed at banishing – through a positive attitude - the demons that plagued his young mind. He writes:

An Imaginary Sickness

If he just imagines 'I am sick'
Or 'Oh, what troubles I face'
Then he should tell himself 'Well, really it's nothing
Soon I will be back on my bike'.
And if he really is sick
Then he should think 'Oh, it is just
Some kind of imaginary sickness'
And much less bad for someone
Who tells himself 'Oh, do buck up,
Soon you can go back out to play'.

L.H. Frijda (this is how it was with him)'

Whether or not Leo can be said to have been 'cured' of what may have been a more deeply-rooted anxiety disorder, it is clear that this time away from home is very beneficial. He seems to revel in the freedom that the distance from his parents and siblings rewards him – whether during the days and weeks spent at the children's holiday home, or during a surprise visit to his grandmother in The Hague, for example, from where he writes to his mother that he had just played draughts with his grandma, spent the afternoon throwing a javelin in the garden, and received a gift of a hockey stick from his Uncle Leonard (a letter home that little Leo ends impishly with the greeting 'a manly handshake'). Let loose, Leo gets the opportunity to plunge headlong into all manner of outdoor activities away from the city, and this enthusiasm and almost boundless energy will become more apparent when he joins the sea scouts, eagerly accumulates proficiency badges, and learns the skills of sailing. He seems to thrive when he has to take care of himself and interact creatively with others, with a purpose, to achieve a goal. At the same time, however, he does not neglect his family: he enjoys writing home and receiving letters in return. In one letter he addresses his parents, brother, and sister separately and – in sending sister Jetteke lots of best wishes – reminds her to play nicely with Nico. He displays a relaxed, informal way of communicating by letter; he is a creative child who enjoys putting pen to paper. In short, he is having fun, and it is easy to imagine that his parents would be charmed by this infectious sense of fun that he crams into his vivid correspondence. So, for example, he writes home on Sunday, 13 August 1933, less than two weeks after his tenth birthday:

'Dear mother and father. How are you? Since I haven't written for a week, I will make this a long letter. On Tuesday we went out early in the morning. We found a great spot to build a boat. We put up a mast, and fixed a tent over it as a cabin.

Meanwhile we were thinking: if only we could sleep here. We had a good time playing. But you can imagine how happy I was when the scout master said: 'Tonight you can sleep outdoors in the tent'. But somebody needed to be on watch. I was on second watch. The password was 'Sea Pines'. Thank you again for the cards. We then went to sleep. That was Tuesday. (P.T.O.)

On Wednesday we went tracking with a lady who used to be a girl guide. That was great. We played for a bit in the camp and went to drink coffee. After coffee, we went to the beach, but it was cold. So we just swam once. Then the lady, who came with us, set us a competition to see who could make the best sand sculpture. I made a boat, the lady made a castle, and then the tide came in and washed away the castle walls, one by one. Then we went home.

(Mother, the food here is very good).

On Thursday I went with two other boys to lay tracks for the others to follow. In the afternoon, back at camp, we made pancakes. Fantastic. Mother, I will now answer your daft questions. As to blowing my nose: <u>I DON'T HAVE A COLD</u> any more. I clean my teeth. We have a bath 2 x week before bedtime. On Friday we spent the whole day on the beach. We ate there and built a really big boat. Wonderful. That was FRIDAY (P.T.O.)

'Saturday the weather was bad, so we stayed inside and did some handicrafts. However, it got better in the afternoon, so we walked to Scheveningen. On the return journey the lady told me a lot about dying, because she had been a pharmacist.

So, seeeeeeee yaaaaaa!

Lots of kisses,

From Leo H. Frijda'

On another such boat trip, after a morning spent fishing, Leo began to get an idea of the spreading reputation of his father as a university teacher and wrote back home with the following news: *'We will set sail again on Monday because today it was too windy. Alongside our boat, father, there was another boat with a gentleman on board who, as soon as he heard that I was the son of the Prof., told me that his son had studied with you and been your assistant. His name is Coupelus'.*

***

It was not a long time after the birth of the youngest child Nico in 1927 that the Frijda family moved home – from the Old South to the New South of Amsterdam, a matter of a few hundred metres across the North

Amstel Canal. The New South was a newly built, coherently planned area of the city in the new style of the Amsterdam School, close cousin of Art Nouveau and Jugdenstil, which flourished between the two world wars. With an aim to create a 'total architectural experience' – interior and exterior - it made Amsterdam the 'Mecca' of new town developments. The houses are typically built of brick, and incorporate complicated masonry to give lines a rounded or organic appearance and an elaborate scheme of building elements, involving arty glass and wrought ironwork. Despite the spaciousness and elegance of the new style, it is too new and exotic for many tastes, and there is no rush to move there. Many of those who did were Jewish, and the neighbourhood became familiarly known within Jewish circles as the 'Jewish South'. So new is the area, that not only is the primary school that the Frijda children will soon attend still awaiting completion, but the very philosophy underpinning the school - 'an open-air school for healthy children' - is in itself rather new and experimental: it claims to provide 'tailor made' education to pupils within a 'challenging, inspiring learning environment' and to inculcate the notion of equal respect for everybody from the start, so that even young children are taught to understand and respect the beliefs and attitudes of their friends and the adults around them. And as for 'open air' – well, it may not offer the wide open spaces of Leo's children's holiday home, but each floor of the new building has large balconies open to the elements, where lessons could be held in the fresh air when weather permitted. This school would appear to offer the Frijda children at primary-school age a style of education in keeping with the young family's modern, liberal, intellectual outlook.

The street on which the Frijda family made their new home is named after the Dutch artist Breughel and, indeed, maps of the area indicate that many other street names consciously pay homage to a roll-call of artists, such as Rubens and Van Dyke, and of classical composers such as Mozart and Beethoven. This is an area of Amsterdam intended to exude an air of intellectual and cultural substance. However, this new district is partly planned with a single structure, and one special event, in mind; a building and event that would put Amsterdam in international focus, presenting a modern, outward-looking style and self-confidence. The names of local streets and some wide, impressive boulevards are a classical nod to this event: Apollolaan, Parnasusweg, Marathonweg, and Olympiaplein.

***

On Saturday, 28 July 1928 the Olympic Summer Games are officially declared open by Prince Hendrik, consort of Queen Wilhelmina, in a new, sleek stadium designed by Jan Wils in the Amsterdam School style that characterises the whole district: 'the most beautiful of any such stadiums across Europe', according to the reporter from the *Algemeen Handelsblad*. Establishing one of several new traditions, an Olympic Flame is lit, and raised on top of a forty-metre high 'Marathon Tower' in front of the stadium, to burn for two weeks in a cauldron that local wags would refer to as 'the KLM pilots' ashtray'. Secured immediately below the cauldron, in the tower's corners, there are four speakers forming part of a Philips-built sound system that ensure performance results and other messages can be boomed throughout the stadium and across the wider Olympic park. Amongst the forty-six participating nations Germany is re-admitted to the 'Olympic family' after a ten-year ban for unsportsmanlike conduct *in re* the First World War: their team of athletes receives the biggest cheer when they troop into the arena at the opening ceremony. The French team has boycotted the ceremony in a Gallic huff, being unsatisfied with the purported resolution of a punch-up between a French athlete and a Dutch gate keeper on an inspection visit of the stadium the previous day. The Americans are sponsored for the very first time by Coca-Cola (as is the Olympic movement): 'men wearing Coca-Cola caps and coats sold the bottled drink to the sporting crowds, while soda fountains near the entrances to the stadium were available to those who preferred Coca-Cola in a glass'. The 280-strong American team, drilled like a military machine, enters the stadium under the stern gaze of its U.S. Olympic Committee President and, in effect, coach-in-chief, General Douglas MacArthur. 'We are here to represent the greatest country on earth', proclaimed MacArthur with no attempt at false modesty. 'We did not come here to lose gracefully. We came here to win. And to win decisively'. Baron Pierre de Coubertin, founder of the International Olympic Committee, had once expressed the Olympic ideal as '...not the triumph but the struggle, the essential thing is not to have conquered but to have fought well'. MacArthur's response was, in effect, a derisory snort.

As a further sign of modernity, women are allowed to participate in athletics and gymnastic events for the first time, to the disapproval of De Coubertin, who warned the organising committee that athletics would be 'too strenuous' for the (presumably) weaker sex.

In an article for the August 1928 issue of US magazine *Harpers*, John Roberts Tunis – 'inventor of the modern sports story' - compares the 'modern' Olympic movement leading up to Amsterdam 1928 with the decline of the games of Ancient Greece and asks openly whether the movement had become too much like a circus, too professional and too cynical to survive. He noted that at the preceding Antwerp Olympics of

1920 local crowds were already becoming distinctly unimpressed by the American team winning medal after medal, with a growing sense that certain countries would stop at nothing to win. He quotes George Trevor, who wrote in the *New York Sun*: 'The history of the Olympic Games since their arrival in 1896 has been marked by sporadic dissension, bickering, heartburning, and one or two old-fashioned rows.'

Nevertheless, these Olympics will produce folk heroes and heartthrobs to remember. On the track, Finnish hero Parvo Nurmi wins a ninth gold medal in the 10,000 metres in his swansong Olympiad. In the pool, Johnny Weismuller (Hollywood's 'Tarzan') wins two gold medals, whilst Swede Arne Borg wins gold in the 1,500 metres freestyle and sets countless pulses racing in a shockingly immodest 'Racerback' swimming costume designed by Speedo that leaves the back and shoulders bare – close-fitting, and offering, according to the manufacturer's catalogue, 'maximum body exposure'. And in the single sculls, Bobby Pearce, Australian flag-bearer at the opening ceremony, goes on to win gold, despite pulling up in his quarter-final heat along the Sloten canal to let a family of mother duck and ducklings pass in single file in front of his boat. And there is also a local hero and family hero, Leonard Frank – Uncle Leo who had presented young nephew Leo with the treasured hockey stick. A talented sportsman in his own right, the first honorary member of the Leiden and Oegstgeest Hockey Club in 1927, and author of a 1933 standard work entitled 'Hockey and How it is Played', Uncle Leo acts as an official in the hockey tournament that is won by India in a final played against the host nation in the Olympic Stadium.

There are also medals to be awarded in the arts for works inspired by sports-related themes across the fields of literature, painting and sculpture, graphic art, and music: 1,150 works from competing artists from 18 countries are exhibited in the local Stedelijk museum from 1 June to 12 August, and are available for purchase. There are medals for architecture and town planning too. The roll call of medal winners reveals a definite northern European bias. To the delight of the home crowd, Wils is awarded gold for his design of the Amsterdam stadium, whilst the German Alfred Hensel wins gold in the town planning category for the overall design of the parkland surrounding the new Nuremberg stadium in Germany. Five years later Hensel would work with Albert Speer in the design of Nuremberg's Party Rally Grounds.

On 12 August, by the time of the Closing Ceremony, the USA has topped the medals table with a haul of twenty-four gold medals. 'Athletic America is a telling phrase', gloats General MacArthur. 'It is talismanic. It suggests health and happiness. It arouses national pride and kindles anew the national spirit.' Ambitious leaders of other countries might well have looked on at the Summer Games in Amsterdam 1928, shared similar sentiments, and foreseen opportunities ahead for their own nations. Roberts Tunis, however, casts a jaundiced eye on this 'national spirit', questioning whether the Olympics had genuinely succeeded in becoming 'a beneficial force in the spreading of peace and good will throughout the world, or [in bringing] together the various competitors in friendly social intercourse'.

III

By train to the USSR, via Berlin

The first 'sacrifice' demanded of them by their Soviet hosts-in-waiting was a photograph of their imminent departure by train from Amsterdam station. And so, on 19 August 1929 Professor Herman Frijda stands at a railway carriage window alongside two suited and hatted fellow travellers, looking straight at the camera, as a small group of family, friends and news reporters prepare to send them on their way across Europe. The other two in the photograph are the 'father of modern Dutch architecture' Dr Hendrik Berlage, internationally renowned for the Amsterdam Stock Exchange on Amsterdam's Damrak, and Holland House in London (but who has recently lost out in a competition to design the Lenin mausoleum in Red Square) and Henri Pieck, painter, graphic artist, and Soviet spy, who would describe the journey with a relentlessly uncritical eye in a journal published early the following year: 'Red Russia in Black and White'. Not that it should be any surprise that any of the group should be a spy: anyone a member of the then Communist Party of Holland owed allegiance to Comintern – the Communist International – charged with creating an international Soviet republic, and thus the following of orders from Moscow.

Another member of the group is Philip Mechanicus, a journalist with the *Algemeen Handelsblad* newspaper. He has had a keen interest in the state of flux within the USSR since the Russian Revolution. He regularly listens to Radio Moscow at home to catch up with the latest news and to practise his Russian which, according to a colleague, he could speak to a 'very reasonable standard'. It is the aim of the director of his newspaper that a tour of the USSR should cure him of his excessive sympathy towards Stalin and the changes wrought on that country and its people. And it would indeed prove to do so, because whereas Pieck extended his stay in the USSR by a few days to get his instructions from his Moscow handlers in the NKVD before heading home, Mechanicus was having none of it: his colleague observed that 'he was too smart for all that, by which I mean too selective, too level-headed. He was much more the humanist'.

The month-long visit has been organized for ten of its members by the Netherlands-New Russia Society, which boasts a total membership of around 400; some Dutch communists, but others simply curious about post-revolutionary Russia. The Society is affiliated to the All-Union Society for Cultural Relations with Foreign Countries ('VOKS') - an entity created by the Soviet government to promote international cultural contact between writers, composers, musicians, cinematographers, artists, scientists, educators, and athletes of the USSR with those of other countries through tours and conferences, with a clear eye to the propaganda value abroad, whilst also serving as a convenient cover for officers of Soviet intelligence to pose as 'cultural representatives' and diplomats.

Stage one of the journey by train takes the group to Berlin, a stopover required for obtaining the visas necessary to enter the Soviet Union (the Netherlands having no diplomatic relations with the USSR). 'Berlin', writes Pieck, 'is a city with two faces: one face looks to the west, and the other to the east. We see these two faces in the bigger political picture'. Under the Weimar Republic – the country's first taste of a democratic constitution - Germany has experienced five years of economic growth, been welcomed back into the international family fold, and formally admitted as a member of the League of Nations. There is still hardship and suffering in Berlin, but it is also the Bohemian, sexually liberated city that enticed newly arrived Christopher Isherwood, with its 'dens of pseudo vice'. Furthermore, despite dire warnings from its communist party's Militant newspaper in early 1929 that unless May Day street protests went ahead (resulting in the shooting dead of 27 protestors on the street by armed police) Germany would soon be enslaved by a fascist terror regime far worse than those of Bulgaria and Italy - in part a shock tactic aimed at overthrowing the Weimar regime and establishing a Soviet republic in Germany - it would be another year before America's Great Depression rounded on Europe and tipped this relatively successful, if precarious, rehabilitation of Germany towards disaster.

The journey continues east, as the train pulls relentlessly across the plains of Poland. A monochrome Polish landscape does little to catch the eye. The weather is miserable and wet, despite it being summer, and the roads they watch through the carriage windows have turned into mud channels. Here and there they trundle past low-roofed poor-looking cottages creeping along the ground. There is a general feeling of impoverishment in the flat, muddy countryside. However, amongst the small contingent of Polish travellers on the train there is burgeoning national pride and patriotism. Poland, like Germany, looks in two directions, explains a Polish doctor they meet in the dining car: 'We Poles are proud that after suffering so much oppression we have our own army now... Our nation must defend itself on two frontiers, against the Bolsheviks and against the Germans'.

The party of ten reaches the Soviet border, marked with a barbed-wire fence, and crosses into the Soviet Republic of White Russia, from where it continues on a wider-gauge railway, and more spacious train carriages, towards Moscow. 'It is a city of workers', writes Pieck as he looks in all directions on the taxi ride to their hotel, a ride that ends somewhat short of the hotel lobby as the cobble stones have been pulled like teeth from the street, its dirt surface waiting to be laid with modern asphalt. 'People on the street give the impression of a sober kind of poverty; their clothing shows no sign of opulence. There is nonchalance in their appearance, but a sureness and vigour in their movement'. Insofar as the streets are filled with any form of advertising, it is 'advertising' focused on social education. The streets, as the shop windows, are at the service of an all-pervasive social pedagogy. 'This enables the man in the street to catch up each and every evening with the latest developments in the nation's industry and trade – the building of socialism.' Their hotel, by contrast, remains majestic for those able to afford the un-Soviet luxury; the still grand dining room boasts immense picture windows that offer panoramic views across the road to the pink Kremlin walls.

What their hosts will not have pointed out to their honoured guests is that Moscow is overcrowded. The newly built Narkomfin building, a celebrated experiment in collective living – a 'social condenser' - boasting communal kitchens, crèches and laundry, together with outdoor spaces, a library and gymnasium – had fallen out of favour almost immediately. Stalin rejected its collectivist and feminist ideals as 'Leftist' or 'Trotskyite', and all available free, open spaces have been crammed with small and very basically equipped new dwellings for the masses of country people who have rushed to the city in search of work. In addition, in this same year of 1929, over 13,000 'Soviet' Germans, many of whom had farmed successfully for generations in Western Siberia, but who were now suffering the effects of collectivisation, gathered on the outskirts of the city to seek permission to emigrate, to return to a country most knew only from inherited family histories. Altogether, just 5,761 of their number, including 3,885 of the Mennonite community, were given permission to return 'home'.

***

1929 is the year in which Intourist – the State travel agency - is founded. It seeks to woo foreign travellers, especially wealthy Americans, by presenting in richly illustrated brochures and posters a tourist paradise wrapped in sleek and sassy art deco lines. Stylised vistas of the Crimean coast try to match everything that posters for the luxury playgrounds of the French Riviera claim to offer their jazz-age hedonist guests. The Trans-

Siberian Express train is a model of luxury, and dining-car tables, with champagne and caviar set upon crisp white linen, are lovingly photographed. But there is reference also to the grandeur of socialist success alongside the grandeur of Siberia's vast wilderness – 'the mighty panorama of socialist construction being carried on across the breadth of this vast country'.

The reality of the speed of change in the USSR is indeed impressive. 1929 sees the Great Turn in economic policy – the acceleration of collectivization and industrialization – and the launch of Stalin's first five-year plan. It requires expertise from outside the USSR to oversee such achievements: Mart Stam, a Dutch architect, would travel there in the following year with a team of twenty from the New Frankfurt project, Germany, to create a string of new Stalinist cities, including Magnitogorsk, heart of the burgeoning steel industry, which would burst out of a small settlement of 100 residents into a city of more than 150,000. Based on the US steel mill in Gary, Indiana, the original plans for the Magnitogorsk plant and the town around it were to follow a linear design, with rows of apartment block accommodation running parallel to, but separated by greenbelt from, the factory – in other words, a modern city that paid respect to the quality of life of those who would live and work there, with open spaces, restaurants, children's crèches, clubs, health clinics and shops. Such plans – to honour the nobility of the worker – would not be followed here or anywhere else. The city inhabitants would be subjected night and day – even in their own homes - to noxious fumes and factory smoke. American John Scott, who migrated to the USSR straight out of university at the age of twenty, and who worked as a welder on the construction of the factory, describes the project as an awe-inspiring triumph of collectivism whilst at the same time detailing the treacherous working conditions, the inefficiency of the system, and the wretched condition of peasants driven from the land in the collectivization programme. Scott observes that Stalin's harsh ideological purges teach the Russian population 'by a painful and expensive process to work efficiently, to obey orders, to mind their own business, and to take it on the chin when necessary with a minimum of complaint'. He describes how one worker complains about hunger, only to contextualize his condition by asserting that 'If we are going to build blast furnaces we have to eat less for a while'.

It is doubtful that the group of ten Dutch guests would have been invited to witness the human suffering and sacrifice on which the Soviet industrial success was built. But even more anodyne situations that might have raised concerns and pertinent questioning amongst more impartial jurors are willingly interpreted by them – at least by Pieck - in the most positive light: in his journal he captions a photograph of a line of people queuing to buy rationed foodstuffs from a cooperative store with an explanation that rationing is more a measure to combat the squandering of resources than the result of any food shortages. Yet there had indeed been significant food shortages in the USSR in 1927, and the Great Famine in which over nine million people would die of deliberately-engineered starvation was just two years into the future. Ironic, too, is Pieck's assertion that 'the prison system in the Soviet Union is not intended to punish the offender, but to educate him into a complete understanding of his responsibility to society based on labour and skills', a view expressed less than two months after the Council of People's Commissars adopted a secret decree for the use of penal labour that would form the legal base and guidance for the creation of the system of 'corrective labour camps' – the Gulag.

A further hole can be picked in Pieck's credibility as anything approaching an impartial witness in his reference to a letter addressed by schoolchildren to author and political activist Maxim Gorky, who had recently returned to the USSR after seven years' less-than-hard exile in Sorrento, Italy. In the letter a group of children of the despised middle classes complain that their chances of a good education and skills training are suffering because of the 'crimes' of their parents. The fact that such a letter could be printed in the Soviet press, argues Pieck, is 'clear proof of the complete freedom of expression existing in the USSR, albeit that no direct attack on the actual Soviet system would ever be tolerated'. He might have added that no attack on Stalin would be tolerated either. On reading Leon Trotsky's open letter of 29 March seeking to 'defend the interests of the Soviet Republic against the lies, trickery and perfidy of Stalin and Company', Stalin takes umbrage, and especially with his enemy's closing remarks: 'Rabid persecution, dishonest slanders, and governmental repressions cannot dim our loyalty to the October Revolution or to the international party of Lenin. We will remain true to them both, to the end – in the Stalinist prisons and in exile.' There was something prophetic in these words; and something utterly naive in his belief that 'It is still not too late to alter the course'. 1929 proves to be a turning point in the Soviet Union: Comrade Stalin drives Trotsky into exile, hunts him down and assassinates him; consolidates his grip on power; and imposes his 'revolution from above' on the Soviet people.

***

The itinerary carefully arranged for the eminent Dutch guests includes, of course, both Moscow and Leningrad, and a ten-hour train journey to the city of Nizhny Novgorod, birthplace of Maxim Gorky and famous for its annual fair at which peoples from the East meet to trade goods with Russians. From there they will take a river trip by paddle steamer 'Karl Marx' – one of over two thousand such steamers operating along the Volga – to visit the cities of Kazan and Samara, ending in Saratov, the home of the descendants of 18th century German immigrants. For a month they will visit what Mechanicus terms 'the focal points of political and cultural life'. The message from their hosts is clear: the Socialist Republics of the USSR are a harmonious diversity of cultures and ethnicities, with respect for all. On the sedate journey down the Volga, however, the overwhelming impression of the landscape on either bank of the river as viewed from the promenade deck of the Karl Marx is not so much of people and diversity, but of 'endlessness and loneliness. The wide expanses of land seem to be uninhabited. Except that on the many river islands there are wild horses, and in the distance loom a couple of men on horseback, alone in the solitude'.

Of all the cities they visit, factories and farms, schools and universities, army barrack and prison yard, Pieck is adamant that at no time was any attempt made to lead him or any of his travelling companions up any country path to a Potemkin village. Nevertheless, there is some disagreement between them as to the extent of their liberty to wander off the beaten track. Pieck is confident that '…we enjoyed every conceivable freedom of movement. Each member of our group could individually visit whom and what they wanted. We could talk in complete openness not just with supporters of the current regime, but also with its opponents.' However, Mechanicus countered somewhat tartly: 'The fact that the borders of the Soviet Union have opened up to foreigners does not mean that foreign tourists can wander around under their own steam; not even those whose names are recognized in the USSR as 'friends of the Soviet Union.' He also reminds readers of his articles for the *Algemeen Handelsblad* that 'We cannot, of course, answer for those things that we did *not* see'.

***

On 6 September, as the end of the expedition to the furthest edges of Europe approaches, Dr Berlage gives a lecture to Moscow's architects at a building of the Central Committee for the Improvement of the Position of Russian Academics on the theme of the connection between architecture and society. It makes a great impression on the audience, as do the lantern slides that present the clear development of Dutch architecture. It is on this occasion that Professor Herman Frijda takes the opportunity to give what Mechanicus describes as a 'fluently delivered little speech' in which he asserts to the audience of Soviet academics that there were many myths about Russia circulating in the Netherlands, and that whilst he must himself accept some share of the blame, he would be happy to help set the matter straight once he returned home. It seems an impromptu, genuinely-felt speech that suggests that Professor Frijda may have seen and accepted exactly what his hosts had intended. Alternatively, or additionally, he may have wanted the opportunity to visit the USSR again for obvious academic interests, and any criticism of his hosts would have weighed heavily against his prospects of being welcomed back. More than most economists of his generation, he had a sense of the shortcomings of the liberal system of free price-setting in the west, and would watch the Russian economic experiment with great interest. Having expressed criticism of theoretical economic models as sometimes being too abstract, and arguing instead in favour of greater respect for empiricism – the acquisition of knowledge through sensory experience and evidence – it is not surprising that he should want to visit the Soviet Union to experience for himself, and report back on, the human effects of the Soviet economic model.

On the overall impression left by their month-long, supposedly 'fact-finding' mission through parts of the USSR, Pieck and Mechanicus are, however, in agreement. Pieck writes that 'Our first impressions of the Soviet Union were of the children [...] The land of the Soviets is indeed the land of children. It is the same wherever we go: what a huge place children occupy in the public life of the Soviet state.' But it is not an image of innocence, of children at play that stays in the mind. Officially disapproved Soviet writer Andrei Platonov had drily commented: 'If kids can forget their own mothers but still have a sense of Comrade Lenin, then Soviet power really is here to stay'. Mechanicus observes that 'The idealism, the fanaticism of young people gives rise to many forms of social stimuli, intended to compel the indolent older generation towards a more rigid economic understanding.' A father is asked what the revolution has done for him and his generation: 'The same as always', he replies. 'I work hard and I survive'. And for his son? 'My son thinks about things very differently. He's looking to the future. He treats me with scorn, even though he never puts it in words. I love him, but I don't understand him... That's how life is now'. Pieck expresses this tension between the generations more brutally still, as a 'fight to the death between the old and the new'. For him 'the young generation in the Soviet Union are tough, pitiless, and fanatical towards their older counterparts. These two generations live next to, and alongside, each other but often in open or hidden mutual hostility. There are without doubt still millions in the Soviet Union who understand nothing of the new world around them. But Youth surges forward. And Youth is life: the Old are dying.'

A few years later, a young Nico Frijda greets his father on his return from a further trip to the USSR, anxiously waiting to learn about the difficult experiences his father might have faced in that turbulent country. Professor Frijda bends down to hug and console his younger son, explains that the streets of Russian cities are very peaceful, and proffers the observation that 'at least the children there are happy'. A few years later still, his father shares an observation with Nico, no doubt referencing his elder brother Leo's current preoccupations: 'If you're not a communist at twenty, you have no heart. If you're still a communist at thirty, you have no brain'.

IV

When students burn books and their teachers flee

In 1932 the University of Amsterdam celebrated its 300th anniversary, tracing its origins to the *Athenaeum Ilustre* in 1632. This was the same year in which Rembrandt painted 'The Anatomy Lesson of Dr Nicolaes Tulp' for the Amsterdam Guild of Surgeons, out of which would grow the university's medical faculty. The University chose to commemorate its anniversary by awarding no fewer than thirty-nine honorary doctorates. One of those eminent recipients of an honorary degree, Sir Dennis Holmes Robertson – Fellow of Trinity College Cambridge and an expert contributor to the field of macroeconomics during the inter-war period - had been nominated by Professor Frijda. And so in June of that year Holmes Robertson was the house guest of the Frijda family; he recalls in a brief note that the Dutch professor and his wife were 'my kind hosts', and that after this short period of hospitality they continued 'intermittently in touch'.

The colourful spectacle of academic processions draws crowds, anniversary ones especially, and Leo was allowed time off school to stand alongside the processional route for a glimpse of his father and those of his father's colleagues whom at some time or other he would have met when they stayed in the family home as house guests. He wrote of the experience in a school essay entitled 'The Procession'.

'When we arrived at one o'clock at the place where we were supposed to be, we searched out a good position. We then had to wait a while. Police officers on horseback and police officers on foot were continuously moving around. Leading the procession was a marching band, with drummers at the front and flag-bearers at the rear, about 30 students. We had to wait another long time and we couldn't resist keep stepping onto the road to watch what was happening... Finally, finally our patience was fully rewarded. A large number of men on horseback passed en masse, followed by two men, each dressed in black wearing a kind of six-cornered hat and long robes. On the robes were the words 'Amsterdam University'. Once they had filed past, then came the professors from abroad, just as elaborately dressed. Some wore robes of bright yellow, some were scarlet, some also had ermine-trimmed hoods, and in all colours. One even had a red gown, with a hood and six-cornered cap of the same colour. Finally came the Amsterdammers in their

academic gowns. They looked almost like nobility. I instantly recognised my father and many others. Then, when the procession was over, I went back to school with my teacher.'

***

1932 saw hyperinflation battering Germany hard as a result of the Wall Street Crash. Child philatelists from abroad may well have soaked from envelopes posted from Germany stamps that they then pasted in their pocket-sized albums: stamps with original face values of ten and two hundred reichsmarks, for example, now overprinted with new values of 800,000 and two million reichsmarks, respectively. In September 1928 there had been 650,000 unemployed in Germany. By 30 January 1933, when President Hindenburg appointed Adolf Hitler as Chancellor of Germany, there were over six million. Within a month, the somewhat pathetic 'lone wolf' act of communist party-inspired terrorism which resulted in the burning down of the German Parliament – the Reichstag – was enough of an excuse to cement Hitler's hold on power and justify the passing of emergency laws to crush political opposition. In quick order, Germany was effectively transformed into a one-party state. What Himmler, Chief of Police, hailed as 'the first concentration camp for political prisoners' opened another month later in Dachau, near Munich, with an initial capacity for 5,000 inmates; vacancies were quickly filled. On 1 April a national 'boycott' of Jewish-run shops, businesses, doctors and lawyers was urged on by propaganda minister Goebbels and implemented nationwide by local Nazi party chiefs. Storm Troopers stood menacingly outside Jewish premises, watching whilst others daubed the Star of David and anti-Jewish slogans on doors and windows in yellow and black paint. Where sporadic violence occurred, the police obeyed orders not to intervene.

On 7 April, new laws for 'The Reestablishment of the Civil Service' barred Jews from holding civil-service, university, and state positions, with immediate effect. The education system came under the direct control of the Nazi regime. Martin Heidegger, rector of Freiburg University, wrote: 'The duty of students as well as professors is to serve the people in three ways – through labour, military service, and scientific service'. Jewish thinking was derided and the poison of conspiracy theorists seeped into academic life: Einstein's theory of relativity was condemned as a Jewish plot aimed at achieving world domination and reducing Germans to the level of slaves. On 10 May, following a proclamation by the German Student Union of a nationwide 'Action against the Un-German Spirit', students lit bonfires in thirty-four university towns across the country for the ritualistic burning of 'un-German books' – a literary purge or

40

'cleansing by fire'. The Union demanded that German universities be centres of German nationalism, and it called for a 'pure' national language and culture, which required that books written by Jews, political dissidents, and corrupting foreign influences be thrown onto the flames. A list had been drawn up by the Nazi Party's Purification Committee and published in the trade journal of the German publishing industry identifying over 2,500 authors deemed fuel for the fires. Work by Bertolt Brecht was picked on, as was that by 1929 Nobel Prize laureate Thomas Mann, whose 1930 novel 'Mario and the Magician' portrayed the dangers of dictatorships. Mann was travelling in France at the time, and, upon hearing the news, immediately sought a place of exile in Switzerland. Works by H.G. Wells and Ernest Hemmingway ('A Farewell to Arms') were listed for burning. Any book, on any subject, by a Jew was deemed 'un-German' *per se* and pulled off all library shelves to be burned. Pacifist literature was to be burned – there was no place in the new Germany for such insipid tendencies. And so, German students paraded through the darkness of the night, illuminated by torchlight, singing, reciting 'fire oaths' and murmuring incantations, in an act of pure philistinism against a backdrop of ersatz pagan ritual orchestrated by a weirdly fetishist Nazi regime. In Berlin alone, a crowd of over 40,000 gathered in front of the State Opera House to hear an address clearly directed at German youth by Goebbels who insisted that the future German would not just be a man of books, but a man of character: 'A young person must already have the courage to face the pitiless glare, to overcome fear of death, and to regain respect for death – this is the task of this young generation. And so you do well in this midnight hour to commit to the flames the evil spirit of the past'. This was Nazism proudly portrayed as a death cult or, as 19th century German Jewish poet Heinrich Heine prophetically expressed the danger: 'Where they burn books, they will ultimately burn people'.

In the first six months of 1933 around 15,000 Jewish people fled across the German border into the Netherlands.

***

In almost immediate response to the German situation, and inspired by the Academic Assistance Council founded in Great Britain in April 1933 by William Beveridge, another helping hand was extended to their dismissed counterparts in Germany by academics in Dutch academia, spearheaded by Professor Frijda and other teachers from the University of Amsterdam, notably Dr Ernst Laqueur (its future chancellor) and Professor Paul Scholten. Uniting to form a 'Committee of Professors for the support of Jewish students and graduates from Germany' they understood the need for practical support to back up moral solidarity, and thus established

41

an 'Academic Support Fund' to provide financial assistance. Professor Scholten was appointed Chairman of the Fund, and Herman Frijda its Secretary. In June, they published an open letter, explaining the gravity of the situation, to solicit donations:

'The measures adopted in Germany have forced a large number of academics there to vacate their positions of professor, lecturer, private teacher or head of a scientific institution. Only a very few of these have any expectations in the short term of finding work within any higher-education institution elsewhere. The financial situation everywhere necessitates the greatest possible thrift, so that it is virtually impossible to count on any new appointments within higher education, and wherever any vacancy does arise, first thoughts must go to an appointment from amongst home-grown candidates.

'Given these circumstances, it is feared that a large number of fine men, including many who through their work have garnered an international reputation, are doomed to an aimless idle existence, and many of them, together with their families, will be consigned to poverty.

'To counter this danger, decisions have been made in several countries to set up an Academic Support Fund to benefit academics who, by virtue of their origins, faith or political convictions have been forced to leave their jobs in their own country.

'The Fund aims to provide financial support to a certain number of academics for a few years, so that they are guaranteed at least a material subsistence and the possibility to continue their academic work, for as long as they are unsuccessful in obtaining new work here or elsewhere.

'We have already been able to provide such assistance to a small number of young academics of exceptional ability.

'We hereby call on all persons sympathetic to the plans outlined above to contribute funds by payment into an account with N.V. Bank-Associatie, Amsterdam, giro number 10303, or giro office of the Municipality of Amsterdam, No. 4327, quoting payment reference: ACADEMIC SUPPORT FUND.'

Attached to the letter is a 'non-exhaustive' list, compiled from various sources, of around 240 higher-education teachers in Germany, together with their locations and academic departments, dismissed or forced to take leave.

In 1923, Dr Laqueur and two business partners had set up a pharmaceutical company - Organon - one of the first companies in Europe to successfully produce insulin on a commercial scale. Not only would the company become one of the main sponsors of the Academic Support Fund, it would also offer positions to some of the academic refugees to work in Laqueur's laboratory in Amsterdam or Organon's laboratory in the small southern town of Oss.

The letter refers to help already provided to 'young academics of exceptional ability'. One such beneficiary of this help was Norbert Elias, who fled from Germany - where he had worked at the sociological institute of the University of Frankfurt - to Paris. There, for two years, he would undertake research on a great work, eventually published under the title 'The Civilizing Process'. In his September 1936 forward to this work he acknowledges financial support for those two years from the Academic Support Fund in Amsterdam and - separately and more particularly – expresses gratitude for the role of Professor Frijda 'for the especially friendly way in which [he] manifested his interest during my time in Paris'. In all likelihood, Herman Frijda supported Elias from his own private funds.

In the main, however, the financial resources available to the Academic Support Fund were insufficient to pay more than travelling expenses to those who sought to travel onwards to Great Britain, or beyond Europe to North America. Or to pay those who remained in the Netherlands such thinly-spread support as provided a monthly subsistence benefit of little more than fifty guilders, and even that amount intended to suffice for a married couple.

***

Most German refugees fleeing across the border into the Netherlands were not, of course, academics and not eligible for assistance under the Academic Support Fund. Within the space of a few weeks of Hitler assuming power, the Dutch government, the Dutch Jewish community, and various left-of-centre political parties were in urgent search of a necessary political, legislative, and social response to the problem. One such response from amongst the Jewish community itself, instigated by Amsterdam University Professor, Dr David Cohen, was to bring together all the various Jewish-interest groups in the Netherlands – all strains of orthodox and liberal persuasion – under an umbrella group, the Committee for Special Jewish Affairs. Out of this organization a second was created – the Committee for Jewish Refugees (the 'CJV') – to take responsibility for the day-to-day running of relief efforts in Amsterdam. Their work was based on three principles: that no Jewish refugee should become a burden on public funds; that any permanent settler should bring business and employment to the country; and that contacts with other Jewish organizations should be used to facilitate this work. Someone who volunteered help to the CJV was Samuel van den Bergh, industrialist and liberal-party member of the Upper House of the Dutch parliament, who in 1930 merged his margarine empire with the Lever Brothers' soap empire to form Unilever. Another volunteer, who would become a good friend of Van den Bergh, was Professor Frijda. Together that year they organized a protest against Germany's treatment of its Jewish population at the RAI exhibition centre in Amsterdam. Herman Frijda addressed a gathering of thousands, condemning 'the plundering of shops, the abuse of Jewish citizens, the mass sackings of Jewish workers, the obstruction of Jews in the conduct of their religious practices, […] the state of utter lawlessness'. And although he insisted that this protest was not directed against the German people, it was clear to Frijda that the Jews fleeing across the German border into the Netherlands were the lesser problem compared to the existential threat of militaristic Germans mobilising on neighbouring German soil.

At the start of the 1930s the Netherlands had become engulfed by a wave of mass unemployment, originating from the 1929 Wall Street Crash that had already swept across the Atlantic to Great Britain and Germany two years before. Even those able to hold on to their jobs had to accept swingeing wage cuts. The Dutch government had no experience or structures in place to deal with large-scale unemployment, and being doggedly conservative would adhere then, and through the rest of the decade, to a staunchly non-interventionist and internationalist strategy, rejecting any pleas for protectionist measures to boost the Dutch economy and create jobs. Harsher still was the way in which the centuries-old Dutch protestant work ethic stigmatised the unemployed. Many groups in society shared an alarmingly illogical assumption that the unemployed were mostly workshy and just needed to get on their bikes to find work: the blindingly obvious fact that there was no work to be had was blindly ignored. Accordingly, income support payments were kept to substance level: an unemployed labourer who had earned a gross wage of thirty guilders per week working at the ports of Rotterdam or Amsterdam, for example, would see his family income halved to fifteen guilders in state support. As if that wasn't trial enough, those receiving benefits had to report twice per day to a government agency, to queue up in seemingly endless lines of the unemployed. And worse: they were required to allow government inspectors to visit them at home and investigate their daily lives, which quickly became a hated practice amongst those whose privacy was thus violated. Further stigmatisation came in the form of subsidised clothing, available only in red, and an official exemption from bicycle taxation, that had to be worn on clothing or attached to the bicycle, which became, as intended, a badge of shame. Where the government did not help, private initiatives and charitable foundations stepped in, but even the most prominent of these – the National Crisis Committee founded by Princess Juliana in 1931 – could only provide sufficient help to take the edge off the suffering.

The inevitable consequence of poverty and unemployment was social unrest. An unrest that was additionally fuelled by a rise in popular support for the communist party at the one end of the spectrum, and the recently-founded Dutch National Socialist Party led by Anton Mussert (amongst at least five other parties that were variations of the same theme) at the other; the one looking to Moscow for inspiration, the other to Berlin, and each sizing up the other with a menacing glare. Anti-fascists made their feelings felt, for example, by chanting slogans and setting off stink bombs in cinemas across the country in protest of the screening of the patriotic German U-Boat film *Morgenrot*; on the streets outside the cinemas both extremes demonstrated and fights broke out. Fascist party meetings were picketed outside the meeting halls in which they rallied, and scuffles broke out and chairs thrown within, to such an extent that it became hard for party organisers to find venues for future meetings. Nor did Jewish groups remain warily passive: when the occupants of one building provocatively flew a swastika flag from a tall flag pole, young Jewish men climbed one upon the shoulders of the other to reach a height able to tear it down. The Dutch intelligence service reported on the weapons of choice for street confrontations: wooden sticks, stones, metal rods, bludgeons, and knives; less favoured, but still used, were beer glasses, bicycle pumps, tear gas, billiard cues, tomatoes, eggs, and buckets of water/waste matter/paint. Most fights erupted when one group or another engaged in distributing propaganda materials on street corners; what may have started out as a scuffle between a couple of hot-headed opponents could grow as an audience of passers-by congregated to watch what was happening, and ended up taking sides, only to be broken up by the police. The mutual handbagging of extremist political opponents was overshadowed, however, by something more tragic. On 5 February 1933, exasperated by pay cuts and poor working conditions, a mutiny broke out amongst the crew of coastal defence warship *De Zeven Provincieen* along the coast of the Indonesian island of Sumatra. The Dutch defence minister authorized an attack by military aircraft and a bomb fell accidentally – or was dropped deliberately, the case is not proven – on to the ship, killing twenty-three mutineers: the survivors surrendered. It was a tragedy that garnered precious little sympathy back home in the Netherlands for the desperate crew members, and mostly served to increase support amongst the Dutch electorate for far-right parties, highlighting their demand for 'law and order'.

Nevertheless, despite this conflagration of stresses, the influx of German refugees into a country experiencing economic depression did have some unexpectedly positive effects. Two reports undertaken by the Committee for Special Jewish Affairs would claim that between 1933 and 1938 German Jews had established 300 businesses in the Netherlands, providing new jobs to approximately 6,500 Netherlanders. Not all refugees could find work – what service would a German lawyer be able to offer in Amsterdam? – but some businessmen with a trade could successfully continue the same businesses in the Netherlands that they had been forced to abandon in Germany. The clothing industry was a particular beneficiary – Amsterdam became a new export centre for women's apparel in Europe, which in turn gave a shot in the arm to the textile industry, particularly the woollen mills of the city of Tilburg.

***

Leo was becoming an accomplished pianist. Some pieces, such as a Beethoven sonata, he could play without sheet music, from memory. The threats from outside the family home - the events as far away as Germany, the events as close as the nearby streets of Amsterdam - were causing anxiety for his parents, and this anxiety permeated the Frijda family home. But meanwhile Leo would sit at the piano and play, recalls his sister Jetteke, in the way that most boys would go outdoors to play football, to release tension, to find an escape from this cloud of anxiety. Another form of – more literal – escape for Leo was his sailing adventures with the sea scouts. But here, too, there were sinister signs of things to come. In a letter home to his father, Leo writes:

'Tuesday

Dear Father,

I wish you a very happy birthday. The journey is going well. I am sitting in the cabin writing this letter as we sail along the Gouwe river. Gouda is already in sight. When we arrive I will post this card. This morning we set sail from Lake Braassem, where we spent the night. The landscape is very pretty around here. I saw the tree nurseries in Boskoop. Super. I had a go at fishing and caught three fish. Here on the water we met a yacht from Dusseldorf flying a swastika flag. However, they were very friendly, gave us priority and waved us on by toasting us with a glass of wine. Now we're nearing the houses on the edge of town.

Byeeeeeee

Greetings also to Mother'

V

The Gymnasium, Mrs Boissevain, and Dr Kastein

In September 1935, a month after his twelfth birthday, Leo begins secondary education at the Vossius Gymnasium, an Amsterdam grammar school that includes the teaching of the classical languages – Latin and Greek - to the most gifted pupils of both sexes in preparation for university education. Vossius is a new school, founded just nine years before Leo's admission, built in the modern Amsterdam style and boasting – unusually for the time – central heating. Headmaster Bruijn, a learned man with an inside-out knowledge of classical literature and the various annotations of Shakespeare, is preoccupied with just one notion: that the school should not become some kind of regimented barracks. As a result, however, its organization occasionally stoops towards the chaotic. The best of its teachers are very able, enthusiastic and relatively young, and continue to explore their own academic fields outside the confines of the school curriculum. Two of these in particular would have a great influence on Leo: teacher of Dutch literature Dirk Binnendijk, and history teacher Jacques Presser.

Alongside teaching duties, Binnendijk is also a poet, essayist, editor of a literary magazine and the arts editor of daily newspaper *De Telegraaf*. Though required to teach his pupils an etched-in-stone compendium of established writers, as a literary editor he identifies closely with, and contributes to, the latest musings within Dutch literary circles of poets such as Hendrik Marsman and Martinus Nijhoff, advocates of a concept akin to 'art for art's sake'. This literary 'new wave' proposes that the purity of a poem lies in its self-sufficiency, existing independently and in isolation from its creator: 'a flower, a plant that has become separated from the ground in which it first grew'. It is the poem that matters more than the poet – 'creativity' weighs more importantly than 'personality'. They claim this exploration of a new freedom of style – expressionist and 'vital' as Marsman describes his work - for a new age. Meanwhile, back in the classroom - Leo's world, offering tantalising glimpses into Marsman's world - Binnendijk's lessons are stimulating and interactive; Presser describes him as 'the best teacher you could imagine'. He encourages his students to read poetry out loud in the class, with the instruction 'You should perform it as a musician, not read the words like someone under duress!'

Historian Jacques Presser comes from a secular, socialist-leaning Jewish family, growing up in some poverty in the Jewish quarter of Amsterdam; his father worked as a diamond cutter. He graduated *cum laude* from the University of Amsterdam in History, Art History, and Dutch. After the war he would veer towards Marxism and write for the communist newspaper *De Waarheid*. By the time of the first year of the German occupation he would have published (under a pseudonym, to disguise his Jewish identity) a history of the Eighty Years' War and almost have completed two more major works; the first a revisionist biography of Napoleon and the second a study of the rise of the United States from British colony to world power. Presser loves teaching, and enjoys the company of his young charges, although his early days on the job were marked by the novice teacher's typical worry as to how to keep order in class. A cynical former colleague offered encouragement: 'Oh, that! Listen, young chap. There's always order in *my* class. 'Order' just means that no one gets murdered during lessons and no one engages in sex'. Through experience, Presser would stretch this elastic definition of 'order' even further: so long as he didn't actually *notice* any such murderous or amorous activity, then that constituted good order in his classroom. Presser could be charmed into submission by the wily ways of some pupils: he recalls a number of lively twelve-year-old Jewish boys able to give him the run-around. Once, when asked a question about work he hadn't bothered to study, one of their number, who had witnessed his teacher moving home into his neighbourhood, replied with the disarming non sequitur: 'Sir, what beautiful curtains you've hung up'. A salvo of laughter whipped around the class, and any thought of penalising the workshy pupil forgotten. Nevertheless, much was learned under Presser's tutelage: a pupil during his early years, Marius Flothuis, recalls Presser's aim of not merely imparting historical facts, but of putting them in relation to each other, and relativising them. 'There has been no person in my life', writes Flothuis, 'who has had more influence on my spiritual development than Jacques Presser'. Teacher and pupils would also gladly spend time together outside school premises, even outside school hours. Together they would walk around the streets of Golden-Age Amsterdam, learning to appreciate their local history from the buildings and waterways around them, and then teacher would test pupils on what they had learned. One of the group remembers when they even got together to enjoy a Chinese meal.

By contrast, as inspirational a teacher as Binnendijk may have been, it was not a job in which he felt able to invest utterly and for always his heart and soul. Or, as Presser more succinctly recalls: 'He couldn't stand either the children or the job'. A pupil once asked him if he would like to spend a day out with a group from his class. His response was blunt: 'Guys, this isn't for me. Please leave me out of it'. Subject closed.

Leo continues to find solace in playing the piano in the family home, particularly works by Chopin; the music envelopes him almost like a comfort blanket. He has also taken up violin lessons with a young female teacher who lives nearby, Miep van Hall. Many evenings after school he practises to the accompaniment of his mother at the piano. Favourite pieces that he loves to listen to - familiar items on the programmes of youth concerts to which either his school organized outings or his mother escorted him - are the violin concertos of Beethoven and Mendelssohn, and Schubert's Unfinished Symphony. As he develops an understanding of the mechanics behind composition, learning also to improvise, Leo would sit down with manuscript paper and pen, and compose simple pieces, including the first movement of a 'Trio in D Major' for strings, marked *allegretto*. 'Opus 3' no less. And signed with a flourish 'Leo H. Frijda'. There is a lot of music in school: Presser recalls the enthusiasm of a physics teacher with great musical ability, and there were always concert events of one kind or another. Leo would join the school orchestra. A girl in his class recalls one such musical occasion when, as a kind of light-hearted interlude, the diminutive figure of Leo, striking a bow across a quarter-size violin, walked through the legs of a statuesque teacher, as though through the splayed prongs of a giant, inverted tuning fork.

***

There is still economic hardship in the Netherlands. There are provincial and municipal elections throughout the country in 1935, and both the Dutch national socialist and communist parties attract significant minorities of supporters, one looking towards Germany for inspiration, the other towards the Soviet Union, but both offering promises of a better future to the nearly half million unemployed in the Netherlands that the government had been unable – or perhaps reluctant - to provide: of a 60 million guilder fund established in 1934 by the State to finance job-creation initiatives, two thirds of this money remained unspent two years later, and only 2,500 of the jobless at most had been helped to find work through the scheme. However, the genuine risks to democracy would be such that the government would be forced to take measures to ensure that this year would be the high water mark for such extremist sympathies, and partly thanks to what would prove to be the beginnings of a slow climb out of economic depression, such fears for democracy would indeed be allayed. A new movement was formed – 'Unity through Democracy' – to encourage the Dutch electorate to vote for democratic parties and to remind them of the Netherlands' 'rich democratic tradition'; the movement's election pamphlet also warned that 'He who defends a dictator strikes at something very much alive in the soul of the Dutch people'. In the 1937 elections the Dutch communist party lost a seat in parliament and the percentage vote gained by the national socialist party - that had campaigned under the slogan 'Mussert or Moscow?' (Anton Mussert being their black-shirted, high-booted leader) - was halved from the previous elections. Reasons may have included the reporting in the Dutch press of the show trials and Great Terror underway in the USSR, and the increasing acts of brutality by German and Italian dictators; but the Unity through Democracy movement also justifiably claimed some credit: 'We've won: it's neither Mussert nor Moscow'.

Behind the statistics of poverty and unemployment are the sorry cases of individual hardship; behind a husband and father scratching around for work is a wife and mother, eking out a meagre income to put food on the table for the family. Where national and local government couldn't - or for political reasons wouldn't – help, individuals banded together to form action groups to provide support where they could. Adrienne Minette Boissevain – 'Mies' for short - wife and mother of five children, was one of those in a privileged position able to help others.

Mies came from a well-heeled and respected family – a Mennonite family - her father was a bank director, and her great-grandfather, Jacob van Lennep, an author and translator of works by Sir Walter Scott and Lord Byron. She met through the Mennonite Church, and married, Jan Boissevain, born in Canada from a long line of Boissevains that had originally settled in Amsterdam in around 1690 to escape Louis XIV's persecution of the French Huguenots, returned with his Dutch parents to the Netherlands. Mies had trained abroad as a nurse, but left her training behind to care for a fast-growing family; her husband Jan ('Jan Canada' to his wider family) worked as a director of a bank that handled German pension funds. In the early 1930s the Boissevain family, spurred on by Mies, was already taking German Jewish refugee children into their home: there were often ten or more laughing faces around the dining table at meal times. One was a young and precocious violinist Theo Olof – 'like a brother' to the Boissevain children – whose first concert as solo violinist would be with the Amsterdam Concertgebouw, aged 11. When his mother could no longer afford to pay for his studies under famous violinist Oscar

Back at the Amsterdam Music Academy, Mies went round with a pot, collecting money till there was enough for the lessons to continue.

There was nothing prim and purse-lipped about the way the Boissevain family applied their religious beliefs to their daily lives. Mies – described by the New York Times during a lecture tour to the USA after the war as 'this tiny Dutch woman' – nevertheless exhibited an almost rumbustious energy to get things done, to *do* good rather than merely preach good. As an avowed feminist, she set out to prove that women could be as successful in business as their male counterparts; she established a successful beauty parlour in the family's stately canal-side home in the centre of Amsterdam, with the motto 'Health + Beauty = Lust for Life', thereby winning a bet with her husband that she could make a go of things. She led a campaign of protest against Government Minister Romme, who tried to ban female employment which, in times of large-scale unemployment, he considered to be 'unnatural' and undesirable. In 1937 she launched the 'Hotpot Club' at which women from all walks of life could get together once a month to eat lunch for next to nothing and exchange ideas, firstly at the family home and then, as the numbers expanded, at Heck's Lunchroom on the Rembrandtplein; and in 1938 she co-founded the Women's Volunteer Corps – 'to prepare for any eventual war and protect the home front'. So, for Mies and the Boissevain family, as with Professor Herman Frijda and his family, resistance to German national socialism began as soon as soon as Hitler came to power.

Though Dora Frijda – through personal choice or sense of duty – played a less overtly independent, feminist role than Mies Boissevain within the family home and beyond, she was not quite, as Nico remembered her, *just* the wife who cooked and sang for her children. In addition to her behind-the-scenes help for German refugees – together with her husband she welcomed many struggling intellectuals into the family home, and supplied them with clothing, food, and a roof over their heads - Dora, who had studied botany at university, had kept up this academic interest and sat proudly on the Ladies' Committee of the Sixth Annual Botanical Congress held in Amsterdam from 2 to 7 September 1935.

***

It was a misfortune that the Olympic Games awarded to Germany in 1931 as part of the nation's rehabilitation following World War I should have lead to the chilling racist bombast of the 1936 Berlin Olympics - a perfect showcase for the 'make Germany great again' spirit. Posters depicting heroic, finely-chiselled athletes claimed Nazi Germany as the

51

rightful heir of an 'Aryan' culture of classical antiquity; indeed, symbolic of such a conceit, this would be the first Olympics in which an 'inextinguishable' flame would be carried aloft by torch relay from the site of the Temple of Zeus, in ancient Olympia, to the host city. And so, on 1 August, the Fuhrer entered a grandiose new stadium to a musical fanfare penned by Richard Strauss. 'An almost religious event' according to writer Thomas Wolfe, 'the crowd screaming, swaying in unison and begging for Hitler. There was something scary about it; his cult of personality'. It was a further misfortune for the athletes entering this sulphurous cauldron, alphabetically by country name, that the official 'Olympic salute' should have born such an uncanny resemblance to the Nazi salute: whilst the US team avoided potential embarrassment by holding their hats against their chests as they paraded by, the Bulgarian team chose to celebrate any ambiguity by coordinating their Olympic/Nazi salute with a meticulously-timed goose-step past the khaki-dressed personage *The New York Times* dubbed 'the new Caesar of this era'. The claim of direct kinship between the heroes of ancient Greece and the heroes of modern Germany was further spelled out by head of the Germany Organizing Committee, Dr Theodor Lewald, who in a speech that was a long time ending declared: 'In a few minutes the torch bearer will proceed to light the Olympic flame on its tripod cauldron, and its flames will rise to heaven throughout the weeks of the festival. It will create a real and spiritual bond of fire between our German fatherland and the sacred places of Greece founded nearly 4,000 years ago by *Nordic immigrants*'.

There had, unsurprisingly, been campaigns to boycott the Berlin Games in response to the blatant human rights issues in Germany, especially vociferous in the United States, Great Britain, France, Sweden, Czechoslovakia and the Netherlands. And whilst the proposed boycott narrowly failed through insufficient backing, the idea of an alternative Olympics in Barcelona, the only other candidate city to earn IOC votes back in 1931, did gain support. The newly elected left-wing Popular Front government in Spain had decided unilaterally to boycott the Berlin Games and organise its own 'People's Olympiad'. 6,000 athletes from 22 countries – selected by trade unions, workers' clubs, and socialist and communist parties, rather than state-sponsored committees - registered to take part, including the USSR, German and Italian teams as represented by their political exiles, and a team of Jewish exiles. Scheduled to start on July 19 and run for eight days, competitors had already begun arriving in Spain to compete in the usual sporting events, as well as participate in a chess tournament, folk dancing, music and theatre, when organisers were forced to cancel the event as the first shots of civil war in Spain fired out.

***

Whereas in 1937 the Dutch electorate had responded to the question 'Mussert or Moscow?' (Germany or the USSR) with the answer 'neither', the struggle between these two powers was played out – at a distance and through third parties – in Spain, where 'neither' would not be an option. A left-wing government faced, in effect, a military coup from right-wing generals, eventually to be led by General Franco. Even though 27 countries – including (cynically) Germany, Italy and the USSR –signed up to an Anglo-French sponsored 'Non-intervention Committee', Germany and Italy continued to send troops and weapons to bolster Franco's nationalists, whilst the USSR offered weapons, advisers and technicians to the republican government, acting in secret to assist communists and their sympathisers to gain key positions in the army and civil service. In September 1936 the Comintern (Communist International) in Moscow felt inspired to create 'International Brigades' – foreign volunteer fighters – to rally to the side of the republicans. In return, the Catholic Church in Spain openly sided with the fascists, blessed military aircraft, and named tanks after the Virgin Mary. As the conflict developed and stories of the horrors of the war filtered through the international press, up to 40,000 volunteers from over 50 countries would respond by making the journey to Spain. In March 1937 a 'Help for Spain' Committee was established in the Netherlands for the purposes of writing and distributing propaganda for the republican cause, providing care for orphaned Spanish children, and raising funds for the supply of food, clothing and medicines. In August of that year a Dutch Brigade was formed. And even though it was enshrined in the Dutch constitution that the joining of a foreign military or civil service without the consent of the State would result in the stripping of their Dutch citizenship – to which the government expressly drew its citizens' attention at the time - over 600 mostly young, idealist souls resolutely headed south. One of these was twenty-seven-year-old Dr Gerrit Kastein.

Kastein had had a strict religious upbringing. He could recite countless psalms by memory. After leaving school, he studied medicine at the University of Groningen in the north of the country, and immediately immersed himself in left-wing student politics. Before long he was hosting 'red lunches' at his student digs each Thursday lunchtime, where social engagement was a recurring theme for animated debate. There were occasional lectures from prominent visiting academics such as Professor Max Adler, a Viennese pioneer of 'Austro-Marxism', who spoke on 'Marxism and Sociology'. In late 1931, Kastein then took a co-assistantship in the psychiatric-neurological clinic of the University of Heidelberg,

Germany, during which six-month period he witnessed at close hand Hitler seizing the reins of power and the burning down of the Reichstag in protest. This engulfing passion for politics and social engagement may have served to compensate for – perhaps disguise – his somewhat low-voltage empathy towards those close to him: in letters to his parents he tended to remonstrate on their shortcomings, blaming them for '…breaches of trust, active interference, trying to stand in my way, change me, forbid me, etc., …', whilst his future wife Ria – a German national – would write to his mother urging her to find ways to help her cope with the pressure-cooker relationship with her husband-to-be. Kastein - perhaps unwittingly – alluded to this side of his character in a letter in which he questioned his future career: 'For a while now I have been realising that I will never be a good doctor. I have far too little interest in the patients… I notice that what attracts me more are the books… and pure manual labour – giving injections, taking blood samples, etc.…' Indeed, Kastein would not only pore over books, but would himself pen a lucid, logical, and science-based debunking of Nazi (and not just Nazi) ideas of racial purity in a book entitled 'The Issue of Race' (*Het rassenvraagstuk*). Taking all emotion out of the argument, he concluded with the crystal-clear observation that racial theories 'are a weapon in the psychological preparation for war'. Kastein is a man of ideas, perhaps a man of the people, but a man who lacked empathy for those closest to him and knew it.

Ria was already two months' pregnant when she and Gerrit Kastein married in July 1935, and their first daughter Ina just four months old when the married couple left her in the care of Gerrit's mother to undertake a month-long trip to the USSR. Ria pined to be with her baby daughter, for which Gerrit teased her. In Leningrad they stayed in the tiny, two-roomed flat of a Russian former fellow student and his wife, but it is likely that the overall purpose of the visit was less to develop his craft as a doctor in that city, and more to consult directly with the higher ranks of his Soviet spymasters in Moscow. Kastein's faith in the Soviet system was utterly slavish. The death sentences passed upon those hapless victims of Stalin's Great Terror were, he claimed, 'the justified verdicts against traitorous elements that sought to collaborate with the German fascists'. It was therefore with the approval of the Dutch Communist Party that Kastein would travel to Spain, arguing that the Spanish Red Cross had fallen largely into the hands of Franco, and thereby pre-establishing grounds for appeal against any attempted removal of his Dutch citizenship by asserting that he had been recruited not by a *foreign power*, but by the Dutch 'Help for Spain' Committee.

Kastein spent just two-and-a-half months in Spain, arriving in Barcelona after a journey by train and plane through France, to offer support as an ambulance medic. He found there a scarcity of hospital beds; in some towns and villages school buildings were hastily converted into makeshift hospitals. Once back home he described in a newspaper interview the pitiful lack of trained medical help, together with desperate food shortages. It was a bloody war, not only in terms of deaths arising from armed combat, but also – and especially – from the number of sickening mass executions on either side, estimated at 20,000 at the hands of Franco's army, and 38,000 by the 'red terror'. Bodies were thrown in mass graves – unknown and sometimes unrecognisable corpses - and over 100,000 missing persons *still* remain unaccounted for, including poet and playwright Federico Garcia Lorca. Writers George Orwell and Laurie Lee would both lament the destruction wrought by this war, the nobility of their cause colliding with the futility of how it all played out. 'To be marching up the street behind red flags inscribed with elevating slogans' wrote Orwell, 'and then to be bumped off from an upper window by some total stranger with a sub-machine-gun—that is not my idea of a useful way to die.' For Lee, who had developed a profound love for the country in childhood dreams, now awakened in his youthful gypsy-like travels from city, to town, to village in the company of his violin, Spain had become sadly, unrecognisably altered. He sensed 'an infection so deep it seemed to rot the earth, drain it of colour, life and sound. The landscape was plagued, stained and mottled, and all humanity seemed to have been banished from it.'

***

Of the three–and-a-quarter hour aerial bombardment of the town of Guernica on 26 April 1937, Times war correspondent George Steer witnessed how '… *the most ancient town of the Basques and the centre of their cultural tradition was completely destroyed yesterday afternoon by insurgent air raiders [...] during which a powerful fleet of aeroplanes consisting of three German types, Junkers and Heinkel bombers and Heinkel fighters, did not cease unloading on the town bombs weighing from 1,000 lbs downwards and, it is calculated, more than 3,000 two-pounder aluminium incendiary projectiles. The fighters, meanwhile, plunged low from above the centre of the town to machinegun those of the civilian population who had taken refuge in the fields.*' Alerted to this report in his Paris home, Pablo Picasso launched into the composition of preliminary sketches for a monumental work: 'In the panel on which I am working, which I shall call *Guernica* … I clearly express my abhorrence of the military caste which has sunk Spain in an ocean of pain and death.'

However, it is not Picasso's work that would link the horrors of the Spanish Civil War in the mind of Leo Frijda to the fate that would soon await the Netherlands, but a painting of another, earlier war – again on Spanish soil - commemorating Spanish resistance to Napoleon's armies during the French occupation: Francisco Goya's haunting 'The Third of May 1808'. The work – 'revolutionary in every sense' according to art historian Kenneth Clark - depicts a group of hapless victims huddled before a group of faceless executioners with bayoneted rifles re-loaded and ready to fire. The process is already underway: a small stack of dead bodies to the left; to the right an agonized line of those awaiting their turn, hiding the bloody vision from their eyes with their hands; and in the middle a smaller group, whose central figure is illuminated by bright lamplight, arms outstretched in supplication or defiance: a simple, sun-baked labourer who is also Christ on the cross. Clark marvels at the intensity of the work: 'With Goya we do not think of the studio or even of the artist at work. We think only of the event'. In this light it is a 'modern' work, therefore, and one that Leo's literature teacher, Dirk Binnendijk, could well have relied on in support of his plea for 'creativity' over 'personality' – though Goya's personality, his passion and rage, soak through the paint and every pore of the canvas. Leo has a reproduction of this painting hanging on his bedroom wall. It is his *memento mori*, but it is less a quiet contemplation of the nature of death, and more a feverish foreboding of the violence of its engineering. He will write a poem inspired by this painting – 'Goya 1941'. The first lines of the poem would be etched on his gravestone.

VI

The Honorary Doctorate and the Pogrom

In November 1937, sixteen years after he established and became head of its economics faculty, Professor Herman Frijda was appointed Chancellor (*Rector Magnificus*) of the University of Amsterdam. In February of the following year he would as Chancellor – in accordance with tradition - give the anniversary lecture. Before a distinguished audience of the mayor and aldermen of the city of Amsterdam, and teachers and students of the university he lectured on the theme 'The Notion of Equilibrium and the Reality'. This year of his chancellorship, 1938 – a year he might justifiably have regarded as the culmination of his years of devoted service to the university and to his students - would coincide with events to commemorate Queen Wilhelmina's forty years on the Dutch throne. Negotiations were already underway between the Palace and the University for a fitting ceremony to award the Queen an honorary doctorate in economics; it would be scheduled just three days following the nation's formal service of thanksgiving for the Queen's long reign in Amsterdam's New Church on 6 September, and Professor Frijda would be Her Majesty's promoter.

***

Leo's adventures with the scouts continue. 'Not just an ordinary troop member', his scout leader would recall after the war: 'He was an outsider, but also – thanks to his engaging character and bright ideas – welcomed as a 'little brother' in our fellowship'. Leo's pet project is his scout troop's magazine, *De Spil*. He sets puzzles and a competition for handicrafts, begins writing a story in serial form that he leaves unfinished (offering a prize for the best ending), launches an old newspaper collection to raise money for new uniforms… 'In short, he tried to breathe new life into his pet project by all possible – and impossible – means'. During scout camps Leo 'unleashed wild mutinies and afterwards apologized with the sweetest of expressions'. This is Leo, honouring his name, bursting with a frenetic energy and vivid imagination, an outsider who never quite belongs yet – paradoxically - becomes the most enthusiastically engaged, always encouraging - indeed inciting - others to journey with him. Then there is Leo the quietly reflective and 'rather frightened boy' who needs to recoup his spent energies and distance himself from his anxieties at the piano keyboard, and later also with pen and paper.

In the summer the Frijda family take a holiday together, accompanied by Leo's maternal grandmother. They travel by car the fifty or so kilometres from Amsterdam to Bilthoven, close to the city of Utrecht. The landscape is of pine trees and rolling sandy dunes, and it is here in this peaceful seclusion that they have rented a large villa set in well-kept gardens, cocooned by trees. Their holiday will last almost a month. It is the perfect opportunity for Leo, together with joint editors Nico and Jetteke, to lay their hands on a typewriter and hammer out – with frequent typos the result of over-enthusiasm - the *Bosch en Duin Weekly News* with which to inform and entertain the family. The first page announces a children's swimming and beach game competition on 24 August at a natural outdoor pool in Bilthoven. There is an instalment of a short story 'Barbas the Sled Dog'; a quiz with a prize of the winner's choice; and a public service announcement on the quickest method of using the Cona coffee maker ('for further information contact Prof. Frijda'). In response to the request for advice submitted from Mrs Charlotte Frank (Leo's grandmother) as to how to avoid mosquito bites, the editors sagely advise that the best repellent is a mixture of peppermint oil, mustard powder and onion juice, smeared into the skin: 'and to escape the aroma of the lotion, it's best to sit for about an hour on a red-hot stove plate. We guarantee that you'll have no further worries about the smell.' Then there was Leo the eco-warrior before his time: under the heading 'The rhyme that doesn't help much' he and his co-editors report that 'The owners of the forests in Bosch en Duin and surroundings who allow the public into their forests find many of the day trippers to be a nuisance. These people don't spend much time thinking about the rhyme: 'Thank the wood owners for the pleasant stay, By not dropping litter along the way'. Instead, they throw all kinds of rubbish onto the ground so that the beauty of this natural environment is lost'. Judging from the tone of the *Bosch en Duin Weekly News* it seems to have been a happy, good-natured summer for the Frijda family; Professor Frijda disensconced from behind his four-inch thick study door to enjoy 'family time', the children allowed their fun and freedom. As the holidays end, the school and university terms start.

***

Theo Hondius is in a class two years above Leo at the Vossius Gymnasium. And though they share the intoxicating thrill for the works of modern Dutch poets, together with a passion for creative writing of their own, a difference of two years is colossal at school age, and fellows like Theo could not be seen fraternising with any of the younger pupils, certainly not one in the same class as his younger sister. So, they would not meet at school. Theo's father – deputy head of the Amsterdam Lyceum, another grammar school in the city - is a renowned classics scholar, graduate of Utrecht University and one-year graduate student at the British School in Athens, and now author of a standard text for grammar-school pupils on the classical world. Theo's parents are divorced and his father remarried, and a stressful home environment is something else he and Leo would have in common. Theo writes for the school magazine *Vulpes* – as in time will Leo - and he composes articles that would certainly have appealed to Leo's sense of humour. With a sly nod to the 'golden age' of English detective fiction Theo sets a competition to complete a short story entitled 'The Mystery of the Double Axe' – entries to be sent to the magazine editors. He explains in a few words how these things generally work: in Part I the body is discovered; in Part II the suspects are rounded up and the culprit revealed. The cast of characters Theo dangles tantalisingly before his readers are Arthur Crabtree of Scotland Yard, Lord Codshead, Professor Milkworth, Sir Arnold Trumpeter and Timothy Weybridge – he apparently dispenses with the peculiar notion of including any female characters. The story thus begins: 'Timothy Weybridge, famous detective and still a popular weekend guest despite the nineteen deaths that had occurred in the last dozen country houses he had visited, hesitated for a moment'.

***

On the afternoon of Friday, 9 September 1938 the prime minister Dr Colijn and his cabinet, members of the upper chamber of parliament, the chancellors of all Dutch universities, and representatives of the various Christian denominations file into the ceremonial hall of the University of Amsterdam, where other guests are already seated. The royal family and other dignitaries then arrive in a procession of horse-drawn carriages, to be greeted by a welcoming party of the university senate. The Queen is escorted by the mayor of the city; Princess Juliana by Professor Brugmans, and Prince Bernhard by Professor Paul Scholten, co-founder with Professor Frijda of the Academic Support Fund. Walking through the seventeenth-century stone gate, the Queen inspects an honour guard of the Royal Student Rifle Association, and turning into the inner courtyard is presented with a bouquet of flowers by Jetteke, Professor Frijda's now twelve-year-old daughter. In the vestibule adjoining the great hall, the Queen is greeted by the Chancellor - Professor Frijda - himself, and in procession they take their places in the hall before over six hundred invited guests. The hall is given additional colour thanks to the brand-new ceremonial robes of the university's academic staff: the traditional black has been replaced by a combination of the city's colours of black and red, together with colours representing their various faculties. The chancellor then takes to the ceremonial lectern. He first gives an account of the history of the university over the preceding three hundred years, and then turns to more current matters:

'The economic problems of the country have always been the concern of Your Majesty. With gratitude we recall the personal initiative taken by Your Majesty in the dark days of 1914 that led to the founding of the Royal National Assistance Committee, which would prove itself of such immense worth. Countless are the issues, often of the greatest complexity, that raise concerns for the development or maintenance of economic prosperity. The great changes that have altered the world order over the last twenty years, and especially since the global economic crisis, have also posed many weighty, extremely difficult problems for our own nation. We know the deep interest that Your Majesty has always shown; we know that Your Majesty has always devoted the greatest attention to these issues, in full understanding of their scale and depth. The Senate of this University, in which the study of economics plays a large role, wishes to recognise this role. It believes it is able to do this by awarding You the highest honour it can bestow, and thus to award Your Majesty an honorary doctorate in economics. It is to the great honour of the Senate that Your Majesty has consented to accept this recognition.'

In reply, the Queen acknowledged the great distinction of this honorary doctorate:

'... and I especially value the fact that it has been awarded to Me in the discipline of economics. It is particularly in these difficult times for trade and commerce, that this, the youngest of your faculties, so very much at home in this great mercantile city, has an extremely important and responsible role to play, alongside its purely academic task, as a voice for those with a position in economic life and as a teacher of those preparing for such position.'

An hour and a half after the ceremony began, the Queen is escorted from the hall in the same manner in which she had been greeted, to take afternoon tea in an ante-chamber. And thus ended 'an unforgettable day for the University of Amsterdam'.

A month later, Professor Frijda and his wife would travel to the south of France as house guests of Sam van den Bergh at his home in Nice – 'Villa Arcadia' – signing his guest book on 10 October. It being school term time, the children remain at home in the care of relatives. The villa enjoyed a reputation as a happy and relaxed place where Van den Bergh's wider family and invited friends would meet, celebrate milestones, and party. A huge terrace, supported by pillars, stretched out over the steep slope of gardens, above citrus, olive and palm trees to offer an uninterrupted view of the Promenade des Anglais and Bay of Nice.

***

There was another fortieth anniversary in Amsterdam that year – a less celebratory one – when the International Law Association met on 29 August for its fortieth conference at the Royal Colonial Institute. There had been world-wide horror and condemnation of the massacre of the villagers of Guernica, the killing of 1,000 civilians in Italian bombing raids on Barcelona, and the aerial attacks on crowded Chinese cities by the Japanese (the fall of Nanking alone was at the price of 150,000 civilian lives), all in the same year. A draft convention by a committee of the ILA followed up on the unanimous resolution of an increasingly powerless and irrelevant League of Nations that called for the protection of civilian populations against bombardment by air.

Article 1 of this *Draft Convention for the Protection of Civilian Populations against New Engines of War* stipulated that 'The civilian populations of a State shall not form the object of an act of war....', and Article 4 that 'Aerial bombardment for the purpose of terrorising the civilian population is expressly prohibited.' However, Article 2 would provide aggressor nations with a very generous legal loophole: 'The bombardment by whatever means of towns, ports, villages, or buildings which are *undefended* is prohibited in all circumstances. A town, port, village, or isolated building shall be considered undefended provided that not only (a) no combatant troops, but also (b) no military, naval or air establishment, or barracks, arsenal, munitions stores or factories, aerodromes or aeroplane workshops or ships of war, naval dockyards, forts, or fortifications for defensive or offensive purposes, or entrenchments [...] exists within its boundaries or within a radius of "x" kilometres from such boundaries.' This would mean, of course, that a city that billeted troops, as Amsterdam would billet troops in the concert hall of its Concertgebouw orchestra, or a city that dug defensive works, as The Hague would dig defensive trenches to protect the nation's government and royal family, would not be *undefended*, and therefore their civilian populations not protected under the rather useless provisions of this convention. And Rotterdam would be protected least of all. In any event, the convention was never dignified by signature or ratification.

As far back as 1932 the threats had been signposted with chilling clarity. On 10 November of that year former – and future re-elected – British Prime Minister Stanley Baldwin spoke in the House of Commons:

61

*'I think it is well also for the man in the street to realize that there is no power on earth that can protect him from being bombed. Whatever people may tell him, **the bomber will always get through**. The only defence is in offence, which means that you have to kill more women and children more quickly than the enemy if you want to save yourselves… If the conscience of the young men should ever come to feel, with regard to this one instrument [bombing] that it is evil and should go, the thing will be done; but if they do not feel like that – well, as I say, the future is in their hands. But when the next war comes, and European civilization is wiped out, as it will be, and by no force more than that force, then do not let them lay blame on the old men. Let them remember that they, principally, or they alone, are responsible for the terrors that have fallen upon the earth.'*

In other words, it is the young – not necessarily the meek – who would inherit the earth, and who would decide how that inheritance be spent.

This year, 1938, would be a year of appeasement, and a year in which international institutions and national political leaders would study the fine print and pedantry of international law, and trust the handshakes of the blood-soaked hands of tyrants, to avoid the effort of meaningful response to acts of inhumanity against citizens of fellow nations. It would also, maybe paradoxically, be a year in which the Netherlands would for the first time try to balance its traditional role of neutrality with a new and urgent need to prepare itself for war; indeed, its perceptible recovery from the preceding years of depression can be attributed in no small part to mobilisation and government investment in the nation's defence. The desire to avoid war at almost any cost is slowly turning into the realisation that a new war in Europe is all but inevitable, and to prepare accordingly.

***

'How can anyone say that Austria is not German! Is there anything more German than our old pure Austrian-ness?' Hitler demanded to know in March 1938, before his troops marched over the border and annexed the country 'as liberators'. Hot on their heels followed the Fuhrer himself, meeting 'such a stream of love as I have never experienced'. Austrian Nazi politician Arthur Seyss-Inquart drafted and signed into law the legislative act reducing Austria to a province of Germany; and once appointed Governor of the newly named territory of Ostmark and given an honorary rank in the SS he wasted no time in dealing with the Jewish population – driven like cattle through the streets of Vienna, their homes and shops plundered, their property confiscated and many of them rounded up and sent to concentration camps. The Dutch government responded by closing their border with Germany to keep out – and send back – 'illegal' German refugees, pleading in its defence the nation's poor economic situation and the cherished principle of Dutch neutrality.

Later that year, on the night of 9 to 10 November 1938 – 'Kristallnacht', the night of broken glass - German and Austrian storm troopers ran amok through Jewish communities throughout their respective countries, destroying over 260 synagogues and approximately 7,500 Jewish businesses, as well as schools and hospitals. Whole streets burned whilst fire brigades, ordered not to intervene, did nothing. The immediate death toll is presumed to have been as high as 1,500, whilst over 30,000 others were rounded up and taken to concentration camps. The events were witnessed by foreign correspondents from around the world. The headline of Dutch newspaper *Algemeen Handelsblad* proclaimed 'One of the blackest pages in the history of the Third Reich'. British journalist Hugh Carleton Greene described the support that the frenzied mob received from ordinary German people: 'Racial hatred and hysteria seemed to have taken complete hold of otherwise decent people. I saw fashionably dressed women clapping their hands and screaming with glee, while respectable middle-class mothers held up their babies to see the 'fun''. And the police, ordered not to intervene, did nothing. A report by the Association of Jewish Refugees in Great Britain would later identify this event as the pivotal moment in the transition from the 'non-violent' war of attrition against the Jews that had preceded it – the boycotts and deprivations of rights - to the use of 'sheer, undisguised violence [that] would lead to Belsen and Auschwitz'. The *Spectator* magazine declared that the word 'appeasement' had now been 'obliterated from the political vocabulary'. In the immediate aftermath fifty thousand more Jewish refugees had rushed to the border with the Netherlands. The Dutch government allowed just seven thousand of them to enter the country, labelling the refugees that had already entered the country as undesirable aliens: it pursued the logic of this policy in February 1939 with a decision to build an internment camp for these refugees at Westerbork.

***

The question plaguing the mind of literary editor Ed Hoornik on a solitary wander through the Jewish quarter of Amsterdam on a grey, grim November day following Kristallnacht was whether to '...close my eyes to the hideous reality that surrounds me and live in my own, imaginary world, or [...] use my talents to stand up against situations that I find inhuman...' As he walked along the Jodenbreestraat (the heart of the Jewish quarter) he felt how close the explosion of hatred in Germany and Austria was to his own homeland, and to his home city – how similar were the streets of Amsterdam and Berlin - and that the Dutch population needed to be 'shaken awake' to the dangers. His poem - 'Pogrom' – counterpoints style with theme to disturbing effect. He adopts a Petrarchan sonnet form, a form adopted and adapted in all western languages and cultures, symbolising, one might say, the refinement of western literary culture over many centuries, in stark counterpoint to the warning he presents of a dark, discordant and destructive machine-age menace. Other, younger, poets would mercilessly deride Hoornik's use of tired and old-fashioned forms and seek to differentiate themselves accordingly, but it may not be too fanciful to suggest that this chosen form paid deference to the long history of a humanist civilising process linking the renaissance of Petrarch to Shakespeare, through to the thriving, three-hundred-year-old communities of immigrant Spanish and Portuguese Jews settled around Amsterdam's Jodenbreestraat; these are links in a chain under attack from a regime that hated culture, that began by burning books, and that was now rounding up people. The final line of Hoornik's 'Pogrom', his sonnet's *resolution*, is a stark prophecy: 'It is but ten hours by train to Berlin'.

As Dutch literary critic Jaap Goedegebuure would later observe, however: 'The written word was not able to avert the threat'.

VII

Vulpes

The main lights in the hall slowly dim, the chattering stops, and from the back of the stage comes a terrifying sound, swelling, growing ever louder, a train, now almost upon us, now rumbling past, and gradually the din draining away: the Ghost Train! This was the impressive start to the festival play.

...at the end, the lights went on and the high tension was broken by huge applause, and there was no one in that hall who did not find it creepy, and who did not look a little pale...

Then, from all sides, people rushed to give their opinions. Teachers and older pupils were unanimous in the view that it had been a long time, if ever, since they had seen such an excellent play at the Vossius Gymnasium. Some of the children remained too overawed to say anything at all, and I even heard that a number of first and second years weren't able to sleep that night.

One of the most important contributions to the success was certainly that of the director, Mr Bob van Leersum, who worked endlessly hard to ensure the success of this production, and was here at the performance itself to ensure that everything ran smoothly...

And finally to the actors. I don't intend to name names; these are listed in the programme. All performers, debutants and experienced hands, were equally good. Perhaps one of them performed slightly better than the other in certain places, but in general there was no weak spot amongst the company and each of them was up to their task.

Review in the school magazine Vulpes of 'The Ghost Train', by Arnold Ridley, performed Saturday 1 April and Wednesday 5 April 1939. Leo Frijda played the role of the Station Master, who warned the passengers huddled and frightened in the station waiting room: 'Folks in these parts runs like mad if they hear a train in the night'.

***

'Tax inspectors', observes Eduard Veterman, novelist and playwright, 'regard houses as dead objects. Real estate. And for as long as their final demands aren't drafted in poetic verse they will wallow happily in this mistake. But we know better. Houses are living beings... and when the time comes, they will speak of profound things with their big window-eyes'. The Frijda family have moved to number 3 Corelli Street. A little later, Jan and Mies Boissevain and their five children move in to number 6 across the road. Daughter Sylvia Boissevain recalls that 'no one wanted to move there, much too modern, and probably much too much glass'. The large windows, however, are to Leo's advantage at least. The two Boissevain girls are attractive and with a pair of binoculars he can look from his bedroom window across to theirs as they undress for bed at night. The two eldest Boissevain children, sons Jan Karel and Gideon, are three and two years older than Leo, respectively. It is not long since they have left school and found jobs. Jan Karel once wrote in a school exercise book: 'Every human life is a brick in the building. At the apex stands Christ. He gives each person a brick and some cement. The cement is the deeds, words and thoughts of this person'.

***

In December 1938, forewarned by the dire events of Kristallnacht, parents Emil and Betty Fryda accompanied their two children Hans, aged eleven, and his seventeen-year-old sister Anneliese on a journey of around one hundred kilometres from their home town of Wattenscheid in Germany to the Dutch border. Once there, father and mother watched and waited to be sure that their children had safely crossed the border into the Netherlands, to seek sanctuary as Jewish refugees. Plans for the parents' own escape would wait. Brother and sister would thereafter be separated due to the gap in their ages; Hans was amongst a first group of forty-five refugee children to arrive at children's holiday residence 'Rivierenhuis De Steeg' near Arnhem on 13 December. Here the children were placed in the care of eight nuns – the 'Frauleins' - all of whom spoke excellent German and provided genuine hospitality. There was enough food to eat (although not kosher), but the weather was cold and the children shivered at night with insufficient blankets: the water in a glass placed on a window sill was frozen by morning.

For financial reasons, the Dutch government decided to close down centres like *Rivierenhuis* for German Jewish refugees and a date was set for all such children to leave – 19 April 1939 – just four months after their arrival, and with few options open for Hans's next port in the growing storm. Anneliese, still only eighteen, had meanwhile married her even younger childhood sweetheart Mauritz Poppers, and was relatively secure living in The Hague. Emil and Betty Fryda had come across Professor Herman Frijda's name in a Dutch newspaper and, because of their shared family name, decided to seek his help for their son Hans. He agrees to do so, perhaps reflecting that Hans is the same age as his own youngest son Nico. By letter to the Refugee Section of the Ministry of Home Affairs dated 5 April 1939 Professor Frijda asks permission for Hans to be placed with a willing carer in Amsterdam; he undertakes full financial responsibility for Hans's care, and discloses as evidence of his ability to afford such expense an income of 10,744 guilders and capital of 101,000 guilders, as included in his 38/39 tax returns. The government bureaucratically dithers about the suitability of the first family willing to offer Hans a home: the mother is a divorcee, provides a room to a single male divorcee as a paying guest, and, more disreputable still, is actively involved with left-wing causes, including assistance to former Dutch 'International Brigade' members returned from Spain. In the meantime, *Rivierenhuis* is closed and Hans placed in Amsterdam's municipal orphanage whilst the search continues. The second home offered to Hans is deemed suitable by the Government for the boy's release into the community, and so after two months in the orphanage he moves into the home of Elie Asscher on Amsterdam's Van Breestraat, an elegant four-storey town house near the Vondel Park, the costs of such care underwritten by Professor Frijda via the Committee for Special Jewish Affairs. The government letter confirming such arrangement, copies of which are so efficiently and scrupulously sent to the Children's Committee, the head of the management board of the orphanage, the chief of police for the area in which the orphanage is located, the chief of police for the area in which Hans will be housed, and the inspector of the population register office, will provide a typically lavish paper trail come the German occupation. The outcome is indeed bleak. Hans and Anneliese will eventually be captured and detained in Camp Westerbork, from where on 8 February 1944 they will be transported by train to Poland and murdered in Auschwitz on 30 June. The same fate will befall Mauritz, the young husband of Anneliese. And in the same year, the parents of Hans, Anneliese and Mauritz will also meet the same dreadful end.

***

Leo decides on a matter of principle to leave his scout troop. He has been reading and is beguiled by the consciousness-awakening maxims of Marx and Engels's Communist Manifesto: 'Let the ruling classes tremble at a Communist revolution. The proletarians have nothing to lose but their chains. They have a world to win. Working men of all countries unite!'. Leo has found new camaraderie with young activists whose political convictions, he explained to his scout master, 'were too much at odds with the scouting movement'. He would later regret the manner of his leaving, but for the present 'With his youthful enthusiasm he threw himself completely into his newly-discovered political consciousness and forgot the important values of the Scout Association'. It is not surprising that Leo would have been attracted by this new camaraderie: his tireless energy with scouting pet projects would mirror the same energy he devoted to extracurricular school activities, but in each environment he participated as a somewhat shy outsider, and perhaps his isolation sometimes hurt. A female student, Hanny Michaelis, recalls the boy with whom she had spent years at school, whom she had mocked to his face and belittled as 'little Leo' and 'the little monkey'. Leo would have felt a much closer bond, cemented by seriousness of purpose and high ideals, with those with a passion for revolutionary politics. Nor was it unusual that someone like Leo should be attracted to communist theory. It was capitalism - the enemy of the proletariat - that the young disciples of Marx and Lenin blamed for the years of economic depression and for stigmatising the hungry unemployed as a work-shy burden; it was the communist International Brigades that had lit their imaginations with their fabled, heroically-failed war against the black-shirted fascists in Spain; and it was the battle cry of youth and progress as voiced in the Communist Manifesto – a work that Isaiah Berlin described as 'a great revolutionary hymn' - that they rallied behind. Most importantly, they believed it was the Soviet Union that would be the most likely to stand up to, and defeat, Hitler's demented racism – at least until the severe testing of their blind faith by the Molotov-Ribbentrop non-aggression pact of 23 August 1939, in which these two powers secretly carved up Eastern Europe between themselves, a relationship that they would further cement by a trade alliance in February 1940. The Dutch Communist Party had some explaining to do: its newspaper *Het Volksdagblad* tried its best, by boasting of 'a victory for the Soviet Union's policy of peace' and 'a blow against Nazi Germany's politics of war'. On the street, recalls Maurice Ferares, one party member would explain it to another with a conspiratorial nod and wink: 'Tactics, comrade'.

***

The start of the new school term coincides with Germany's invasion of Poland, the bombing of four Polish cities, and the declaration of war against Germany by Great Britain and France. The Dutch newspapers reiterate in ever more desperate headlines and in mounting type size that the Netherlands will remain steadfastly neutral. Leo receives an official card through the post signed on behalf of the mayor of Amsterdam; it requires his early attendance at the police station in Amsterdam's Leidseplein to sign up to the local section of the LBD, a nationwide air-raid defence force; an organization largely comprising volunteers established within the framework of the country's general mobilization. Meanwhile, classicist Dr Hondius has been offered the headship of a grammar school in The Hague, and so his son Theo will leave his studies at Vossius gymnasium and his life in Amsterdam, and sit his final year at a new school in a different city before going on to university. The Vossius school newspaper *Vulpes* loses the writing talents of Theo, but gains the galvanising writing and editorial skills of Leo.

At cinemas throughout the Netherlands the emotions of many filmgoers, especially the younger generation, are stirred by the internationally lauded British film 'Goodbye, Mr Chips'. The title character, a beloved, dying schoolmaster, overhears on his death bed the melancholy conversation of friends who express sadness that their colleague had never had children of his own. He responds: 'I thought you said it was a pity, a pity I never had any children. But you're wrong. I have! Thousands of 'em, thousands of 'em...' This film causes Leo to reflect on life at his own school and, perhaps, also on his life at home – on parents and on those *in loco parentis* - and he expresses his thoughts in a short article in the November edition of *Vulpes*:

Mr Chips and the Dutch School Spirit

by L.H. Frijda

In response to the film 'Goodbye, Mr Chips' we are confronted with the following question: What are the factors that prevent the spirit that lives in British schools from also thriving in Dutch schools? I understand, of course, that it is significant factor that such schools are boarding schools. However, why is it not possible for the relationships amongst the pupils themselves, and between the pupils and the teachers, that we see so powerfully explored in that film, to exist in the Netherlands?

One might have been pointed out to Leo that relatively few British children attended boarding schools, or had the good fortune to be taught by someone with the fatherly care of an idealized and idolized Mr Chipping. One might also have reflected that families that could afford to send their children to boarding schools were not those likely to have a well-thumbed copy of the Communist Manifesto on their book shelves. Nevertheless, Leo's concerns are clear: against the background bellow of air-raid drills at home, warring ideologies across Europe, and the fading hope that the Netherlands could retain for long its 'neutral observer' status, there is a lack of *esprit de corps* amongst fellow pupils at school, and not much in the way of wise reassurance from their teachers that is able to lift spirits for the troubled times ahead. Leo had a point. History teacher Dr Presser describes reading the announcement in the evening paper of the death in March 1937 of Dutch poet and literary historian Albert Verwey, a great national figure credited with the revival of the Dutch literary scene in the 1880s. Presser persuaded headmaster Bruyn that Verwey's cultural legacy should be appropriately recognized, a legacy and loss of such significance – he felt - that it should unite the whole school in an act of remembrance. The response was immediate: the very next morning, pupils of all years and all the teaching staff assembled in the hall to hear a 'magnificent' eulogy from literature teacher Binnendijk – a eulogy that Presser recalls simply bowled him over. But what about when war erupted in Europe in September 1939 – was there the same urgency to bring the school together in some kind of collective contemplation of *this* grave turn of events? What words were said in the school hall when on 9 September 1939 the Dutch minesweeper *Willem van Ewijck* hit a mine and 30 of its 51-man crew perished – honoured by newspaper *De Nieuwe Rotterdamsche Courant* as 'the first Dutch victims of this war'? And although one might read into Leo's article nothing more than the plaintive gripe of an introverted, insecure young man feeling isolated at home due to his father's fixation on work and the atmosphere on the sidelines of his parents' embattled relationship, he did indeed strike a chord with many readers: the debate continued in the December 1939 edition of *Vulpes*, albeit that the conclusion shared by the contributors seems to have been recognition and resignation that the Dutch system was what it was.

The Dutch school system tries to prepare its pupils for higher education or for a job in society; and it therefore attempts to impart as much knowledge to the pupil as possible. By contrast, the British school system endeavours to prepare its pupils for life, by teaching them manners, etiquette, etc.

Where can etiquette be better learned that in sport? There is not a school in Britain that doesn't have its own, often wide, expanse of playing fields, tennis courts, and even swimming pool. And the tasks of the teacher in Britain also extend to sport, although one shouldn't think that the teacher is only involved in sport because it is their job to be so. On the contrary, the teacher in Britain has a sense of the sporting honour of the school, as does the pupil, and will therefore train school teams much more than a teacher here in the Netherlands would do. A cricket match is as tense and exciting for the teacher as it is for the pupils. It should go without saying that this contributes greatly to the understanding between the pupils and their teachers.

However, this spirit is further encouraged by something that in other countries is generally disparaged, namely the school uniform.

This uniform, worn in the past to distinguish the rich from the poor, encourages the wearers to identify themselves with their school, especially since it is also worn outside school. In this way life outside school is still to some extent governed by the school spirit, whereas in the Netherlands it is conversely home life that has much more influence over school life.

In my opinion it is these major distinctions between Dutch and British schools that make it impossible for us to adopt the school spirit that exists in Britain.

And in March 1940 the debate advanced further:

It may be true that in British schools the pupils are not fed enough knowledge, but a lot of attention is instead focused on character forming: great value is attached to nurturing and strengthening a community spirit...

The 'hall' (our 'aula'), which is still regarded in our system as a luxury, is the focal point of a British school. It is here that teachers and pupils come together and the teachers address the school on current affairs...

From all this it is apparent that the British school is not just a place of education with the sole purpose of imparting knowledge, but a place for nurturing in the widest sense of the word, and a place that plays a much bigger role in general life than our schools.

In April 1940, Leo, now editor-in-chief of *Vulpes*, interviews Hildo Krop, the sculptor of a new statue of Rotterdam-born Erasmus, renaissance theologian and social critic, to be placed at the entrance to the school. In recognition of the second anniversary of the school magazine, a prize competition is set:

'Explain the connection that exists between Erasmus and the gymnasium, and refer in this context to the nature of the education provided by a gymnasium and its exclusivity.'

Tip: We are not interested in the year in which Erasmus was born, nor in the year in which he died. The intention is that you should relate what you know about Erasmus to the gymnasium (why is his statue at the entrance to our school?) and offer your own interpretation of the purpose and nature of the education provided by a gymnasium.

The jury shall consist of Dr J.C. Bruyn, Dr J. Presser, and Dr J. van Liempt.

Was this competition perhaps a means to focus the question of education as debated in the pages of the school magazine back upon that which Dutch grammar schools did well – scholarship and learning – whilst avoiding the unfavourable comparisons with what the British public school system claimed to do best – preparing its pupils more holistically for the world outside? One wonders, given events happening over its border, whether any competition entry dared to reflect on the observation by Erasmus that 'He who allows oppression shares the crime.'

***

In April 1940 the Dutch government declared a state of siege after the foreign correspondent for *The New York Times*, Vladimir Poliakov (writing under the pen name Augur), spread the fake news that the followers of Dutch Nazi leader Mussert were preparing to kidnap Queen Wilhelmina as part of a coup. The spring weather was beautiful, and the holiday resorts along the Dutch coast were packed with those seeking to forget the political turmoil through the heady mix of sun, sea and sand. The early days of May 1940 may have 'breathed sunshine', according to the local newspaper of seaside town Zandvoort, but there were tensions there, too, beneath the surface. Zandvoort was pro-German. There were many German tourists who occupied the local hotels and lounged in the beach chairs, and many German girls who worked in the hotels and married local Dutch boys. In the 1935 municipal elections a bigger proportion of the town's electorate had voted for the Dutch Nazi party than any other municipality bar one. But there was also a sizeable Jewish enclave in Zandvoort, and there was a synagogue. The fascist, pro-German residents complained of the 'hordes' of Jews in the town they labelled the 'Jewish aquarium'.

On 10 May 1940, the day that Germany launched its invasion of the Netherlands, the panicked journey by car of Professor Frijda and his family to the port of IJmuiden to board any ship headed for England proved futile. They drove back to their home on Corelli Street, to confront their future in a country no longer their own. The Queen issued a proclamation that same day promising that she and her government 'would do their duty', and she urged the same of her people: 'everywhere, and in all circumstances', and with the 'greatest of vigilance and with the inner calm and dedication that results from a clear conscience'. Three days later, with she and her government having favoured sanctuary in a friendly country over surrender to a hostile occupying force, the Queen issued a further proclamation from London via the BBC: 'Where the usurper is in control, local civil government must continue to do everything in the interests of the people and in the first place to cooperate in order to maintain calm and good order'. She ended with the plea: 'Do everything possible in the nation's clear interests'. Was this a clear instruction or a mixed message? Was the Queen advising her subjects to keep calm and carry on, and all those in public office to carry out their duties under the instructions of an invading force? On 20 May Prime Minister De Geer also spoke to the Dutch people by radio from London, asserting the duty of the administrative bodies – local government, the policy, judiciary, public records offices – 'to cooperate with the German authorities and thereby assist the population as much as possible'. Perhaps, despite years of evidence of tyranny from across their border, and the droves of German Jewish refugees that actually crossed that border in fear of their lives, the Queen and her government really did believe that this administrative collaboration with the enemy would be the best way to ensure victory in the long-run, with as little loss of Dutch blood in the meantime. For neighbours Professor Frijda and Mies Boissevain, the assistance they and their families had provided to Jewish refugees from Nazi Germany for the last eight years would now continue as acts of resistance, and therefore be punishable with the utmost severity. They had every reason to be fearful.

Within the first two months of the occupation Leo, having returned to class 5B of the Vossius gymnasium, must sit his school exams. The circumstances could not be more stressful. His mother has now left home. His parents had virtually separated at the start of the year and divorce papers filed. Dora Frijda would have such problems with her mental health that she could no longer provide proper care and support for her three children – Leo, Jetteke and Nico – who therefore remained with their father in the family home on Corelli Street. Indeed, she would leave Amsterdam altogether and find lodgings in Utrecht where, for a full year, she could receive expert treatment for a neurotic disorder under internationally-renowned professor of psychiatry at Utrecht University, Dr Henricus Rümke. And so, in July 1940, Leo, who had acted in a school play, plays violin in the school orchestra, plays school hockey with the hockey stick given him by his Uncle Leonard, and writes and edits the school magazine, takes his end-of-year exams. What else could he do? Fears of an uncertain future could be shut out by searching for a certainty and normality in the present. Maurice Ferares, a Dutch Jew of Leo's age and similar political persuasion, a student of the violin at the city's conservatoire, wrote: 'It is hard to imagine that we simply refused to think about our future. It never occurred to me to consider whether it made any sense to continue studying the violin. It just went without saying'. But Leo fails his exams. Apart from a high score of 8 in history, all other subjects are marked a rather mediocre 5 or 6, and in physics a 4. The consequences would be dramatic. There was no chance of re-sitting failed exams, or of re-sitting the entire academic year. He would have to leave the Vossius gymnasium, without the school examination results to qualify him for university entrance: that much of his future, at least, would appear to be certain.

VIII

The Temple and the Cross

Creating – that is the great salvation from suffering, and life's alleviation. But for the creator to appear, suffering itself is needed, and much transformation.

Friedrich Nietzsche: 'Thus Spoke Zarathustra'

In September 1923, the year in which Leo was born, his literary hero Hendrik Marsman published at his own expense, and in a print run of just one hundred copies, a collection of thirty poems that his young generation of fans would come to revere as 'the little red book'.

Marsman sought to write in free verse, in expressionistic style, with a rhythm that reflected modern life. Clarity was also important. 'A poet', he wrote, must be someone who 'speaks infinite tenderness with a crystal-clear voice'. He was discovering this individual voice even as he adopted some of the tenets of a movement in poetry known as 'vitalism' – a desire to experience life as intensely as possible, to the extent of 'living dangerously'. Unsurprisingly, perhaps, this was coupled with an intense fear of death: the more one fights, in Thoreau's words, to 'suck out all the marrow of life', the more one has a sense of the finite time we are allocated on this earth, and a dread of what awaits us beyond. 'Vitalism' was also a protest against society; a philosophy absorbed especially by those who felt pinned down by all the norms, rules and regulations of society. Both these elements – an awareness and fear of death, and a refusal to 'toe the line' – would resonate with Leo.

However, by 1934, Marsman had already rejected vitalism as a part of an earlier life that he had outgrown: 'I am now aged 35 and [...] still I have the feeling that only now is my life beginning. I hope that I have a long life ahead of me, for my work too.' He made trips around the lands, the sites of ancient civilisations, that circled the Mediterranean Sea and there he discovered the warmth and intensity of the life that he had been struggling to find.

Marsman had been somewhat reluctantly coerced into joining sides with his friend - writer, literary critic and Leo's school teacher – Dirk Binnendijk, in the debate within Dutch literary circles that endured between the two world wars; a debate that poet J.C. Bloem characterised as a rather binary choice between what he called 'form' (creativity, the ability of a poem to stand alone, 'art for art's sake') and 'fellow' (the poet, the person behind the work, their ideas and influences). An earlier standard-bearer on the side of 'form', Edgar Allen Poe, had written around one hundred years previously: '...under the sun there neither exists nor can exist any work more thoroughly dignified, more supremely noble, than this very poem, this poem per se, this poem which is a poem and nothing more, this poem written solely for the poem's sake.'

Thus, Marsman appeared to side with those who championed 'form'. Insofar as this somewhat re-hashed debate would put the role of the poet and of poetry in society – indeed the value and very purpose of arts in society - under a spotlight, it could be valued as a timely and valuable introspection in the light of political developments in neighbouring countries. Insofar as it focused too closely on this unsophisticated binary choice, however, it rather missed the point - as Marsman, who had read and translated the work of Friedrich Nietzsche, perhaps already understood: in his work 'Twilight of the Idols' Nietzsche described 'art for art's sake' as 'a worm chewing its own tail'. He claimed that no such thing existed: 'A psychologist [...] asks: what does all art do? Does it not praise? glorify? select? highlight? By doing all this it *strengthens* or *weakens* certain valuations [...]. Art is the great stimulus to life: how could one understand it as purposeless, as aimless, as *'l'art pour l'art?'*

On one aspect of this debate various past and present voices within Dutch literary circles and abroad were united: the need for poetry to be clear to the reader. Marsman's call for a 'crystal-clear voice' was echoed by Binnendijk: 'Muddled writing is muddled thinking'. Nietzsche wrote that an artist should be a 'genius of communication'. George Sand held that a true artist had a 'duty to find an adequate expression to convey [their art] to as many souls as possible'.

***

Hendrik Marsman drowned at sea on 21 June 1940, aged forty. He and his wife were passengers on the S.S. Bérénice, a ship that sailed from Bordeaux in German-occupied France towards a safe harbour in Great Britain. On reaching the English Channel the ship was torpedoed by a German U-Boat which – in pursuit of another vessel – had lost track of its intended prey under a blanket of early morning fog. Marsman's wife survived; wearing a life jacket, she had been on deck about to take breakfast at the moment the explosion threw her overboard and away from the burning wreck. Her husband, she recounts, 'Couldn't hold on' for the rescue ship to arrive, and his body was never recovered.

The S.S. Bérénice would not have been torpedoed were it not for mistaken identity: are then the twists and turns of life, even the time and manner of one's death, 'merely' a matter of chance – a throw of the dice? In a literary example of even more outrageous fortune Jean-Paul Sartre recounts in his short story *'The Wall'* – set during the Spanish Civil War and only recently published - how a captured Pablo, enduring interrogation to disclose the whereabouts of his still-at-large comrade Ramon Gris, suggests a location where he is absolutely certain Ramon will not be found: *'I consented to die in his place; his life had no more value than mine; no life had value. They were going to slap a man up against a wall and shoot at him till he died, whether it was I or Gris or somebody else made no difference.'* However, prankster fate intervenes to place Ramon at that very location where he ought not to have been - hiding out in a cemetery – and enemy soldiers are able to encircle and entrap their hapless prey. Ramon is duly executed. Pablo's life is spared; and when he learns of the reason he 'laughs so hard that he cries'. Leo would read this story and publish his translation in the underground literary magazine he would work on with his friend Theo Hondius.

Then again, far from being a sardonically played game of chance, life may be predetermined, it's destination and route carefully plotted on nautical charts with divider and sextant. Early in his literary career Marsman himself had written no fewer than six poems about the sea, linking water, or a journey by water, to death. It is possible to find evidence here of the poet predicting the manner of his own death. In one such poem - *'The Crossing'* - Marsman identifies himself as a frightened passenger on a 'black and lonely boat':

> *'I wept for the bright land,*
> *that slipped below the horizon*
> *and I wept for the dark land,*
> *that soon on the skyline appeared.'*

In the final stanza of another verse - 'Sinking Ship' – there could not be a more direct premonition of drowning:

> *'a sinking ship*
> *a chilling moon*
> *two voices rising from the reef:*

oh, save us, we are doomed.'

***

'He knew that he would never survive the war', recalls Rita Klijzing of a conversation she had with Leo, 'because he said to me: 'Will you come to my funeral?''.

***

'The Temple and the Cross' – Marsman's final collection of fifty poems published shortly before his death, a summation of his life's experiences - explores parallels between the personal struggle of the poet and the struggles confronting western civilisation in 1930s Europe. The temple represents the pagan, polytheist beliefs of ancient civilisations, whilst the cross represents two thousand years of Christian belief. The poems pit chaos against order, fear against hope. A ship that ventures over uncertain seas in search of land and safe moorings. A journey across an almost mythical Mediterranean Sea from the temporal to the eternal. Here along its shores the Classical, the Christian, and the modern worlds meet. In the last poem of the cycle, entitled 'The Sea', Marsman brings together the western world's ancient beliefs, and its three great modern religions, in which the temple is now the Jewish temple:

> *Riding the night waves the Dionysian ship*
> *roaming from Hercules' Pillars to the Hellespont*
> *from Damascus to Etna's mount,*
> *from whence sprung the fountain zenith-high*
> *spewing its rainbows towards the shores,*
> *to the mosque and temple, and to the cross.*

In an earlier poem in the cycle, Marsman fears the ability of the poet to lead an autonomous existence: instead he is forced to lead a life determined by the prevailing culture. In the last stanza of 'The Sea', almost in the poet's dying breath, there is, however, hope: *'As long as the European world survives / and bleeding, dreams its reckless dream / [...] the lights of the creative spirit will drift above this sea.'*

There is hope as long as European civilisation survives.

'The Temple and the Cross' was one of the last great works of Dutch literature to be published before the outbreak of war in the Netherlands. It was also one of the last works to be critically reviewed in the Dutch newspapers a few days before the German invasion effectively censored the newspapers and the arts. The following review appeared in the *Nieuwe Rotterdamsche Courant* on 4 May 1940:

Culture as a source of inspiration

H. Marsman – 'The Temple and the Cross'

Marsman's now collection of poems, one of the most striking examples of self-renewal I know of in our literature, in its entirety and in its more obvious meaning, cannot be better characterized than as homage to a dying culture...

The theme of 'The Temple and the Cross', as the title would suggest, is Classical-Christian culture in which here 'eternity' is professed. A philosophy that cannot otherwise be expressed without the aid of a body of concepts has here been transformed into poetry by the simplest means; a poetry that extends strong roots towards a European philosophy of life (Nietzsche's influence is detectable here: the significance of 'eternity' – death and eternal recurrence – self-deification) but whose personal character is fully assured, thanks to both the autobiographical episodes and the direct tone of despair, assertiveness, or ecstasy.'

IX

The First Drops of Rain

Each act, each occasion, is worse than the last, but only a little worse. You wait for the next and the next. You wait for one great shocking occasion, thinking that others, when such a shock comes, will join with you in resisting somehow.

Milton Mayer: 'They Thought They Were Free'

In summer 1940 the two eldest Boissevain children, Jan Karel and Gideon ('Janka' and 'Gid'), formulate a daring plan to escape by boat to England, from where they would join forces to fight for the liberation of their country. They construct a makeshift vessel from two wooden vermouth casks, one for each of them, complete with mast, a place for food supplies, ballast, a firework for use as an emergency flare, and two square peep-holes. With the surreptitious help of the municipal cleansing service they are able to transport the vessel – named *Diogenes* (self-proclaimed 'citizen of the world') - from its dry dock in the basement of the family home to a quayside from where, despite its conspicuous appearance, the boys succeed in navigating the craft through locks on the outskirts of Amsterdam into open water. Their aim is to sail a passage between the Wadden Islands before heading out to open sea. However, the wind changes and they are stranded on a sand bank near one of the islands, a prohibited area. An English pilot spots them from above and believing them to be in danger, seemingly adrift on choppy waters, reports the sighting to the Director of the North and South Holland Coastguards - someone happily known by the two boys as 'Uncle Tom' and possessing the authority to ensure they are kept out of trouble. So, with a convincing charade of having ventured out on nothing more than a drunken, laddish escapade, Jan Karel and Gideon are 'rescued', avoid arrest, and return home safe.

'Home' behind the large, all-seeing windows of 6 Corelli Street is a happy place. 'There was a lot of laughter', recalls younger brother Frans, 'even though we were brought up in an extremely sober manner. Father was a deacon of the Mennonite church and made a note in a pocket book of the exact amount of every item of expenditure. We never had sweets at home. If we ever ate cake or bought sweets, then we were asked 'How could you get such foolish ideas?' It was a real treat to be given an ice cream.' Jan Karel, who survived on one kidney, and had spent a lot of his childhood bed-ridden, physically weak and often in pain, had found work with the telephone service after leaving school. At home, with a love of astronomy, impressive engineering skills and a spirit of determination, he had set himself the task of designing his own precision instruments for star-gazing. With the outbreak of war, however, the enticing space of the 12 metre-long basement to the family home becomes his workshop. He and Gideon will also construct a false wall and secret hiding places to store large quantities of TNT and nitro-glycerine for the manufacture of time bombs, together with the weapons they have retrieved from the ditches and dykes in which they had been secreted by the Dutch army before capitulation. Over the next two years large numbers of telephones, connection boxes, and timers from lampposts would unaccountably disappear from various buildings and streets of Amsterdam, and find their way into this workshop, to be ingeniously recycled by Jan Karel into the tools of sabotage. Not only this basement, but the entire house, is full of telephones and radio sets, and in virtually every room, thanks to some expert, rather surreal tweaking, one can listen to the BBC broadcasts of *Radio Oranje* on the telephone, and listen in to telephone calls via the radio.

***

The house across the street, the home of Leo and his family, is not such a happy place. Now without his wife Dora at home and divorce proceedings filed in court, Professor Frijda must struggle to combine his academic work and his concern for the increasingly precarious position of Jewish people in the Netherlands with attempts at more interactive parenting of his children. There is, at least, a housekeeper to do the cooking and cleaning - whose pretty young daughter catches Leo's roving eye. The first priority this summer is to find some way for Leo to be able to continue in education, despite failing his end-of-year exams. Professor Frijda urgently consults with the head of the Vossius gymnasium, Dr Bruyn, and together they decide to approach the head of the Amsterdam Lyceum and its founder, Dr C.P. Gunning, with the question whether he would accept Leo into his school as a final-year pupil. Drs Bruyn and Gunning speak by phone on 17 July and agree that Leo be provisionally accepted. Dr Gunning receives a visit from Leo the following day and notes how young he is compared to the average age of year-six pupils – not even seventeen until August! He notes that Leo is bright – but lazy; a poor list of exam results. Arrangements are made for him to have remedial lessons during the summer holidays in areas where he is weak: biology and chemistry. On 17 July Professor Frijda writes to Dr Gunning:

Dear Sir,

I enclose the form to register my son Leo as a student in class VI of the Amsterdam Lyceum.

As you know, I was grateful for the opportunity to speak in advance with Dr Bruyn. I am pleased to say that there are no objections on his part to the transfer of my son to the Lyceum. Dr Bruyn will confirm this to you himself.

If I am not mistaken, I may now telephone Dr Kettner in order to determine what work my son will need to prepare for biology classes.

I look forward to your response.

With the greatest of respect,

H. Frijda

On 18 July Dr Gunning replies as follows:

Dear Professor Frijda,

Mr Kettner has just informed me that your son Leo is rather a long way behind in a number of subjects. He will certainly need to have lessons in these subjects during the summer, namely in analytical geometry, solid geometry, and biology. I think it best that he does this under the guidance of Mr Onland (I gave his address details, etc. to Leo). I look forward to welcoming Leo to our school on Wednesday 28 August at 9.00 a.m. I confirm that I am prepared to accept Leo into our class VI on a provisional basis. We will afford him the opportunity up to 1 December to catch up in areas where he is behind. In any event it will be necessary for him to have two lessons a week in chemistry with Dr Van Den Broek after 1 September – I trust that you can agree to this. If by 1 December Leo has reached the required level, then he may remain a student with us and take the school exams. I sincerely hope that this will be the case.

I enclose the documents for the definitive registration of your son at our school.

With the greatest of respect,

[...]

On 14 October 1940 Leo's teachers at the Amsterdam Lyceum write a report on his first six weeks at the school. It concludes:

This report covers only a short period, and therefore we have little information at our disposal. From the above comments, however, it is clear that we are not at the present time dissatisfied. Nevertheless there are a number of subjects in which Leo is weak. He will therefore need to knuckle down and work with care and determination across the board if he wishes to get a good report in November. We trust that he will do so.

***

Arthur Seyss-Inquart, Austrian Nazi leader who had played such a significant role in the German annexation of Austria, and then acted as deputy to Hans Frank in the General Government of Poland, had been appointed Reichskommissar for the Occupied Netherlands in May 1940. Responsible for directing the civil administration, with creating close economic collaboration with Germany and with defending the interests of the Reich, his broadcast address to the Dutch people sought to assure them that the German presence in the Netherlands served as a 'protective' force intended to guarantee the country's continued 'neutrality'. He promised them that Dutch newspapers and radio stations could remain independent and uncensored, provided that they were not anti-German in their reporting of news - something, surely, of an oxymoron. The choice for a civilian government of the Netherlands had been Hitler's: on largely ideological grounds he considered that the Dutch were a 'racially related kindred-people' and therefore had to be 'won over' to national socialism. The government of Seyss-Inquart would cast doubt, however, on how much emphasis the occupying force truly placed on winning the hearts and minds of the Dutch people. At his trial in Nuremberg after the war, Seyss-Inquart would sneer at the provisions of the 1907 Hague Convention that safeguarded civilian rights in wartime as 'obsolete' and confirm that his task in the Netherlands had been to 'annihilate' all opponents. And whilst he certainly avoided the language of terror in 1940, he was sincere in his belief that the Jews were the enemies of the Reich with whom 'no armistice or peace could be reached'. And so, the process of Nazification of the Netherlands began immediately, assisted by the civil servants, police and judiciary whom both the Queen and her Prime Minister in London had asked to remain in their places to carry out their tasks as instructed.

Leo is a first victim of the sequence of anti-Semitic laws in the Netherlands that would begin like a few drops of rain and end in a monsoon. Having already been informed that Jewish members of the air-raid defence force need not report for further duty, its members were then asked to sign a form indicating whether or not they were Jewish – a status defined by German law as requiring at least three Jewish grandparents. This was the first group of people required to sign the 'Aryan Declaration', and the vast majority complied; innocently and truthfully, and ultimately with fatal consequences. In July, their declarations having been processed, those who were Jewish – including Leo - received formal notification of their exclusion.

Other anti-Jewish measures would soon follow. Later that summer, masquerading as an 'animal-friendly' law, the ritual slaughter of animals is banned in the Netherlands, a clear attack on the dietary rules of religious Jews. This is followed by a ban on any further recruitment of Jewish people within the civil service, or the promotion of any Jewish person already so employed. There is a ban on all Jewish newspapers, with the exception of the Jewish Weekly News (*Het Joodsche Weekblad*) which claims: 'It is our intention to fill in the gaps left by the many Jewish associations and institutions that have ceased to carry out their work'. In the meantime, an SS unit has been billeted in the casino of the tourist resort of Zandvoort and in the early hours of 5 August 1940 the town's synagogue is blown up: witnesses from nearby homes hear two explosions and the rattling of their own furniture from shock waves. The 'investigation' into the attack proves, of course, futile and the perpetrators are never identified – either from amongst the local membership of the Dutch Nazi party or the members of the locally billeted, death's head adorned SS unit. It is a reminder of the wanton destruction of Kristallnacht.

On 5 October 1940 Professor Herman Frijda, as a university teacher – a public servant - is required to sign the Aryan Declaration. On 4 November he receives notice that all Jews employed by the government will be suspended from work with effect from 21 November. This suspension would quickly translate into dismissal. It is therefore perhaps not surprising that when on 23 November he receives the good news from the headmaster of the Amsterdam Lyceum of the decision approved by a meeting of the teachers to admit Leo as a full member of the school – expressing the confidence that 'all will be well that ends well' – it takes him a week to reply:

Amsterdam, 30 November 1940

Dear Mr Gunning,

It is due to current circumstances that I have not written sooner to thank you for your letter of 23 instant, in which you inform me that Leo will be permitted to remain in the sixth-year class as a full member of the school. Naturally, I am very glad to receive this news. I am especially pleased that my son feels so happy in your school, which is clearly making such a very positive influence upon his character.

I am convinced – especially given the current climate - that my son will continue to do his very best and that he will not shame the trust placed in him by your school.

Yours most respectfully,

H. Frijda

***

There were no colleagues of Professor Frijda to protest on his behalf at Amsterdam University. There was more resistance, however, at Leiden University, the oldest university in the Netherlands, symbolically born of the nation's liberation from Spanish occupation under William of Orange. It is here in Leiden where Professor Frijda had first studied and then taught at the start of his career. On 26 November, Professor Rudolf Cleveringa, Dean of the Law Faculty, turned up at the appointed time to lecture in the Great Auditorium in place of his revered mentor, Professor Eduard Meijers, dismissed from his post under the same circumstances as Herman Frijda and all other Jewish teachers.

The doors to the auditorium were held wide open so that students who spilled out onto the corridor could hear his address. Cleveringa had already packed a suitcase, anticipating arrest, but he had also drafted a carefully worded speech, highly charged in its delivery precisely because of its apparently measured but barely submerged undertone of contempt, yet on paper worded in a way that legal minds could perhaps argue offered some points of mitigation against imposition of the harshest penalties. Cleveringa gave, in effect, a eulogy for Meijers; as for the strength of his own feelings, he referred to them in no uncertain terms only to brush them to one side, a smart rhetorical sleight of hand:

'It is this Dutchman, this true and noble son of our people, this man, this father to his students, this scholar whom the usurpers that now rule over us 'relieve of his position'! I told you that I would not speak of my feelings. I will keep to my word, even though such feelings threaten to burst like molten lava through all the fissures that at moments in time I feel could crack open my head and my heart'.

It was a magnificent performance. Later that day and all through the night a band of students, stiffened in resolve through supplies of beer, worked hard to type up around fifty copies of the speech for distribution amongst the nation's universities, each of these to be copied again in their hundreds for distribution by underground resistance movements. There were no similar orations at other universities by other professors to copy and distribute; this one document, splendidly isolated, was to speak for all

Dutch academia. The next day Cleveringa was arrested and Leiden students promptly went on strike: in no-nonsense retaliation, the Germans simply shut the university down. Whilst having quietly fumed at Nazi injustice and total disregard for the rule of law, Cleveringa had also cautioned against reckless action in response: 'We have no other option - without resorting to futile foolishness, against which I must urge you most strongly - than to bow before the force of circumstances'. Was his message to 'resist' at the level of remaining true to one's beliefs but to all outward appearances submit meekly to the usurpers? Or had he surreptitiously, through his carefully-controlled rage and references to the 'unspoken understanding' that had crackled like electricity between himself and his audience, urged a more active resistance? Hetty Cohen-Koster, a Jewish law student, attended that lecture and wrote much later of 'the enormous impetus this gave people to carry out *real* acts of resistance. It was this, as well as other sources, that led to the stencils and underground newspapers, to falsifying identity documents, searching for hiding places, stealing ration cards, acting as secret couriers, to all that hidden work that would eventually save my life and the lives of so many others'.

***

Notwithstanding the non-aggression pact between Germany and the Soviet Union, the Dutch Communist Party, banned by the Nazi occupying forces in July 1940, continued as an illegal organization and actively engaged against the regime. Its underground newspaper *De Waarheid* (The Truth) – 'published intermittently' - first appeared on 23 November 1940, and on its front page:

The Road to Peace and Freedom

We now find ourselves in the middle of the most terrible and wide-scale slaughter of peoples that the world has ever known…

The Netherlands must become a free, independent, and socialist state, governed by and for the workers – those employed in the factories and those on the land. What can we do under the current, difficult circumstances to chart this course?

TO BEGIN WITH, WE MUST CONTINUALLY STRENGTHEN OUR MENTAL RESISTANCE TO THE FOREIGN NAZI INFLUENCE!

No fascism in the Netherlands! None of the racial hatred or anti-Semitism used by the Nazis to poison our people! No understanding with the occupying force!

***

The pressure of circumstances at home and events outside weigh on Leo. These, combined with the need to acclimatize quickly to a new school and to focus on the class work and the passing of exams that would open his way to university, served to push him deeper inside himself. Nevertheless, his twin passions for political engagement and poetry continued to fire his imagination, and a somewhat frustrated desire to communicate his ideas. Leo was rather trapped by shyness: it is often the introvert more than the extrovert who – when they can discover their voice – have the most worth saying. Leo befriended another Jewish boy in his class, Henri Vleeschdraager. It was perhaps the fact that they were both a little introverted, remembers Henri, that drew them together. Of course, they would talk together about the pressures facing any student looking ahead to end-of-school exams. Leo would also try to talk politics, but apart from the anti-German sentiment and big pinch of patriotism, Henri could not share, or even take seriously, Leo's interest in 'Trotskyite slogans' and he would laugh off Leo's attempts at proselytizing. Poetry, however, was a different matter: 'In the field of literature he introduced me to a completely unknown world: poets and prose writers whom we never heard spoken of during Dutch literature lessons: Marsman, Slauerhof, Du Perron, Ter Braak, etc. They were rather like forbidden fruit'. Henri remembers little acts of rebellion by Leo: he once got into trouble with a teacher for writing an essay deliberately in the style of one of the new poets, an erudite kind of one-upmanship apparently frowned upon. On one occasion Henri was invited back to the Frijda family home on Corelli Street, but he did not like Professor Frijda when they met, and suspected that Leo did not like him either. Henri thought there was something arrogant about Leo's father, a chip on his shoulder, trying to compensate for his lack of height. He never visited again, and had the idea that Leo did not often invite friends home.

***

Only nine days into the new year 1941 there is a further, incremental humiliation of the Jewish population of the Netherlands who are now banned from visiting cinemas and theatres; not that there was much that a ticket to the flagship Rembrandt Theatre or indeed any other cinema would entitle you to see, other than sentimental German comedy romances glittering with torch-song brandishing stars like Zarah Leander, buttressed at either end by hard-edged German propaganda films, courtesy of the German Nazi party owned UFA. One infamous film screened at the Rembrandt Theatre was 'Süss the Jew', considered 'one of the most anti-Semitic films of all time': twenty million people flocked to see it in Germany. This small indignity would be overshadowed, however, by the following day's menacing decree that all persons with at least one

Jewish grandparent must register with the local records office: no more than twenty of those affected are claimed to have refused, compared to the 160,820 that quietly complied. Tensions erupt, sporadically, between the younger generation of Jewish men emboldened and empowered by growing anger and resentment, and the WA - the militia of the Dutch Nazi party - that seems to have no purpose other than to parade bullishly through Jewish areas, intimidating and threatening the locals, and instigating scuffles.

On 11 February, Leo, studying hard for the exam results that will be his passport to university, reads the latest proclamation that the doors of higher education have now been slammed shut to him: Jewish students are henceforth prohibited from attending university. Leo's father cannot teach at university; Leo cannot enroll to study. The very next day the area of Amsterdam inhabited by most of the city's Jews – the lively, working class area of tradesmen and dealers and market-stall holders near to where Rembrandt once lived and painted at his easel – is encircled by barbed wire fences and sentry posts, whilst bridges over canals are raised to isolate the district even more. Leo, armed with his Leica camera, visits the area and takes photos of the barbed wire and the signs all around the city, in the windows of bars and restaurants along the Nieuwe Herengracht, that proclaim: 'Jews not welcome', and 'Jews prohibited'. It was a very risky thing to do, which Leo knew perfectly well. It was something that would cause his father deep anxiety, and he knew that too. His brother Nico remembers it as 'a very headstrong, unorthodox... and risky way to behave; for a Jewish boy in particular, he was rather daring'. And when Leo came home one day with the photos, Nico recalls that 'we all practically died of shock'. The tension between father and elder son would thereafter grow insidiously.

X

Strike and Counter-strike

In the first days of February 1941, under the heading 'Mussert must go', underground communist newspaper *De Waarheid* reports on the attempts of the Dutch Nazi leader to ingratiate himself with the German occupying forces by swearing allegiance to Hitler and seeking to assure him that he had no cause to worry about the Netherlands in the event of any German offensive against Great Britain; the Germans would require the means and manpower to suppress still further any troublesome Dutch rebel elements, and Mussert was keen to lend a heavy hand in support of such a project. His assurance, claimed the article's author, would mean a yet more deadly terror against the Dutch people, and in his desire to 'fight to the death' to unite the country within the Greater German Reich, 'Mussert will not hesitate to surrender our young people to Germany...'

The thugs of Mussert's national socialist party's 'defence section' were soon flexing their muscles in the centres of Amsterdam, burned-out Rotterdam and The Hague, forcing reluctant hotel and restaurant owners to put signs in their windows stating that Jewish customers were not welcome. On 8 February there were riots in the Rembrandtplein in Amsterdam when café owners and militia exchanged blows. Café and variety theatre 'Alcazar', a venue friendly to, and often frequented by, Jewish patrons, was destroyed as the police - forbidden by law from interfering – stood at a safe distance from flying glass and the hurling of chairs through windows. It was a matter of pride for the black-shirted fascists, whose comrades-in-arms had commandeered the old Moorish palace of Alcazar during the Spanish civil war, to now lay claim to a café of the same name in Amsterdam. A few days later the riots spilled into the nearby Jewish Quarter. National-socialist newspaper *Het Vaderland* reported the fake news of the 'continuous attacks' by Jews on national socialist families living amongst them, including innocent children. Many were bruised and bloodied in the pitched battles, but the serious injury and subsequent death of one, Dutch Nazi party member Hendrik Koot, 'beaten, and literally trapped, by a thirty-strong Jewish horde' according to *Het Vaderland*, would be the excuse the Germans relied on to engineer the process that would lead to the destruction of the Jewish community in the Netherlands.

***

The immediate response to the riots was to hermetically seal off the Jewish quarter; no traffic would be allowed to enter or leave until order had been restored. All non-Jewish inhabitants were to be re-housed outside the quarter as soon as possible. Then, at 4.30 p.m. on 12 February 1941, Hans Böhmcker, the special commissar responsible for anti-Jewish measures in Amsterdam, met with the small group of prominent Jewish citizens he had summoned together, and ordered them to form a Jewish Council, tasked with facilitating communication between the German forces and the Jewish community, and with keeping good order amongst the latter. The Council were to inform and instruct the Jewish people as directed by the Germans via the pages of the *Jewish Weekly News*. Present at the meeting was diamond merchant and former President of the Dutch Jewish Congregation Abraham Asscher who, having consulted with the two rabbis present, indicated that he, together with Professor David Cohen, would assume joint chairmanship of the Jewish Council; they and the two rabbis would together nominate other members. Asscher and Cohen had headed the Committee for Special Jewish Affairs and its offshoot the Committee for Jewish Refugees set up with government support in response to the Jewish refugees fleeing Germany from 1933 onwards. Now their first task, according to an official memorandum of this meeting, was to restore law and order in the Jewish quarter and, to this end, to immediately call upon the local residents to surrender all clubs, blades and firearms to local police stations: 'It should be considered a great concession that this way of handing over the weapons was chosen instead of a police search of the Jewish quarter and punishment of those who illegally owned weapons'. Remarkably few weapons were handed in. The order was repeated in more ominous tone, with a new deadline of 21 February, but the result was no different, interpreted either as a message of defiance or the simple fact that there were few such weapons actually being hidden. The Jewish Council was then to immediately issue special identity cards to all those Jews who in future wished to enter the Jewish quarter. Most significantly, it would only be through the Jewish Council that any Dutch Jew – irrespective of status - would be able to contact any Dutch agency or official; attempts at direct contact would be rebuffed and labelled an unacceptable 'impertinence'. It was historian Lou de Jong who, assessing the role of the Jewish Council, would observe after the war that 'the path of collaboration … is a most slippery one'.

Professor Cohen and Mr Asscher may well have convinced themselves that acceptance of their chairmanship of the Jewish Council was about making the most of an impossible situation, and they may well have also convinced themselves that the best way to protect Jewish interests was to comply with all Nazi orders; nevertheless, there was one individual – Israel Voet – who, having accepted a position on the Council, was soon plagued by doubts (and, as a pretext, by ill-health) and resigned just one week later. Furthermore, there were two significant figures asked to join but who point-blank refused. The first of these was Lodewijk Visser, the recently dismissed Jewish presiding judge of the Dutch Supreme Court, who wrote to the Council's leaders: 'It is possible that in the end the occupier will achieve his aim [in relation to the Jews] but it is our duty as Dutchmen and as Jews to do everything that will prevent him from achieving that aim, and to refrain from anything that will pave the way for him'. The second such notable person to refuse was Professor Herman Frijda, who predicted that the Council would become a tool of the Germans. The minutes of the inaugural meeting of the Council on 13 February 1941 read:

The Chairman focuses especially on the order to form a committee of 15-20 Jews, which is the reason for the convening of all those present. He calls upon all those present to join [the Council].

It turns out that all, except Prof. Frijda, are ready to do this…

Visser's calm, measured, but very clear exhortation to Dutch Jews to do everything to prevent the Germans achieving their aims was diametrically opposed to the rationale underpinning the Jewish Council, whilst Herman Frijda's 'prediction' of future collaboration was no prediction at all but simply an observation of the immediate present: the Council was transparently a tool of the German occupying forces *ab initio*.

***

On 19 February the German police stormed the Koco ice-cream parlour, one of a small chain of ice-cream parlours in Amsterdam owned by German-Jewish refugees Alfred Kohn and Ernst Cahn, venues popular with Jews and non-Jews alike. The ice cream was reckoned to be the best in the city, and there were a variety of enticing flavours to choose from, including advocaat and 'Cosy' – a rich concoction of rum, raisins, chocolate, shards of nougat, and mixed fruit. As their company logo made clear, however, it was also the place to enjoy a nice hot cup of coffee. The owners were celebrated locally for their informality and charm, and regular customers would meet to discuss in a relaxed atmosphere the burning topics of the day. When war came, Kohn and Cahn knew to expect the worst and prepared accordingly; their ice-cream parlour would become a focus of aggressive anti-Jewish sentiment from the German occupiers and local Dutch Nazis alike. Together with some of their regular clients, they therefore organized a defence force, purchased flashlights and made weapons of gas pipes fitted with handle straps. Cahn procured a bespoke 50 centimetre metal gas canister filled with ammonia gas – a gas used in the process of freezing ice-cream - which he attached to a back wall of the parlour, ready and accessible. On the said date, the police raided the premises and opened fire in the direction of those inside. One account states that a stray bullet hit the gas canister, another that the canister was deliberately opened by one of the defenders of the parlour and the escaping gas directed towards the attackers before making his escape; either way, a Nazi agent sustained severe burns to the face and several police officers were injured in fights with young Jewish vigilantes.

Hanns Rauter, chief of the German SS in the Netherlands, immediately reported back to Himmler on the events of that day as well as the death five days previously of Dutch Nazi Hendrik Koot. In response, Koco's joint owners Kohn and Cahn were hunted down and arrested. Kohn was sent east and would ultimately perish in Auschwitz three years later; Cahn was first brought to prison in Amsterdam, then transferred to the prison in Scheveningen nicknamed the 'Orange Hotel' - short-stay accommodation for arrested members of the Dutch resistance awaiting execution. Cahn was tortured with the intention that he should give away the name of the person who had manufactured the metal gas canister, but he refused to speak. He was executed by firing squad on 3 March in the nearby dunes of the North Sea coast, the first resistance fighter in the Netherlands to be executed in this way. It was never discovered who did manufacture that gas canister, but if it wasn't made to order by the inventive Boissevain brothers in the basement of their family home on Corelli Street, it was made by others with similar aims and ideals in what would have been a very small-scale and secretive cottage industry.

For Rauter, however, it was not enough that only the two owners of the ice-cream parlour should be caught and punished. He demanded, with the encouragement of his masters in Germany, reprisals much greater in scope. There then followed, over a period of two days, a grotesque round-up of hundreds of Jewish men in the streets of Amsterdam.

***

On 22 and 23 February the German police entered into the sealed-off Jewish quarter. The 25 February publication of the underground newspaper *Het Parool* reported the full horror of the events:

94

Countless persons were seized and driven away. The number of arrests climbed into the hundreds.

On the street a painful drama played out. Weeping mothers held tightly to their sons, but the Prussians came between them, using their fists. Occasionally a gun was fired into the air. A man carrying a toddler on his arm as he walked alongside his wife, was also grabbed. The child was handed to the mother and the man pushed into a car. A pharmacist was dragged out of his shop and forced to crouch down on the ground for as long as one and a half hours. A young man, scarcely yet an adult, with a speech defect, was hit time after time in the face until all of a sudden he was able to find the words to answer whether or not he was a Jew. Many others were hit so that the teeth fell out of their mouths, and with bloodied faces were taken away.

Twenty-one-year-old Sara Menco, living in the Jewish quarter with her parents, witnessed similar events that she described in a letter to her future husband Bert: 'Today a number of Jews were mistreated in their own community and in an extremely barbarous way dragged in front of the synagogue. Then, forced onto their knees, they were ordered to shout out that they were 'filthy Jews''.

A total of 425 young Jewish men aged between 20 and 35 were rounded up – many from the streets, but Nico de Vries and a couple of friends, for example, were dragged out of a gym where they were training - and taken in army trucks to a prison camp in Schoorl near the Dutch town of Alkmaar. A few, due to their injuries, were permitted to return home. The vast majority of 389 were deported by train to Buchenwald, and then transferred in May of the same year to Mauthausen concentration camp in Austria, where they endured brutal treatment in the infamous stone quarry. Some were executed; others committed suicide by jumping hand-in-hand over the edge of the quarry to the broken rocks far below. Within a few weeks they would all be dead.

***

An open-air meeting was organized by the outlawed Dutch communist party for 24 February to protest against this pogrom and other measures taken against the Jews. A call to strike the next day was printed and distributed throughout the city. Mien Pooters, who was from a communist family and who - along with her brother (nicknamed 'Pam' from his initials P.A.M.) and sister Nel - undertook resistance activities from the start of the occupation, helped distribute a pile of the leaflets. 'I was scared to death', she later explained, 'but it needed to be done.' The leaflet urged those who had read it to then pass it on to others, or to post it where others could see it, but to be careful. It implored action:

ORGANISE A PROTEST STRIKE IN ALL WORKPLACES!!

Shut down the entire economy of Amsterdam for one day; the docks, the factories, the workshops, the offices and banks, the municipal services and employment projects.

Join in solidarity with our badly-treated Jewish workers.

STRIKE!!! STRIKE!!! STRIKE!!!

Release the enormous power of your united effort!!!

This is many times greater than the German occupying force!

Be united!! Be courageous!!!

The first workers to strike were the city's tram drivers, followed by other city services, the Bijenkorf department store, and schools. Mien Pooters, employed as a seamstress, stood by the window of the atelier when the strike began. Her husband stood on the street below to keep an eye on whether the city really would take up the call to strike; if he raised his thumb, that was the sign for Mien to act. When the sign was given, Mien addressed her co-workers: 'Ladies, everyone is out on strike, because they are taking our people away and we won't stand for it'. Everyone put down their work and went outside; all except one young woman who was dating a German soldier. 'All of us headed to the Noordermarkt', recalled Mien. 'The entire population had taken to the street. It was marvellous'.

By lunchtime 300,000 people had joined the strike, which had already begun to spread out from Amsterdam in all directions to Zaanstad, Hilversum and Utrecht. SS Chief Rauter gave orders that troops should be kept at the ready on the outskirts of the city, and that in the meantime the Dutch police authorities should be induced to act effectively against the strikers. When this proved to be ineffectual, the two leaders of the Jewish Council, Asscher and Cohen, were summoned before the German authorities and notified that unless the strike was over by the next day, another 300 Jews would be arrested. That same evening German motorized units entered the city and vans with loudspeakers announced that all those out on the streets needed to be back home by 7.30 p.m. The strike continued the next day, and with even more effect in the expansive industrial area known as the Zaanstreek to the north of Amsterdam. At eleven that morning, however, Rauter got serious and imposed martial law. The Germans sped through the streets in police vans, breaking up gatherings of workers and firing guns randomly into the air: nine people were killed by stray bullets and around forty wounded. The Mayor of Amsterdam called upon the people to return to work immediately, and referred to 'very serious measures' if they did not. A proclamation by the Commissioner for the Province of Utrecht dated the same date elaborated on those measures:

Striking is sabotage; it is forbidden and will be punished accordingly by the German Government. I give warning of the serious consequences of such irresponsible conduct. These are:

Unpaid Wages and Hardship

Financial assistance will not be provided. The innocent will be punished just like the guilty. Anyone who causes disruption and gives encouragement to strike will be most severely punished.

RINGLEADERS WILL BE SENTENCED TO DEATH.

***

Alongside the terrifying introduction of unannounced pogroms that now made any Jew anxious to be out on the street, the constant trickle of punitive, demeaning measures against the Jewish people living in the Netherlands continued apace. Within the next three months alone a series of proclamations appearing on the front page of the *Jewish Weekly News* would prohibit them from owning radio sets; from visiting markets; from using swimming pools and accessing beaches; and, for those living in Amsterdam, from moving home outside the city. All around them, in all aspects of their lives, a ligature was being slowly and inexorably tightened.

The front pages of Dutch newspapers dated 2 June 1941 announced that 'Germany, Italy, Finland and Romania are at war with the Soviets'. By radio broadcast Queen Wilhelmina condemned the 'unexpected and treacherous' invasion of the Soviet Union, though in truth Operation Barbarossa would be a beneficial turning point in the war. On the home front, it had two effects. On the one hand, insofar as Dutch communists had held back from resisting occupation through observance of the pact between Nazi Germany and Stalinist USSR they were now released from any such moral scruples. On the other, the night of 24/25 June witnessed 400 communists being dragged from their beds and arrested. Over the next year 1,500 Dutch communists would be arrested. On 31 August 1941 communist newspaper *De Waarheid* wrote: 'We are no supporters of the House of Orange. However, we have no reason for animosity towards the Queen.' They called on that date for massive street demonstrations to celebrate the Queen's birthday 'in such impressive and overwhelming numbers that the Nazis and their Dutch Nazi party poodles will get the fright of their lives'.

***

Milly Kaufman was in the same final-year class at the Amsterdam Lyceum as school friends Leo and Henri. Her family lived on Euterpestraat, opposite the Gestapo headquarters. On the occasions that she saw through an upstairs window an unusually large number of uniformed personnel scurrying around the front of the building and vans lining up like coupling train wagons, she understood that a pogrom was in preparation and would telephone those she knew to be in the greatest danger to warn them to stay indoors. The dangers were very real. Simon Kalf, young husband of the Frijda family's maid, recalls that a young Nico was arrested twice, simply in the course of walking along a street – the wrong place at the wrong time. Nico managed to duck and dive, and run away on each occasion. Milly also remembers that during the final examinations in summer 1941, headmaster Dr Gunning – a 'fantastic man' – allowed the Jewish boys to sleep overnight and eat all their meals at school. Leo would visit her home - rather more often than she ever visited his - and their friendship would continue after they both left school. She remembers him as shy and introverted, though generally liked at school. She knew that Leo enjoyed photography but their conversations avoided anything too serious so they never shared his passion for the new poets, or his politics. Leo passed his exams that summer with good grades across the board, with only slightly less impressive results in French and English. Dr Gunning had expressed the hope in the early months of Leo's academic year at the Lyceum that 'All will be well that ends well' and to the extent that the school had done what it could to help Leo, and that Leo in turn had knuckled down, studied hard and achieved good grades, this was the case. But what now, when Leo, as a Jew, was barred from studying at university?

For a short time, however, such worries could be put to one side as the entire class of VI-a were invited by the parents of one of their number, Clazien van Baumhauer, to spend a week at their country home in the village of Vierhouten, nestled in the rolling heath land and dunes of the Veluwe countryside, in the east of the country. The spacious villa contained seven bedrooms and twenty-five beds, into which accommodation a small number of Jewish families that had decided to go into hiding would soon thereafter be welcomed as guests of the host family - Clazien's father, an Amsterdam lawyer and former president of the

98

Holland-America Chamber of Commerce, and mother. The family would later oversee the digging of a 150-metre escape tunnel from the basement of the villa out into the nearby woods, in which in 1943 they would create a hidden encampment of tents, barracks, and underground facilities to become known as the 'watch-out camp'. They would engage trusted tradesmen to install water, electricity, and other necessities to enable over a hundred people - Jews, non-Jewish resistance workers and Allied pilots – to live in some comfort as forest outlaws. However, for that one week of summer in 1941, basking in their examination success, Leo, Clazien, Henri, Milly and the rest of the newly graduated class of VI-a could enjoy the freedom of the villa and its surroundings, the beautiful sunny weather, and a break from the angst-drenched streets of Amsterdam. Milly took photographs of the entire class in swimming costumes alongside the outdoor swilling pool, the girls sitting by the edge, legs dangling in the water, the boys standing protectively behind. Leo is smaller than all of the other boys, slender and younger-looking, and he gazes downwards, as though shy of the camera's eye, in contrast to the self-confident posing of the other boys. Henri remembers the time there as a real celebration. At the end of that week Henri and Leo hire a holiday cottage in between Amsterdam and Utrecht and for two weeks they sail in Henri's boat on the Loosdrecht Lakes. It would be a fine, rather elegaic end to a final holiday for Leo, and as summer turned into autumn, Henri and Leo would gradually lose contact.

XI

Theo's lodger

At number 3 Corelli Street, Professor Frijda and his children reluctantly accept that Leo, having left school and somewhat of a law unto himself, is also now old enough to become semi-independent, leave the family home, and thereby reduce by a few notches the tense atmosphere within its walls contributed to by the clashing personalities of father and eldest son. With their father now separated from their mother for a year and a half, it would be sixteen-year-old Jetteke who would strive to keep the remaining three members of the family together, whilst also studying hard at school. A proclamation of 1 September 1941 requiring all Jewish children to attend exclusively Jewish schools means that at the start of this autumn term Jetteke would attend the newly constituted Jewish Lyceum, sharing a class with best friend Margot Frank; one of their teachers would be historian Dr Presser, no longer permitted to teach at Leo's former school, the Vossius Gymnasium. The Montessori Lyceum has tried to hold out against such measures but on 11 September, in an attempt to loosen the yolk around the school, the head teacher supplies the German authorities with a list of twenty-two Jewish pupils - full names, dates of birth and home addresses; a list that includes younger brother Nico. The Jewish children are allowed to remain at the school until 1 October. The head teacher decides to constitute a Jewish Montessori School and new premises are sought. Eventually a home for the small school is offered by lawyer Leonard Frank, Leo's uncle, at the Frank family home; appointed as chairman of the management board is Professor Frijda.

Leo, prohibited by the anti-Jewish measures from attending university and his hopes of studying medicine thereby thwarted, is instead permitted to enrol at the nearby Central Israelite Hospital to train as a medical analyst. Many Jewish students removed from university medical schools pursue this same path. Leo scours newspaper ads and seeks the advice of friends and acquaintances in search of a room to rent. He discovers that Theo Hondius, the brother of his former classmate Lot, and fellow former editor of their school magazine *Vulpes*, has returned to Amsterdam and is possibly willing to share the cost of renting a room. Theo had left Amsterdam following his father's new teaching post to spend his final school year in The Hague and in accordance with his father's wishes had then enrolled at Utrecht University – his father's alma mater – where he began studying law and joined a student fraternity. He hated life there, hated the study of lawyer's Latin, disliked and fallen out with many of his fellow students, and lasted no more than three months before returning to The Hague, to then register for admission to Amsterdam University this autumn of 1941.

Theo had found a room on Amsterdam's Herengracht, the oldest of the three majestic canals in Amsterdam, dating from the city's 17th century Golden Age. He records the events in a diary:

At the time I was living in a house on the most beautiful canal of Amsterdam. My rooms went from the front through to the back, and the inside walls sloped to allow light into what had once been a dressmakers' atelier. [...] I inspected the bathroom and found it small but clean. I sorted out the gas and electricity with the owner, an extremely small, businesslike and melancholy Jewish woman. She sat down on a low, uncomfortably sprung Louis XVI ottoman left by friends who had just moved on. She needed just five minutes to value the meagre furniture, write out a receipt for the rent and ask about everyone in my family up to six times removed. Then she stood up, scurried to the sliding door by the staircase, turned round over the step and disappeared with a peculiar exaggerated swivel of her heavy body above her short legs.

Meanwhile, I arranged my few possessions to their best advantage around the twelve by five metre floor and alongside the rippling flowered wallpaper. An enormous glass orb lit the room right into the musty corners; with my first month's allowance from home I bought some brick red curtains which divided the floor space arbitrarily in half. My bohemian neighbour came round on the second day to borrow a saw; after one week I knew all my neighbours on either side and inside a month I had rowed with all of them except the neighbour who had borrowed the saw.

Theo's 'bohemian neighbour' was Gisèle van der Waterschoot van der Gracht who had moved into an adjacent third-floor apartment at the start of the war. As an aspiring artist from a very distinguished and well-travelled family she had studied for a year at the Paris Ecole des Beaux-Arts till funds dried up at the start of war. At the cosy, canal-side home she code-named *Castrum Peregrini* (Pilgrims' Fort) she took into hiding five young Jewish students and sold paintings in secret to wealthy Dutch patrons to raise the funds to maintain her adopted bohemian 'family'. In more desperate times the sale of her mother's expensive fur coat raised enough funds for thirty bread rolls. The saw borrowed from Theo would have helped with the carpentry work involved in creating hiding spaces for the Jewish 'family' members in the event of a police raid: there was room for one to hide in the pianola (once its working mechanism had been taken out), cupboards were built into a lift shaft, and a double crawl space created in the attic. The entire 'family' would survive the war by ignoring the manifest deprivations – the accommodation lacked any proper kitchen and bathroom - and by focusing on art and literature instead; the apartment was a treasure trove of books, paintings and mementos of different places. One of the family, Manuel Goldschmidt, recalls this experience as the time of his life: 'I was introduced to poetry and literature. We read Goethe, Hofmannsthal, Hölderlin, Baudelaire and the Tachtigers. That is when I started to live. That is the world I still live in.' Time was spent drawing, painting, reciting poetry, and writing, so that freedom was something that could be experienced by the mind, if not the body, although gymnastic sessions were also fitted into the daily activities to ensure physical as well as spiritual well-being.

Theo, too, preferred a more bohemian lifestyle to that of a hard-working student: the few scheduled weekly lectures began so early in the morning that he admits to becoming a stranger in the part of town that was home to the university. Any pretence at devotion to studies was further stymied by the unfortunate breaking of his alarm clock during the first housewarming party he held. 'Artistic evenings formed the central point of my existence', he recalled. 'Even though what I had to offer by way of refreshments consisted primarily of a substitute for tea, the flow of friends who came round steadily increased'. To this number would be added Leo, although his shyness would keep him in the background, quiet and separate, when others visited. Theo recalls the introduction:

In the autumn I received a short letter, written in red ink and fiercely clenched letters, reminding me of the school we attended together and a few literary frills. A vague, diminutive figure came to mind; yes, I was able to recall the story of how Leo Frijda, the writer of the letter, as a young child standing upright and playing on his quarter-size violin, walked between the spread legs of a grown man – a story told to me by my sister, who, like Leo was in the class two years below me. We couldn't at the time associate much with the nippers below us, but now I wrote a short reply and the following evening Leo appeared. The purpose of his visit was quickly explained, with the same short, nervous choice of words he used in his letter. Due to disagreements at home and for reasons of safety after curfew, he wanted to find somewhere else to live, or at least somewhere to spend the nights. He didn't stay long; it was Saturday evening and he didn't want to miss his weekly bath that evening. What purpose this necessary ablution served for him I would later fully discover for myself; but then it seemed just a reason to make a scathing observation on my part about the bourgeoisie in general, and more in particular those who wish to know exactly when it was that they had last bathed. I accepted the proposal there and then; it would mean a small relief to my financial position, although I received more than enough (250 guilders per month) from home.

Astride a wobbly delivery bicycle and bundled inside grubby blue overalls, Leo procured over the course of the next week a bed, a rickety table and a few chairs, and a rented piano with yellow keys. And so, every evening thereafter he would arrive just before the dark hours of curfew and set down a bag with some slices of bread. Sometimes he would then spend a half hour playing at the piano, or sit at the rickety table composing verses, pulled off his rubber boots to lie on the creaking bed, falling quickly into a deep peaceful sleep. His dark grey suit was laid out next to him folded over the piano stool, a shirt with a soft collar, no tie – the ensemble topped off by a shapeless grey workman's hat with a flattened down brim. I thought Leo was a medical student, although now he appeared to be working in a hospital. In the mornings he had always left before I awoke.

Occasionally he also made limited use of his fairly sizeable book collection, or sat silently in a corner when my friends, sitting over their orange-red cups of tea, got heated up about the problems of the world and the literature of the day, but some degree of trust only became forged when, arriving home earlier than normal, I allowed him to read my verses. He took hold of the elegant book with its beautifully typed white sheets of paper, began to walk up and down the room as he was wont to do whenever he was deep in thought, knitted his blond eyebrows into a scowling line above his pale blue eyes and read half out loud a line here and there.

The reading lamp on the barrel by my bed was switched on. I thought he had gone to sleep, until I heard his voice from the darkened rear of the room.

"Aren't you asleep yet?" I asked. "Is my lamp a problem?"

Leo didn't reply, but continued speaking, and I now heard that it must have been a poem, even though the lines were very uneven and did not rhyme at the end. But the rhythm of the rising and falling words sounded so insistent, and so intense, that I listened enraptured till Leo had finished. Then he laughed, loudly and rather ironically.

"That was poetry" he exclaimed, a little too loudly in the still of the night on the Herengracht in Amsterdam. Then, excusing himself: "It wasn't mine, but that's the way I am going to write in the future. Sleep well!"

"Sleep well". I switched off the light and the lights from the cars along the canal side crept across the ceiling. Leo's bed continued to creak restlessly until he was silent, apart from the heavy, regular breathing of a contented child.

That was in the autumn...

The winter of 1942 would be particularly hard. The canals froze early, which enticed the young and energetic to skate on the ice and gush smoking breath into the brittle air like wheezing steam engines. It was especially hard for unemployed Jews now faced with another proclamation ordering that they be transferred to labour camps in the east of the country – one stop on the longer journey further east that would await them and their families. 'It was like a Russian winter', one survivor recalled: 'The snow lay metres deep on the tracks and froze over. To be there felt like we were overwintering in Nova Zembla'. But it was also hard to keep homes warm in the tight-knit houses of Amsterdam. Supplies of gas and electricity had been rationed for a year already, and it was hard to come by bits of wood to burn in a kitchen stove. Theo recalls that winter:

Month after month a fierce north wind attacked the poorly fitting sash windows to the front of the old, lopsided studio. The small supply of coal had been quickly devoured by the heating stove, public transport came to a virtual halt and fuel couldn't be bought for even ten times the price. And it became strangely silent in our 12 x 5 room. To begin with, I sought refuge away from home in lecture halls or the university library, but when the Christmas holiday arrived I sat at my desk as immobile as possible in hat, coat and scarf. When I needed to turn a page in my study book I removed a glove and put it back on quickly. Once every hour I heated some water on the gas and refilled the small canister I kept inside my coat. When it reached minus fifteen, I no longer bothered with keeping up appearances and simply didn't get out of bed. The water pipes from the sink and WC had been frozen for a long time, so that I had to use the iron dustbin in the corner of the room.

Leo came back each evening and occasionally so did C. or H. who provided me with something warm to eat or drink. Leo also brought some blocks of wood from home, which burned with a glow at the bottom of the heating stove. Crouched wide-legged over the stove I singed the legs of my pyjamas just as I used to do with the linings of my day-to-day suits.

Often I stayed dozing as I heard the rubber boots climbing the wooden stairs and beneath the felt rim of the hat the round, flushed face appeared at open door. With hands in the pockets of his short grey winter coat, Leo prowled across the room reciting poetry. From one blacked-out window to the other and between the sparse items of furniture. If he saw that I was still awake, then he would head straight for my bed, leaned over me with wild gestures and sprayed the verses in my face. His eyes peered threateningly into mine:

'...and your mouth is wholly of its own

and your blood swathed by your own blood'

He bit off the words, clipped and fierce, and yet this voice was like a song as no other poet had ever sung before. Leo stood upright and strode across the room with the heavy tread of his boots.

That's how Theo got to know the poetry of Marsman, just as Leo had introduced school friend Henri to Marsman.

***

Leo never showed me his own verses: some time later I realised that after each new attempt he destroyed all previous lines. Sometimes in the cinder tray of the heating stove I found a half-blackened piece of paper amongst the bits or remaining wooden blocks. I would smooth it out flat and gradually built up a collection of lines of verse from which I grew to know the man. And like the man himself they were wild and fiery and full of song – not one word too many. The lines were regular across the page, sometimes forming into a harmony, where the disunity of the rhyme found its master. And I recognised that it was angst and uncertainty that were the propelling forces in his life. He demonstrated this angst one evening when two police officers suddenly stood in the doorway: he turned white and clutched a hand to his heart. I was left to do the talking and it appeared that on the floor below a connecting door to the neighbouring house had been left open. The police officers left with apologies and a cigarette; Leo sat motionless on the couch. We took our jackets off and I put out the light. Marsman remained silent and the following day too I waited in vain for the voice I feared and loved, that later I would never hear again.

When a short time later the curfew was brought forward to 8 o'clock for the whole of Amsterdam, following some attacks on the occupying forces, we were completely thrown into each other's company. The consequences soon made themselves felt. Blazing rows erupted for the most trivial of reasons, physically I was the stronger, but Leo's arguments were also weaker than mine. What attracted me least to Leo were his domineering outbursts that scarcely seemed to fit his small, slim frame.

We were happy when our neighbour on the other side of the dividing door sought refuge with us. This new medic, a former law student, quickly and accurately diagnosed me as having a harmless strain of dysentery; more importantly, he knew how to get hold of some tea and rusks. It was seldom that we had any fruitful discussions; C seemed to think that Leo harboured a secret fear of him, especially after the occasion when C and I burst in one evening making a great racket. C had earned some money writing a newspaper article and invited me to join him for a few drinks. We staggered together through moonlit Amsterdam and after a drunken lurch landed against a German soldier and a difficult journey across the frozen waters of the canal, arrived home again. We crashed up the staircase banging stolen beer bottles and forced open the locked sliding door. Leo lay still and trembling in his bed. Through almost squeezed shut eyes he followed our blundering movements around the room. C began to curse him as a 'vile Jew', but when he saw that his jokes brought no response, he returned next door where he lived in an attic room at the top.

My sympathy was split evenly between my two friends. I was attracted to C's self-assurance and his free and original way of living, which made him known and celebrated from everyone in his circle; but Leo had given me the gift of Marsman's voice.

And we shared even more in common.

XII

People departing

On 13 March 1941 fifteen Dutch resistance fighters and three communist leaders of the February Strike were executed in the sand dunes that meandered between The Hague and the North Sea, the first mass execution of occupied Netherlands. Writer Jan Campert's poem 'The Song of the Eighteen Dead' inspired by the reports of their arrest published in the underground newspaper *Het Parool* in February 1941 would be clandestinely printed and sold as a single sheet for a small price to raise money for resistance activities, but only after the writer's own death in a German concentration camp in January 1943. The poem's lines are spoken by one of the eighteen prisoners awaiting death, who observes in the dark hours before dawn: 'A prison cell is but two metres long / and scarce two metres wide / But smaller still the patch of ground / that lies I know not where / a nameless grave that gives me rest...'.

In the 'Jewish block' of the Weteringschans prison in Amsterdam such a four-metre-square prison cell, absent of any sanitation, would at certain times crush sixteen Jewish prisoners within its walls.

A cell may be so small as to provide standing room only; a limp and exhausted body pinned upright by other bodies pushed against it. A prison, however, may be the size of a country; the size of half a continent. Jewish people would be rounded up across Europe and the timetables of a continent-wide rail network dedicated to transporting them to their death. In the early months of 1942 Jewish people as were not being picked off the streets in brutal round-ups and reprisal actions were being confined within the Jewish quarter of Amsterdam that had become, in effect, a ghetto. Jewish families from the rest of the province were told to pack their bags with three days' notice of their imminent relocation within its barbed wire perimeter. Escape was becoming an increasingly remote opportunity. Their bank accounts first depleted, they were then compelled to hand in all their gold, silver, antiques and works of art. Without subterfuge and without contact to their potential saviours in the underground resistance, it thus became impossible to afford and plan an escape route abroad – to neutral Switzerland, or south to Spain and then by boat the England - or to pay the asking price to those who might have provided them with a hiding place at home, right under the noses of the Germans trying to smoke them out. Private travel had become impossible with the prohibition on Jews owning or driving motor vehicles. As regard public transport, simply being in the vicinity of Amsterdam's central rail station, let alone boarding or alighting from a train, was fraught with danger, especially after June 1942 when a proclamation issued the Jewish population with a total travel ban. Across the imposing station façade that stood guard at one end of the Damrak, the avenue linking city, station and – behind the station - harbour, a banner proclaimed 'Victory: Germany is winning for Europe on all fronts!'. A symbol of the occupier's strength and presence, a shadowy place where the Gestapo, working closely with the Dutch police, loitered menacingly at the foot of stairs that lead up to platforms, the station building also served as a danger-fraught meeting place for Jews who had adopted false, Aryan identities and for members of the Dutch resistance.

Escape by sea - even access to beaches along the North Sea coast – fast became a hopeless dream. In spring 1942 the Germans – now fighting on both western and eastern fronts - began construction of the Atlantic Wall fortifications that would make beaches and adjacent dunes prohibited areas, even in once fashionable seaside resorts. Initially, 350 houses in Scheveningen would be evacuated and demolished; later that year around 30,000 more homes demolished and 50,000 trees cut down in nearby parks and forests. On the razed ground encircling the former holiday town like a firebreak they dug an anti-tank ditch more than five kilometres long. At intervals along the entire Dutch coast they built concrete bunkers, fenced off the beach with rolls of razor wire shivering like trapped tumbleweed in the winds blowing off the sea, and buried mines in shallow graves in the sand. Along dikes, dunes and beaches armed German soldiers patrolled day and night. Many of those local residents ordered to evacuate their homes would have read the advertisement placed locally by J.B. van Veen, dealer in second-hand furniture, with premises in The Hague and Rotterdam: 'If you have to EVACUATE, let us value your surplus furniture! We buy entire or part household contents, china, Persian carpets, etc. Telephone 33.19.00 (before 5 p.m.)'. To make it clear that the coastal area that had once been their home and livelihood was now a no-go area, wooden signs warned starkly that 'anyone caught veering off public highways or footpaths would be **immediately** shot at'.

***

Leo remained in contact with his former class friend Milly Kaufman. At the hospital where he was training as a medical analyst Milly was training as a nurse. He would visit her at her home, they would talk casually about nothing in particular, and he would take photographs of her in her nurse's uniform with his Leica camera. They were not romantically linked. Milly had a boyfriend whose framed photo stood on the dresser and who had already escaped to Switzerland, and Milly sensed that Leo understood, although it was never discussed between them, that she and her family would attempt the same escape route under the necessary false identities, for her to be united with the man she loved. When it became time for Milly to undertake this risky journey all arrangements were in secret; no one was told, and no goodbyes said. Looking back, she feels for the young Leo who must have called at her home one day to find it empty, its occupants gone, and with no means of knowing whether the abandoned home signified escape or capture.

***

Leo continues to share the canal-side attic room with Theo for several more months, through an historically cold winter that saw the ships in the port of Amsterdam trapped against the quaysides in the vice-like grip of thick ice. The curfew is draconian – after 8 p.m. windows had to be closed and even leaning out of a window could be punished severely. During this time they grow to understand each other better, appreciate each other's qualities, and thereby cement their friendship. As Theo recalls, they shared more in common than the memorised lines of Marsman:

The war completed its third year. After the defeat of the days in May and the novelty of foreign troops, peace was initially restored under a new form of administration. The number of dead on our side was limited, there was sometimes a lack of food, here and there resistance briefly broke out which resulted in severe measures being taken, and victims fell. During the short war betrayal by our countrymen had indeed startled us, but as far as appearances were concerned, not much had changed.

Later, people began whispering that workers were being deported, hostages were being taken from amongst groups of former leaders, there was no lack of disquieting rumours – but arms fire across western Europe had grown silent and university life continued as normal.

During our discussions from morning to night, however, a new tone was added. After the poetry we exchanged confidences about our wretched experiences of love, our criticisms of our parental homes (his mother was divorced from her husband, mine died shortly before the outbreak of hostilities; a housekeeper managed the home of the professor, his father, whilst mine wasted no time marrying one of his teachers, a cold miserable woman). Without knowing many of the facts, we aimed our sharp scorn at our separated elders, stirring up each other's feelings of hate,

111

combined with sultry, unworldly and inexperienced poetry. Our images were given form and colour; green, yellow and brown, and the contours of a country that lay closed, sweet and unapproachable within itself. In the world atlas our eyes scanned the borders of the great powers and every unoccupied day the oppression increased as a tight bond between us. The currents of the sea marked on the coloured paper gradually became familiar to us.

When winter was over, and green buds sprouted on the trees along the canal, we found the courage to act. I said my goodbyes to my family, friends and country in a long poem. It was a Saturday evening; the sun poured basking rays onto the window ledge, the birds were hushed and everywhere was scented. Leo returned from his weekly bath, appearing with a radiance and handed me a sheet on which a few short lines were scored into the paper. Now I showed him my poem – and it seemed that at pretty much the same time we had committed our thoughts on the same subject to writing. The bonds between us were complete; I gave notice to quit my room, and we remained a few more happy weeks in our Pact.

Gradually I moved my furniture to C's attic. Leo got into his overalls and transported bed, table and piano, with some of my smaller things, to the home of his girlfriend. To begin with he did not want to tell me the address, but after a short quarrel, which reduced us to the childlike state of former times, he gave in.

Leo and Theo have plotted their escape by boat to England, a plan buoyed by their blossoming friendship and the emergence from a bitterly cold winter of the first signs of spring. They won't need to live in the attic apartment on the canal any more. Leo moves his belongings to the home of a friend, Mien Harmsen, a young woman eight years his senior, someone he has met through his contacts with young communist party members and others committed to resisting - through evenings of ersatz tea and shared political discourse, as well as through more tangible acts of resistance - the will of the Nazi occupiers. It is therefore perhaps not surprising that he should have been cautious about revealing her address, even to Theo. Preparations gather pace:

We purchased waterproof clothing and placed an advertisement to find a sturdy boat. I tied up my poems into a tight bundle, and added the fragments of Leo's fantasy that I had saved; we were travel-ready. All that remained was for us to actually make our farewells and plan the route.

Leo had some knowledge of sailing, his father had transferred money abroad and, I believed, had quite a few colleagues from the academic world to which he could have access. I would take charge, and be responsible for arranging provisions. We fixed our departure date for the beginning of March, expecting the sea to be fairly calm at that time of year. Furthermore, during that period there were holidays, so that the first few days of our absence would go unnoticed.

My sister's birthday would provide a reason for returning home and withdrawing some money without arousing suspicion. The birthday party itself provided me with an unfamiliar sensation of approaching separation and quiet superiority.

As if naturally, for the first time I behaved properly and in an obliging manner towards my step-mother, and it bothered me a lot that my stay in the family home was made instantly more pleasant as a result, given that on previous occasions I had never been able to hold out for longer than 36 hours. But I stuck to my decision; I would meet Leo early the next morning in Leiden, and so I bid farewell to my few remaining possessions in that house on Kanaalweg and in the morning silently left. Mists hung low over the patch of grass in front, veiling the trenches that had been dug into the ground. Tram rails glistened dimly and in the distance the blush of a rear light, and I – shivering in my thin raincoat – waited for the next tram to arrive.

Leo was already waiting by the station, stamping his boots impatiently. I suggested that we should first get something warm to drink in the buffet, but he immediately and angrily rejected the idea. And so we set off on our journey, half-frozen, angry and picking on each other. We took the tram to Katwijk and from there we walked. Eventually we reached the strip of sand dunes, ritually called out to the classical sea goddess 'Thalassa, Thalassa', and climbed down onto the beach. Here the cold wind bit ferociously into our unprotected faces. We continued in silence, side-by-side along the wet sand, where the high tide had receded. To our right the wild seas foamed and to our left the rising sun glowed through a shroud of grey clouds. Shells cracked underfoot. My stomach was rumbling impatiently, and I began to increase the pace. It was difficult for little Leo to keep up with his shorter legs, sucked deep into the soft sand. Quivering flocks of foam scattered towards the dunes. The south-westerly wind began its rampage; with a little difficulty I reminded myself of our objective. Dejectedly I directed my companion's attention to the revolving glass turrets; machine gun posts every two or three hundred metres along the beach. I had the feeling that there wasn't a second when we could walk without being watched. After half a kilometre we had our first encounter with a dog. The roaming animal suddenly raced up to us and, growling, started to sniff the boots of my companion. We heard a piercing whistle, and immediately the dog turned back so that we could continue our journey untroubled. We now walked over the dryer sand higher up the beach to make it easier for Leo, but even so he quickly fell behind by a few metres.

I waited for a few moments so that he could catch me up. Unusually calm, he went in search of a parallel path in the dunes. We ran up a wicker-laid path to meet a narrow, tarmac road that ran along the coast. We came to a standstill alongside a wooden hut. Grasping onto my clasped hands, Leo climbed up onto the roof. The view we got was of the usual landscape of sand dunes: hills, patched with sand grasses; here and there a small bush, and a solitary group of pine trees in a sheltered bowl. The fierce wind blew sharp grains of sand in our faces. The cold

113

lunged through our clothes and against our bodies and tanned our skins and spat a thin layer of salt on our lips. Thirst mixed with fainting pangs of hunger.

I caught sight of the sentry guard looking through binoculars. I alerted Leo, and he jumped down from the roof and sprained his foot. With a determined expression he trotted off ahead. Half-turning in my direction he reported briefly on his findings: deep rungs of a defence system extended far back into the hinterland. He avoided spelling out the simple conclusion, but the sense of disappointment hit us hard, now that we knew our escape had so unmistakably failed. Everywhere we looked now, we came across interconnected trenches, supported by wooden planks; there were look-out posts at regular intervals, and occasionally a larger commando hut.

Now it was my turn to take the lead again; Leo followed a long way behind, struggling along with his injured foot. Reaching a slight bend in the road I looked back to see him as a small ant in the distance, shortly afterwards, a wider bend hid him from view completely. I was now walking as fast as a speed walker and within the hour I stood next to an abandoned café that I recognised from the past: the town couldn't be more than another quarter of an hour away, but the mist had thickened and hid the townscape from my view. I decided to wait in a sheltered spot and after a while I did indeed hear the familiar tread and watched the hunched figure pushing slowly against the wind, a grey coat hood covering much of the face.

I ought to have called out to him – wasn't I the one in charge, the expedition leader? But a profound denial and an indescribable pity grasped my throat. The boots trudged as heavy as lead over the tarmac, his right leg still limping. He had now reached the place where the roads crossed, furtively lifted his head to take one look around – that, dear, dear face – and then vanished back into the mist.

Scrambling to my feet, I suddenly felt the tiredness in my legs. At the junction I quickly debated with myself and then walked straight ahead on the off-chance – it was the trusted route home...

It was by the viaduct on the edge of town that I eventually caught him up. We continued in silence. I carefully adjusted my pace to his heavy gait and once or twice gave him a sideways glance, fearing that I would detect the hate that I could barely suppress myself. If he had spoken just one word I would have burst into tears, but his lips stayed firmly pressed together. Oh God, how I wish I could have held him in my arms and carried him like a child, but – so close to him that our arms brushed together – a chasm had grown between us, and a sheer, heaven-high wall.

We separated at the tram stop, the same stop where this morning I had just missed the first tram. I don't know if we said anything – words had lost all meaning. Leo sank down onto a bench; I walked first slowly, and then faster and faster until the *tram stop disappeared between the trees. There was the bridge, the grass bank with the trenches dug in zig-zags alongside the barbed wire, and there the house that I had wanted to leave for ever, and that now accepted me back as if had never been away. At that moment, father came down the stairs for the midday meal.*

***

Mien Harmsen rented rooms in a large house overlooking an Amsterdam canal that she described as 'lugubrious'. Its other occupants – Jewish families - had all been removed. It was here where Leo found a place of refuge, and where he began a process of going into hiding, or at any rate hiding his true identity. He would continue to be registered till the summer of 1942 as a trainee medical analyst at the Central Israelite Hospital, and continue to be registered in his own name as living at the family home at number 3 Corelli Street. But meanwhile he obtains forged identity papers that provide him with a new identity. 'He was a more of a brother to me', recalls Mien. 'In the neighbourhood he was believed to be my brother. He was blond and so was I. And he used my brother's identity card'. Mien marvelled at Leo's talents, but found his personality difficult: 'He was the most brilliant man I ever met. Without doubt. He could do anything. He studied medicine, he wrote, he composed - and knew a huge amount about - music. [...] He could create anything. Anything. He was fantastic. But he wasn't, of course, a nice person. The two things don't go together.'

'Leo lived like an animal in a cage. He couldn't deal with the isolation', Mien remembers of those days. 'I once heard him say: 'If I could get my hands on a machine gun I'd go out onto the street in broad daylight and shoot down all those jackboot-wearing scum'.'

PART II

'Disobedience – that is the nobility of slaves'

Friedrich Nietzsche, Thus Spoke Zarathustra

XIII

'It is a lie...'

Art is always criticised and always an outsider gets the blame.

Ville Valo

The rise to power of Mussolini in Italy in 1922 saw the swift emergence of Dutch fascist parties in enthusiastic response. Up to the end of World War Two there would be no fewer than sixty of them. Hardly a united front; their various self-serving leaders often worked against each other rather than together. The first off the starting blocks was the *Verbond van Actualisten* (Union of Actualists). On 9 December 1927 a new Dutch fascist movement *De Bezem* ('The Broom') launches a magazine with the same title – subtitled 'Fascist Weekly News for the Netherlands' – aimed at the poor, working class at a price of just seven and a half cents per issue. An illustration in a later edition of the magazine would depict a broom furiously sweeping away a communist hammer and sickle with the words 'Away with the pig filth'. Other publications representing various apparently divergent fascist parties in the Netherlands, such as the 'Dutch People for Fascism' and the 'General Dutch Fascist Union' – some being reincarnations of, or split-offs from, previous iterations - follow suit with rather obvious titles such as 'The Dutch National Socialist' 'The Black Front' and 'The Fascist'. Most well known is the publication of the movement led by Anton Mussert, entitled *Volk en Vaderland* ('People and Fatherland'). There are efforts to attract a young, energetic following to the fascist cause, and one product of this membership drive is an offshoot magazine of *De Bezem* aimed at younger readers - *De Flits* ('Lightning Flash') – 'Organ for the Fascist Youth Movement in the Netherlands'.

'In the end, only fascism will be able to form a bulwark against this Marxist plague!' claims the Black Front. But of course the USSR under Stalin, the supposed natural enemy with which they share many common traits, serves as a useful existential threat by which the various haggling fascist parties in the Netherlands hope to obtain power, remain in power, and extend their power. Though they purport to hate communism, they raise no cheers for democracy either. What they seek – *'without terror, if possible'* - is:

1. An end to the parliamentary system;

119

2. Invigoration of a national consciousness and closer bonds with the Royal House of Orange-Nassau;

3. Government intervention to combat the threats to the working classes by parties that call themselves 'socialist' and the communist party.'

The same magazine quotes the words of German historian Oswald Spengler: 'There are two types of government: one that puts the common good above all else, the other that does not put the common good above all else. A 'democratic' government always belongs to the second type'.

In 1932, journalist, poet and publisher George Kettmann Jnr., chief editor of *Volk en Vaderland*, together with his wife Margot, found a Dutch national socialist publishing house, the *Amsterdamsche Keurkamer*. In time Kettmann would become one of the most fanatical supporters of the New Order, beyond the pale even for Mussert, who would expel him from his Dutch national socialist movement. Thus disowned, Kettmann would proudly sign up to the Dutch SS and travel to the Eastern Front as a war correspondent. The *Amsterdamsche Keurkamer* would go bankrupt in September 1944 but, until its demise, it boasts that the only culture it is willing to disseminate is *'the people's culture'*. Kettmann lauds the right of authors published by his publishing house '[...] to represent our culture at a moment when our people must rediscover their creative energy through a renewal of this culture, which will then cross outdated national borders to unite a diverse Germanic world'. He asserts here a clear connection between culture and politics, in which culture is to be at the service of politics: culture as state propaganda. Furthermore, by emphasising the culture of 'the people' he is consciously attacking the notion of an elitist art that celebrates the individual self-expression of the artist. It is something that Nietzsche warned of: 'Being nationalistic, in the sense in which it is now demanded by public opinion, would be for us who are more spiritual, it seems to me, not merely insipid but dishonest; a deliberate deadening of our better will and conscience'.

***

The prayers of Dutch fascists are answered when on 10 May 1940 German tanks trample over the Dutch border and German paratroopers spew from the sky over airfields close by the seat of the Dutch government. Alongside the censorship of information – cutting the supply of reliable news - censorship of the arts begins almost immediately: the occupiers have at hand the lists of books and authors banned years previously by the eager censors in Germany. On 7 September 1940 the

Police Commissioner for the town of Deventer, for example, notifies all publishers, printers, bookshop owners and librarians under his jurisdiction that an edict from the Rijkscommissaris for the occupied Dutch territory now bans the buying, selling or lending of any written work whatsoever that opposes or is disloyal to 'the German people, their leader, the German national socialist workers' party, the German state, the German government, or the German army'. Any such books are to be taken out of circulation and 'stored under lock and key'. In 1941 alone, over one hundred such circulars are issued, each containing a new list of outlawed works. Soon after the invasion we also begin to witness the steady water-torture drip of anti-Jewish measures by which the voices of Jewish artists – creative writers and journalists, painters and sculptors, film and theatre directors, performers, composers and musicians – become muzzled.

Since the middle of the nineteenth century Dutch policy had remained consistent: according to the dictum of Dutch government minister Johan Thorbecke 'The arts are no business of government'. Those who now rule over the Netherlands beg to differ. In November 1941 all artists, Jewish or not, are finally brought to heel with the introduction of the Dutch *Kultuurkamer* (Culture Chamber). Consisting of six 'guilds', one for each field of art, including journalism, the *Kultuurkamer* is part of the project to nazify the Netherlands, modelled on the original instigated by Goebbels in Germany in 1933. As an artists' union it is a closed shop: anyone producing any kind of artistic work who has not signed up to the *Kultuurkamer* is liable to pay a crippling fine of five thousand Dutch guilders. Those who join are also required to sign an 'Aryan declaration' as proof of their racial purity.

Whilst one could nominally join the *Kultuurkamer* as an artist or musician, for example, and then as a matter of principle not write or compose anything for the duration of one's membership, the same could not be said of those contemplating membership of the guild of journalists: they were the employees of newspapers, paid to produce copy, day in, day out. They may have toed the Nazi party line through gritted teeth and some sense of shame, but toe the line they mostly did. Ed Hoornik, editor of the *Algemeen Handelsblad*, wrote in a letter to a friend on 8 December 1941: 'I have had to become a member of the Union of Journalists in order to keep my wife and children (and myself!) alive; however, I am not prepared to make any further concessions'.

***

The first President of the *Kultuurkamer*, Tobie Goedewaagen, is effusively thankful that 'the New Order, the focus of our attention, will result in the artist once again becoming one of the people'. As editor-in-chief of *De Schouw* - a cultural magazine launched in January 1942 as the 'Organ of the Dutch *Kultuurkamer* / Dedicated to the cultural life of the Netherlands' – Goedwagen proclaims: 'Our culture stands at a crossroads, but the choice is not difficult. To the left Death awaits; to the right, Rebirth'. He parrots the Nazi/Stalinist cult of youth - the 'idealism and fanaticism' that Professor Frijda had identified on his first visit to the USSR in 1929 - at the expense of a moribund older generation: 'Before us lies the still unexplored land of rejuvenated Dutch culture, revitalized by the test of world revolution that will scourge and purify body, soul and spirit'. Soon a feeding frenzy of articles from various contributors to *De Schouw* are honing in on both the individual creative writer and the 'wrong' kinds of groups of writers like sharks encircling their next meal.

The process towards political control of the artist's voice is in three stages. Stage one, censorship: the requirement for artists to sign the Aryan declaration and embrace the *Kultuurkamer* before they could continue to ply their trade. Stage two, self-censorship: approved artists (members of the Aryan *Kultuurkamer*) would learn the kind of work required of them and churn it out accordingly. Stage three, *no* censorship: in a utopian dictatorship all artists would instinctively sing in harmony as loyal servants of 'the people' (a euphemism for 'the machinery of the state').

A poet of course has creative freedom, opines Dr. J. van Ham in elaboration of stage two, but 'freedom without responsibility is chaos'. The poet must search for a 'good way of life'. Some groups, however, could *never* adopt good ways of life. The Jews, for example. 'From both a psychological and artistic point of view', writes Ham, their work 'occupies an unnecessary page in our literary history'. Ham et al. didn't think much of homosexuals either: another contributor to *De Schouw*, Andreas Glotzbach, criticises the 'outpouring of personal hyper-sensitive emotions and sentiments' and asserts that these new times demand a poet who should write with 'a broader, manly expression, open but at the same time resilient; a replete, fierce and muscular energy'. No effete drama queens, then.

Almost exceeding their dislike of certain obvious *groups* of writers, the contributors to *De Schouw* also salivate in their contempt for the idea of the loner poet as a cherished individual spirit – the egocentric poet. Professor Jan de Vries, Vice-President of the *Kultuurkamer*, denounces past displays of 'bizarre exhibitionism' by poets whose work was 'so unreal and insubstantial that it had lost all meaning to society'. Similarly, Roel Houwink attacks 'navel-gazing' with the warning that 'we should not separate art from life'. Another author, Ger Griever, concludes that 'the

122

writer must, in the first instance, regard himself as a *servant* of his people'. The problem with identifying the poet as a 'servant', however, is that a servant is there to do as he is told: his opinions and ideas are never sought, and are not welcomed if volunteered.

If you turn a writer into a civil servant – worse still an underling servant - you stifle the creative spirit. Those not prepared to compromise values they hold true either refuse to join the *Kultuurkamer*, or else nominally sign up and thereafter refuse to produce any work. Those, by contrast, who champion the *Kultuurkamer* and endlessly drivel their ideas across countless pages of *De Schouw* (churned out twice monthly) tend to be wholehearted supporters of Nazi Germany and adopt a sycophantic attitude towards their German 'conquering heroes'. They could not seriously be considered as amongst their nation's greatest writers or thinkers; many were second rate at the very best. Nevertheless, it would have been foolhardy to underestimate the Nazis on the basis of their loutishly unsophisticated appreciation of the arts. Christopher Isherwood had raised the alarm in his 1939 semi-autobiographical novel 'Goodbye to Berlin' when he warned: 'The Nazis may write like schoolboys, but they're capable of anything. That's just why they're so dangerous. People laugh at them, right up to the last moment...'

***

Willem Arondeus, openly homosexual and therefore psychologically unsuited to producing the type of art demanded of its 'peoples' artists' by the Nazis, started out as a talented and successful painter and graphic designer, and then turned to creative writing. With a somewhat never-satisfied, self-pitying demeanour - he complains in his diary of longing for love when alone, and feeling stifled by love when offered it by another - the wartime occupation somehow focuses his general anger and disenchantment in life where it can actually be productive: he is one of the first artists in the Netherlands to join the resistance movement. His decision is perhaps not so surprising: openness about his sexuality in the 1920s had been an act of defiance to prevailing morality: in Leo's words, he refused to 'toe the line'. In spring 1941 he is writing and distributing illegal pamphlets that impassionedly urge his fellow artists to join the fight. A year later, in March 1942, he addresses them on the insidiousness of the *Kultuurkamer* in one of his clandestine 'Brandaris' letters ('Brandaris' being the name of a radio station broadcasting from London to Dutch ships at sea, which in turn took its name from a sixteenth-century lighthouse on the Dutch island of Terschelling). Arondeus writes:

It is a lie that our nation will ever be let free by a conquering Germany. [...] If Germany wins, our nation will become a German colony, our people coolies, and our art reduced to 'Kultur'. We will lose everything that we value, that we pride ourselves in, and that makes us strong: freedom of conscience and freedom to live![...]

It is a lie that there has been any people's revolution in the Netherlands. [...] This was not a revolution, but a robbery perpetrated through treachery and lies, sustained by the weapons of the enemy.[...] [Amongst those who have joined the Kultuurkamer] there is not a single architect, painter, writer or performer of any rank; they are just second-hand-bought renegades who have signed up out of vanity or greed.[...]

It is a lie that this Kultuurkamer is established to serve the arts and artists. It is nothing more than a spiritual prison guarded by national socialism. [...]

Therefore do not collaborate, do not respond to any request, do not accept any commission, boycott anything that comes from the Nazis and that has anything to do with the Nazis and the Kultuurkamer: everything, everything!

Lies and compulsion will never win! The forces gathered in the world to fight them are growing in strength and will soon have the upper hand. Our future is freedom! The future of the Nazis is oblivion!

Drive them out! Away from our people, our culture, our work!

Arondeus honed in immediately on what lay in store: when artistic expression is controlled, the human spirit is controlled; when the human spirit is controlled, the whole person - body, mind, and soul - becomes enslaved. In this 'Brandaris letter', which would later become incorporated in the clandestine publication *De Vrije Kunstenaar* ('The Free Artist'), Arondeus's call to 'drive them out' uses the pen to incite use of the sword. He was neither saying nor doing anything new. The *Vrije Kunstenaar* observes: 'An artist who temporarily sets aside their work to play an active role in the struggle for freedom is something that is as old as art itself'. It is a struggle taken up by Arondeus that would result in him being arrested and sentenced to death. It is a struggle that he would describe in a farewell letter written on the eve of his execution, even as he was sharing out small slices of a cream cake – his last request from his prison cell - amongst his condemned comrades, as 'a time of joy and happiness that I had never before experienced in my life.'

XIV

A wave of the hand / a clenched fist

On 29 April 1942 a notice published in the *Jewish Weekly News* announced the mandatory wearing, as from the following Sunday, of the 'so-called Jewish star'. The yellow cloth stars would be issued by the Jewish Council, a maximum of four per person – in exchange for one clothing coupon on the ration card plus a payment of four cents per star. Each star was to be trimmed and sewn to a garment such that all six points and the black outline were visible on the clothing. The word 'Jew' was printed in the middle of each star in a new typeface intended to mimic Hebrew calligraphy. Jetteke Frijda remembers that her mother – who had returned from a period of psychiatric treatment and convalescence in Utrecht to live near, but detached from, the family home in the New South district of Amsterdam - supplied her with the requisite number of stars. Seventeen-year-old Jetteke, being the woman of the home now, was charged with sewing the stars onto clothing, and recalls: 'Yes, I thought it was weird and I didn't really like it – but because all of us, I think, who were at the Jewish Lyceum and many others wore the star, somehow I never really felt that bad. A lot of people were in the same situation.'

The Jewish deportations began in earnest. During the short life of the Jewish Lyceum – the makeshift school designed to concentrate Jewish children into one place of learning - teaching of a kind was provided to several hundred schoolchildren over varying lengths of short stay. Here historian Jacques Presser could continue his passion for imparting knowledge to his young charges, and Jetteke could continue her friendship with Margot Frank, elder sister of Anne. Perhaps ironically, given that it was a school for Jewish children only, the school was something of an innovative melting pot. It included the children of German refugees, and it included local children from all social strata. Jetteke remembers one of the girls in her class coming from the Jewish working-class district of Amsterdam: it presented a different and unfamiliar world to her. 'It wasn't that you discriminated, but you were brought up to be aware of your status. My parents were excessively worried that I might begin to talk with a broad Amsterdam accent. They were always correcting me if I said something that they thought didn't follow the etiquette.'

Despite describing the situation at the school as 'absurd', Presser did what he could to provide an education that also offered some kind of escape from constant anxiety: for example, he gave a course on the theme of Romance, explored through a series of readings, special lessons and musical performances. It was the first time in senior school that Jetteke had attended a mixed-sex class, and with boys outnumbering girls by three to one she loved the attention paid by potential suitors and soon found an admirer. But Jetteke had to walk the journey to and from school - Jews were by now banned from travelling by public transport or riding bicycles - and the walk through the streets of Amsterdam felt threatening; there was a new regulation affecting Jews almost by the day, and Jetteke often sensed that she might 'suffocate with fear'. On some days, if the tense atmosphere on the streets was heightened by the brutal chaos of a further round-up, there would be empty chairs where pupils remained at home for their own safety. But there were other, more sombre, justifications for absenteeism. There were mornings when the attendance register was called and a pupil would indicate the reason for a school friend's absence with – as Presser recounts - 'a few seconds of silent mime, repeated on dozens of occasions': a slight wave of the hand to indicate the child had gone into hiding, or a clenched fist to indicate their capture. But even so, as Jetteke recalls, 'it wasn't as bad then as it was later to become'.

Although Professor Herman Frijda had declined membership of the Jewish Council on the basis that its principal purpose was to assist the anti-Semitic policies of the German occupying force, there were departments within the Council that could be used – secretively - to actually help Jewish people stay alive. He served, for example, as Secretary of the Committee for Administering Funds – a committee that his brother-in-law, Leonard Frank, chaired: funds were always needed to help people go into hiding. The two men were also severally involved in committees for support and social work, socio-economic affairs, and personnel. Frijda also had contacts with some trusted members of the Jewish community involved in resistance activities, and allowed his home telephone number to be used to pass on warning messages whenever a new round up of Jews was imminent. Leonard Frank's unauthorized – underground – activities as a lawyer working *pro bono* for desperate Jewish clients, and his devotion to the patients and staff of the Jewish psychiatric hospital of which he was a dedicated board member, would lead directly to his arrest, deportation, and death.

This is how Herman Frijda immersed himself in work once relieved of his academic post; and since Jetteke was still studying at school and unable to assist with many domestic chores, it was necessary again to search for domestic help following the enforced departure of a *non-Jewish* maid (now prohibited by yet another decree) who had been with the Frijda family since 1938. He placed an advert in the *Jewish Weekly News* of 8 May 1942: 'Seeking: capable young woman, for household chores, live-in or out. Apply: Prof. Frijda, Corelli Street 3, Tel. 28612.' Although Professor Frijda invited replies by telephone, within two months the authorities would even forbid Dutch Jews to use a phone. And before the end of those two months number 3 Corelli Street would be deserted.

***

The seemingly random round-ups of Jews from the streets of Amsterdam by day, and the jack hammering on front doors theatrically lit by the headlights of leering trucks in the dead of night, were eventually replaced by a more coldly bureaucratic method of selection for deportation. A department of the Jewish Council responsible for 'emigration' arranged letters to be sent family by family, name by name, in alphabetical order, requiring that they report to a stipulated location on a specified date and time for eventual transfer to the transit camp at Westerbork, and thence, subject to being declared medically fit, to German labour camps to work. Some with suspicious minds might have questioned what kind of work was envisaged, given that men and women of all ages and infirmities, children and babies were being called up. The letter posted through their letterboxes contained a short and very prescriptive list of items they should pack into a strong case or rucksack, including just two pairs of socks and underwear, two shirts, two sheets and blankets, a towel, toiletries and a bowl, cup and spoon. There was considerable pressure to comply. On 14 July 1942 an extra edition of the *Jewish Weekly News* announced that:

The Security Police have informed us as follows:

Approximately 700 Jews have today been arrested in Amsterdam. If the 4,000 Jews who were this week given notice to report for transfer to labour camps in Germany do not do so, the 700 arrested persons will be sent to a concentration camp in Germany.

The joint chairs of the Jewish Council for Amsterdam.

A. Asscher

Prof. Dr D. Cohen

An interesting feature of this announcement is the distinction drawn between 'labour camp' and 'concentration camp', with the clear implication that the latter would be a significantly worse fate than the former, which raises the question as to what readers of the newspaper thought the conditions of a concentration camp might be like. And such a question leads inexorably to the endlessly anguished-over question as to what Jewish people actually knew, or at any rate might have reasonably concluded, would be their fate on the available evidence. Nico Frijda remembers that elder brother Leo taught him a song written by prisoners in Nazi labour camp Borgermoor as far back as 1933 – a protest song known as 'The Peat Bog Soldiers'. One of its verses paints a bleak picture of what a 'labour camp' – the lesser evil - actually entailed:

> *Up and down the guards are marching,*
> *No one, no one can get through.*
> *Flight would mean a sure death coming,*
> *Guns and barbed wire block our view.*

***

News of the first mass deportations was slow to reach London – secret lines of communication still painfully inefficient. When Dutch prime minister-in-exile Pieter Gerbrandy did receive the reports, he was anxious to immediately address the people of occupied Netherlands. On 25 July 1942 via the BBC's *Radio Oranje*, some ten days after the first train containing 1,135 Jews had departed from Westerbork with a final destination of Auschwitz, his voice was heard over the radio back home:

Fellow citizens,

[...]

As disturbing as these reports may be, they are not entirely unexpected, either for you or for us. When one reviews the various regulations that the enemy has enforced upon Dutch Jews over recent months, they all point in the same direction. The enforced relocation of Dutch Jews to Amsterdam, the physical identification of the oppressed by means of the un-Dutch Jewish star, the ban on Jews entering the homes of their non-Jewish neighbours, the travel ban, the ban on ownership of a bicycle... all these measures point to the clear intention to fasten a noose around a group of 180,000 Dutch citizens, with the intention in turn to carry out the outrage against defenceless people intimated over recent weeks in one fell swoop.

[...]

*People of the Netherlands! It is fitting at a time like this to pray to our Heavenly Father who suffered for **us all**. We know that these terrible events cause all of you immeasurable sadness. This will spur on those remaining to greater steadfastness.*

128

Have faith and persevere. The weapons of tyranny shall not always overpower the spirit.

Meanwhile, however, cattle trucks fully loaded with frightened people were setting off from Camp Westerbork in the east of the country, week in, week out, to arrive days later at Auschwitz or Sachsenhausen concentration camps. And the Jewish Council offered little solace, less still salvation, to those in receipt of letters requiring them to report, for example, to the Holland Theatre in Amsterdam – renamed the Jewish Theatre in 1941 – and which, by 1942, had become an overcrowded holding pen of stalls, grand and upper circles for thousands of Jews awaiting the first leg of the journey to Camp Westerbork. On 16 October 1942, in response to a letter from a Mr Louis Polak begging for help, a representative of the Jewish Council's Exemption from Deportation Committee wrote:

Dear Sir,

With reference to your letter of 13th instant regarding an exemption from deportation for Mrs E. Cohen-Leeuwenstein, I must regretfully inform you that there is nothing that I am personally able to do.

Yours faithfully,

A. Krouwer

On 7 August 1942 the *Jewish Weekly News* conveyed a further notice from the German authorities:

1. *All Jews who fail to respond immediately to a notice to report for transportation to Germany for work will be imprisoned and sent to Mauthausen concentration camp.*

2. *All Jews who fail to wear the Jewish star will be transported to Mauthausen concentration camp.*

3. *All Jews who move home or residential address without permission from the authorities – even for a temporary period - will be transported to Mauthausen concentration camp.*

Jewish people were now excluded from all economic life. They had no rights left, and no possessions. On 24 September 1942 German chief of police in the Netherlands, Rauter, wrote to his boss Heinrich Himmler: 'On 15 October the Jews in Holland will be declared to be as free as birds'.

***

129

Nietzsche wrote: 'He with heart is one who knows fear, but vanquishes it'. Both Herman Frijda and his eldest son Leo knew a great, sometimes paralyzing fear. And if, perhaps, Leo would ultimately vanquish his fear in a way that his father could not, neither of them permitted such panic attacks and constant dread to deter their steadfast, active opposition to the policies of the Nazi occupiers of their country. Nevertheless, the tense atmosphere at home at 3 Corelli Street was becoming unendurable. Jetteke recalls that 'If someone rang the doorbell, my father wanted to jump off the balcony and I […] had to pull him back. […] He used to go on to the balcony and climb over with one leg. Of course, every time it was a frightening situation. Or he would go to the bathroom and open the medicine chest, and I would have to follow him. Those sorts of things, you could have cut the atmosphere at home with a knife, there was shouting and screaming. It wasn't a pleasant situation. [My father] shouted but we couldn't understand him. He was afraid.' Jetteke was not at home the day that the wagons pulled up on Corelli Street and the security police pummelled on their door. Professor Frijda and Nico had managed to climb into the attic and hid there until all was clear. It was a sign of an urgent need to find somewhere safe to hide - not for a few tense hours, but for the foreseeable future. It would not be easy to arrange, and it would not be an easy time to endure, not least because each member of the Frijda family would now become separated from the rest.

In the summer of 1942 George Puchinger, a twenty-one-year-old history student at Utrecht University, received a visit from a banker from Amsterdam. His visitor had learned of Puchinger helping a couple of Jewish families go into hiding and urgently sought the same help for his former teacher, Professor Frijda, and two of his children. Puchinger was as worried that word of his illegal – and therefore dangerous - activities had apparently spread to Amsterdam, as he was irritated that as a student of Utrecht University he was being asked to help a professor from Amsterdam: 'Couldn't those left-wing Amsterdammers do something for their own professors?' he wrote scathingly in his memoirs. He recounts that Herman Frijda felt similar antipathy to his university and expressed the view that once the war ended he would have little appetite for returning to an institution whose members had left him to his fate. Puchinger first visited Frijda at the family home in Corelli Street, then at another, safer, contact address in order to make preparations. Frijda's aim was to secure hiding places for Jetteke and Nico; he wanted to continue to work for the committees of the Jewish Council through which he (and Leonard Frank) could be of real service to the Jewish population; Puchinger advised him that it was safer, however, for them all to go into hiding. Leo was already working in the resistance under a false identity, and Dora, Professor Frijda's now estranged wife, had made plans to escape to Switzerland with a man she had fallen in love with and was living with, Dr Fritz Aron. Her own need for safety had become urgent – having received the letter requiring her to report for deportation – and she spent four weeks in hiding with Aron before undertaking the dangerous journey. Once in Switzerland she would explain in a written statement to the authorities in Berne that she had planned to bring her children with her, but that her ex-husband had acted too quickly in arranging for their hiding, so when the time came to take them to safety in a neutral country they could no longer be reached. Nico and Jetteke would hide 'in plain sight' in the small town of Zeist - Nico eventually with Puchinger's own family - and be given false names and background histories so that, subject to great precautions, they could venture out onto the streets. Each, however, would change address frequently at the start of the process in a manner that was disorientating – Jetteke five times in quick succession. The process was nightmarish; it involved a secretive chain of resistance workers negotiating arrangements right up to the last moment. Nothing was certain until it happened. In her diary, Hanny Michaelis describes waiting for news that she had been found safe hiding: 'Since nine thirty I have been sitting waiting in a strange room for a telephone call to tell me that the address where I might be offered safety will actually take me. It's important enough – by two o'clock this morning I am supposed to report to the Holland Theatre for transportation'. The recognisability of Professor Frijda, however, amongst a great many of his students and former colleagues, as well as those who may have seen his face in the newspapers, created even more of a problem. Nevertheless, a safe place was found for him in the Frisian town of Leeuwarden, at the home of a Mrs Van Diemen, and it is care of her address that the rarely-permitted correspondence between father and his three children could pass.

***

Shortly after Professor Frijda, Nico and Jetteke had discreetly left their home at 3 Corelli Street the authorities, finding no signs of current occupation at that address, sent in the removal firm Puls. Managed by long-time Dutch Nazi party member Abraham Puls, this family-owned company had been hired by Herman Frijda to move his family's belongings into their new home in 1939. Now the same firm had been given the task of stripping to the bone the homes of Jewish families, a small number of whom had gone into hiding, but the great majority of whom had compliantly reported themselves for deportation to the east. Puls's team worked with vulture-like efficiency – nothing going to waste - and such was the firm's notoriety that the business name became used as a

131

verb to describe their specialist work: around 29,000 homes are reckoned to have been 'pulsed' in this way. The intention of the German occupiers was for all these household contents to be shipped to Germany to provide for the German people, especially those bereft of their homes and possessions through allied bombing, as well as to help finance their war effort. Often, however, neighbours got there first and picked out some choice items - as did Puls's own employees - and many goods were snapped up by Dutch dealers. Homes could be ransacked even before the food left on the hob had grown cold: mattresses would fly down staircases, out through front doors, and tumble onto streets. Sometimes the neighbours would first ask for permission: 'If you do have to go away, could I have some of your stuff?' but often, as Katharina Blog-Suesan recalls, it was the 'so-called 'good Dutch' who were out to get the belongings of Jewish people. They sneaked off with chairs and tables; even entire three-piece suites were stolen. That, too was *pulsing'*.

Leo would shortly learn of how his father and brother had hid in fear for their lives amidst the roof timbers of their home and of how Puls would eventually remove from the rooms below everything that his firm had transported there three years earlier. On visits to the Boissevain home at 6 Corelli Street he would gaze across the street at his empty and forlorn family home. He would write about such feelings in a short prose work published under his pseudonym Edgar Fossan in the monthly underground literary magazine *Lichting* that he would create with Theo Hondius and other students from Amsterdam and Utrecht.

The House

This is where I was born. It was my home for eighteen years. When I turned six I would walk down the small street each morning to the school on the corner, just there, on the left. By the age of sixteen, I had begun to resent this journey, every day the same. My fantasies craved variety, excitement, danger. Two years later, reality wove itself into my dream. Terror now roamed the streets like a slithering, grey serpent. Discharged bullets, now pale shards of metal, drifted around on street corners. It was always like this when late in the evening the door bell would ring: from home after home families would be taken out and pushed into the waiting police wagons, always with some degree of violence. From most of them, nothing more was heard of again.

One evening, they rang our door bell too. Over time we had come to learn all that this would mean, and we did not go to answer. The door broke into splinters under the blows of a crowbar. But the hunters had to return empty-handed; for they hadn't lived eighteen years in this house and they had overlooked the small wardrobe at the back of the attic above their heads. A few weeks later lorries with foreign-sounding place names pulled up quietly in the street. Within a few hours the house was stripped bare.

One night, many months later, I was once again back in that house. It was a clear night, the moon almost full; the roads in the neighbourhood were almost deserted at that hour. I walked along the silent street and stopped opposite the house, hesitating. Motionless in the midnight blue moonlight lay the corpse of a small mouse by a lamp post. Its tail and hind quarters had rotted away. It gazed across at the dead black windows and did not move. By its side lay a small bottle and a piece of cloth. It must have been polishing the door bell; a shaft of light tied it to the door. I lay my hand across its back. Its wary eyes shifted from my face back to the windows; it seemed to draw groaning breaths, almost to raise itself up a little. Then it gave a faint sign towards the door, with a gaze that travelled parallel with the line of light.

I crossed the street. And the door stood ajar, waiting for me. Cautiously, I pushed it open and climbed the bare wood staircase. After a short while a boy came down, nodded briefly as a sign of recognition, and then disappeared again. They had also taken away the mirror half way up the stairs. I wandered through a few empty rooms to the continuous creaking of wood. I knew its stories. I could not tolerate it for long. Up another staircase. I wandered around, searching. On one of the doors was a metal name plate. I traced around the engraved letters, feeling an E and then an L, and then a long scratch. From somewhere a gramophone began to play and I listened to a melodious, monotonous song, perhaps a song from the east. I entered my room. It was still completely furnished. In the corner the floor lamp was lit and in front of it my deep, comfortable chair. Then I noticed the bed, the piano, the writing desk. But my attention finally rested on the armchair, an attention that my armchair certainly demanded.

For in the armchair, curled up snugly, that is where I found you. At first I saw only the patch of light there where the glow of the desk lamp shone through your blond hair. You spoke only with your eyes. And they were so full of words that we shall never understand. They were so full of distance and that, I remember, was the first thing that attracted me to you, back then. You were a person filled with the melancholy of what lay far off, in place and time, and with a longing to be home. And now, too, you were the very image of the entire universe, for your eyes were also warm and glowing. They were also dead, of course, but I did not then realise that.

I sat down by your side in the chair, and leaned against your shoulder and fell asleep. And the dead mouse came back to my mind. It was cold outside. I threw a cover out to out. "Has he been officially appointed to stand on watch, or does he do it of his own free will?" I asked. You didn't know and shook your head with a smile, looking towards the lamp, the fire in the corner, and the small, crouched-to-the- ground bed.

On the wall on the left all the wallpaper had been torn away in strips and bits of broken plaster lay across the floorboards. Someone had turned over the gramophone record. It played the same song.

I took a book from the cupboard and read you a poem; I don't recall which one. Only that it was passionate and rebellious in the beginning, turning bitter and cynical in the last verses. I read it several times over, and then when you had learned its lines you went over to the window and gazed out onto the noiseless street, full of deep shadows cast by the full moon. On the pavement opposite a man walked by, out too late: every footstep was a venture. You lay your arm on my shoulder and I wrapped my arm around your waist, and that is how was stayed gazing out into the night, and you pointed laughing to the sky, where the stars were only faintly to be seen through the clear moonlight. I squeezed you tighter and the light continued its embraces inside and around my head.

The song had become very soft and deep.

The night breeze played with the curtain. With a deep kiss it dissolved into some elongated form like a stack of books or a casket, and flew upwards, straight into the heavens, and disappeared from sight.

My footsteps back through the empty house clattered hollow and the whole street shook when the door fell shut behind me. I looked carefully around me and then walked in haste back to other, unknown streets of Amsterdam.

XV

Leo, Lichting, and CS6

'The individual has always had to struggle to keep from being
overwhelmed by the tribe. To be your own man is a hard business. If you
try it, you will be lonely often, and sometimes frightened. But no price is
too high to pay for the privilege of owning yourself'

Rudyard Kipling

During his time as a trainee medical analyst at the Central Israelite
Hospital – in April 1942 he is granted a waiver for part of the 'general
analyst' exams and in July is issued with a certificate by the hospital
director confirming his status as an employee - Leo met and fell in love
with Irma Seelig, a German Jewish refugee seven years older than himself.
Irma had grown up with her family – parents and elder sister – in the small
city of Homburg in the Saarland, where her parents owned a shoe shop.
The Nazi boycotting and looting of Jewish businesses caused her father to
fall into a deep depression and he was admitted to a psychiatric institution.
Fleeing Germany in April 1934, Irma first registered in the Dutch
municipality of Apeldoorn. Here she obtained work as domestic staff at a
large psychiatric institution - *Het Apeldoornse Bos* - having been refused a
permit to train at the institution as a nurse. In 1938 she was registered as
having moved to Amsterdam and eventually, sometime after the German
invasion of the Netherlands, was allowed to take a course at the Central
Israelite Hospital as a medical analyst. It was here, after her relationship
with a doctor had broken up, that she got to know and fall in love with
Leo.

Life was dangerous at the hospital. Leo still worked there under
his own name, and was still registered at the family address on Corelli
Street. Resistance workers acting in loose coalitions and some posing as
medics – including, almost inevitably, Mies Boissevain and her twenty-
year-younger sister Hester - were sometimes able to rescue Jews who were
locked inside the holding pen that was the former Dutch Theatre awaiting
deportation to the east by carrying out 'routine' examinations of the
inmates, certifying selected persons as sick and in need of urgent

treatment, and bringing them to the hospital where they could stay in relative safety till a more permanent hiding place could be found. However, there were frequent German raids to endure. On one occasion a doctor at the hospital, Maurits Poons, had just enough time to hide ten 'patients' in a lift that for the duration of the raid he was able to render out of action.

In summer 1942 Leo therefore leaves the hospital and goes further underground, using his assumed name as the brother of Mien Harmsen to find employment at Teerbedrijf Uithoorn, a coal tar processing plant located just north of Amsterdam. Its Catholic owner Frans Van Seumeren was sympathetic to the plight of German Jewish refugees and willing to help them and others facing hardship when opportunities arose, but always did so anonymously: he taught his children that 'only arrogant people give money in a public way'. In 1939 he offered work to such a refugee, Sebald Müller, whose twenty-five years' experience in the tar-producing industry in Germany before his escape would prove a huge asset to his new boss and company. To protect his identity, Müller worked under his first name of Sebald – and only his employer knew him by his German family name. With such paternal management the factory was therefore a relatively safe place of work for Leo, too, even when an inspection and requisitioning spree known as a 'Rüstungsinspektion' conducted on behalf of the German army turned up at the factory premises to order that the company's products be sent to Germany to aid the war effort. Over the next few months, however, Leo's chosen life of resistance work would occupy more and more of his waking hours, so that he would also resign from this job. His entire life is now lived in secret; it was a transition that resistance member Maurice Ferares described as a 'leap into the dark'.

***

The Boissevain and Frijda families had been helping German Jewish refugees virtually since Hitler's rise to power, and they redoubled their efforts after the invasion of the Netherlands. Indeed, when family head Jan Boissevain was arrested in March 1942 and transported from prison camp in Amersfoort to Vugt concentration camp – his second arrest following a three-week detention in December 1941 for being caught lending money to Dutch Jews – youngest son Frans recalls that 'the floodgates opened'. Mies Boissevain described her sons as 'infuriated' by the arrest of their father. Circumstances were necessarily different for the Frijda household, tagged with the yellow star on their outdoor clothes: once Professor Frijda and his younger son and daughter had gone into hiding, and Dora Frijda had found sanctuary in Switzerland, it was left to

Leo - living 'underground' and with his false identity - to 'refuse to toe the line'. For the Boissevains, it was rather a matter of hiding in plain sight. The windows of the family home were large and let in light, and gave no clue as the activities conducted by the Boissevain boys in their secret workshop. Furthermore, their mother 'rented out' properties on Corelli Street vacated by Jewish families to members of the German security service on the basis, perhaps, that keeping close to one's enemies offered some kind of protection. The boys in the basement – Gideon and Jan Karel – were joined by their younger second cousin, Louis, a student at engineering school, and by Sandor Baracs, a Hungarian Jew who came to Amsterdam in 1927, acquired Dutch nationality, and would eventually fall in love with the boys' young aunt, Hester, whilst living in hiding in her canal-side home on the Keizersgracht from September 1942 onwards. A decade previously, a young German friend had given Baracs a gift of Hitler's 'Mein Kampf': she insisted that he read it to understand Hitler's ambitions for the country and for Europe. Baracs overcame his initial hostility to reading the book, became convinced of the extent of Hitler's maniacal tyranny, and undertook a mission to warn all his friends and colleagues. 'But most of them did not listen', he recalls. Baracs understood the need to oppose Hitler with *armed* resistance – an out and out fight to the death. And so, in the basement of Corelli Street 6, where a firing range had been constructed, he gave instructions on how to fire weapons to the young men and women slowly coalescing over the mid-months of 1942 into a resistance group.

'The sons of plutocrats', was how the national socialist press derided the exploits of the nineteen resistance fighters executed on 1 October 1943. They had a point. Guido van Suchtelen, for example, would refer to, and eventually come to reject, the 'aristocratic humanism' of his father. The group's membership of young men - and women - some still in their late teens, increased through the recruitment of former school or university friends; many had attended together the two or three schools in Amsterdam that fed their charges almost as a matter of course to Dutch universities, to train as doctors, lawyers, accountants, academics, or business leaders, as younger clones of their fathers. With former school friends, recalls Sylvie Boissevain, sister of Jan Karel and Gideon, you knew where you stood. The group had a liberal, left-wing outlook with ambitions for the sort of society they were fighting to create once the war was over – by no means a simple return to the *status quo* before the occupation. In a few short months they would form contacts with the military wing of the outlawed Dutch communist party, which would instil in them the need for a more professional, military discipline. However, although the group would regularly hold propaganda classes for small and intense groups of adherents, and preach Malraux's novel 'Man's Fate' - about the 1927 failed communist insurrection in Shanghai - almost as their Bible, what mattered was not whether the group's members were paid-up communist party members, but that they were committed to the cause of resistance, and had skills that were of use to the group: the Boissevain family shared, after all, a deep Christian faith; Jan Verleun had been a Catholic altar boy; whilst 'Pam' Pooters - a slightly older, married, leading member of the group with a reassuringly laid-back charisma - had been thrown out of the Dutch communist party having been denounced as a treacherous Trotskyite.

Jac van der Kar, a Jewish resistance fighter, recounts how in the early days of the occupation he received help for his own resistance activities from 'the Boissevain group'. In the latter half of 1942 the name 'CS6' would be coined and over the following months acquire a reputation that would spread across the country, particularly amongst student resistance groups in other Dutch cities. The code name was most likely inspired by the Boissevain family address of 6 Corelli Street, which became a kind of headquarters and spiritual home for the group: Mies Boissevain – 'Mammie' - would become a surrogate mother to many of the young members. However, not all group members understood this name association: Marianne van Raamsdonk was amongst several who maintained that CS6 stood for *Centrum Sabotage 6,* whereby the number six referred either to its six founders (as claimed by Marianne) or to the five previous incarnations of the group (as claimed by another member): in any event, so they agreed, any link to the address on Corelli Street was mere coincidence. To have conflicting beliefs as to the derivation was advantageous: the risks of succumbing to brutal interrogation if captured were such that the less one knew about the group the better.

Notwithstanding the munitions factory below stairs at number 6, the initial – and continuing – concerns of the group were not primarily the imminent waging of war against the occupying tyrant, but rather the saving of Jews from deportation and the finding of ways to support them and those willing to hide them with food and other necessities. It wasn't just Jews that needed help. The Germans had introduced the forced deportation of men from occupied territories across Europe to Germany to help work in the factories and fields – the *Arbeitseinsatz.* If, perhaps, a husband and father refused on moral grounds to report for transport, the only option was to go into hiding, and that meant reprisals against his family such as the withholding of ration coupons, and thus hunger. The father of a twelve-year-old girl called Anneke went into hiding to avoid such deportation, and it thus became very hard to feed the family. Anneke recalls how her mother sent her out one morning on a long walk (bicycles had been confiscated) over many kilometres to the farm of her aunt and uncle to ask for food. The journey there and back took the whole day. She returned home in the evening dejected and in tears, a bag of potato peelings in her hand; it was all that her relatives were willing to spare. So CS6 distributed ration cards and false identity papers. Gideon Boissevain procured a printing press, and Johan van Dijk, a photographer's son and friend of brothers Gideon and Jan Karel, was tasked with taking passport photographs intended for the forged identity papers of resistance fighters and those wishing to hide in plain sight: one hundred and sixty rolls of negatives would survive the war, along with records of particular commissions and those who commissioned them – including Jan Karel himself - but there are very few names to put to the thousands of now unknown portraits.

Young people joined the growing snowball of CS6 as 'couriers', to pass messages and deliver documents and illegal newspapers from one person to another, from one part of town to another. One of this burgeoning number was seventeen-year-old Theo van Haaren, a born rebel who had been invited to leave his strict Catholic school after pleading the case for Nietzsche in class, and who had been recruited through his older cousin and senior member, Jan van Mierlo.

Another such courier was Bert Schierbeek. To the disappointment of his parents, Schierbeek twice failed his final-year exams, preferring to read 'pointless and dangerous' philosophers instead of doing his schoolwork. A new arrival in the city from a farming community in the east of the country, his eyes opened wide to an exciting, slightly decadent metropolitan world: 'Despite everything it was a good time, a really good time. Never before had I come across gay men, but they turned out to be extremely nice people, and I spent evenings talking with them'. With an ID card confirming his profession as farm labourer, and with a weathered, lined face that fitted the job description yet concealed his insatiable consumption of literature and philosophy, Schierbeek was introduced into the group by Leo Frijda, Hans Katan, and Reina Prinsen-Geerligs. He was useful to them: 'I certainly didn't form part of the hard core of CS6. At Emmastraat 1, where I lived, they did once meet to draw up plans. My activities? A friend of mine, Jan Pape, had a dairy in the town of Boekelo, the place where I grew up. Jan collected ration cards from the farmers. He would pass them on to me and I would then distribute them amongst the various addresses across the city where people were in hiding'. Schierbeek became particularly friendly with the half-Jewish, and thus expelled, biology student Hans Katan, who would drop by his home with the latest news: 'We sat for hours discussing what should happen after the war. [...] He was a communist, a template for a serious, left-wing intellectual. He did possess, however, a necessary dose of cynicism, and you could enjoy a laugh with him, but that didn't happen often'. Together they also discussed philosophy, and agreed that 'the truths posited by most philosophers are not so hugely important; however, what is important is the method of their discovery. It is this that creates freedom!'

Schierbeek would later express the belief that fellow members of CS6 had nothing to do with literature: 'People within my resistance group', he wrote, 'had no connection at all with literature, not even Reina Prinsen Geerligs – a girl of about eighteen or nineteen, who wrote nice pieces, but these had more to do with 'fundraising efforts' in those times than with literature'. Schierbeek was wrong. Nonetheless, his claim showed the extent to which group members compartmentalised their lives, deciding what parts of their lives they were willing to share, and with whom. Mien Harmsen, who provided a roof over the heads of Leo, and later of Hans Katan and others, knew better: 'They were wonderful young people. In the intensity with which they lived their lives, they wrote poetry and essays, which they published in an illegal magazine'. The magazine that Mien was referring to was called 'Lichting'.

***

In the autumn of 1942 Theo Hondius, the friend with whom Leo had attempted an escape by boat to England, received a visit from Gerrit Jan de Jongh, an arts student he knew from his own short time as a law student at Utrecht University. De Jongh threw down a challenge to Hondius: 'Listen. I think we need to become more pro-active. My idea is to create a magazine'. Hondius responded enthusiastically. They agreed on joint editorship of the magazine, Hondius operating from Amsterdam, and De Jongh working in Utrecht, where he could access the now idle stencilling equipment from the outlawed Utrecht Student Corps in order to make copies of the magazine. They chose the name 'Lichting', which played on the meanings of the words 'luchting' and 'lichting': a clearing in a forest into which light could fall, and a new class or generation - 'the class of '42', so to speak. Was it a political gesture, an act of resistance? Inevitably so, as De Jongh indirectly confirms: 'The original idea was not meant politically. At the time we formulated plans for this magazine, our intentions were not *primarily* political'. Since November 1941, however, the creation of any 'cultural product' by a non-member of the Dutch *Kultuurkamer* was a political – and criminal – act. Initially the maximum imposable penalty was an eye-watering fine, but the authorities would later get tougher still with harsh prison sentences for some miscreants. To emphasise the political element, another of the magazine's contributors, Govert Gezelle Meerburg, recalls:

I mostly contributed to Lichting through my personal contacts with De Jongh. We often discussed aspects of literature, and it annoyed us that some writers collaborated with the Kultuurkamer on publications that received the blessing of the occupying forces. I thought it was great that De Jongh had contacts in Amsterdam with Leo Frijda and other poets. Consequently, I regarded Lichting mostly as a protest against the occupying forces and against collaborators.

Hondius approached Leo Frijda to contribute to the magazine, confident of an eager response. Leo agreed, and indeed he became, in effect, a third editor: De Jongh would later recall that Leo was present at all meetings at which editorial decisions were taken, and expressed his opinions. It was essential to adopt pseudonyms, and Leo chose the name Edgar Fossan. De Jongh chose a name for Gezelle Meerburg – which started out as A.G. de Meester Landsdorp - before the writer himself selected the more manageable name of Allard Landsdorp. It was also essential that none of the contributors knew the identities of the others. Only Hondius knew the contributors from the Amsterdam 'centre' and De Jongh those from Utrecht. And so, the first edition of fifty stencilled copies of the magazine subtitled 'Literary Monthly Journal for Young People' appeared in November 1942. It was thirteen pages long, in folio format. Hondius, writing under the name of H. ten Doohuis - an anagram of his real name – wrote a defiant introduction to the magazine:

This is not about drawing up any authoritarian programme, or creating any premature 'generation'. However, the editorial board, remaining anonymous just like our contributors, call upon anyone who wants to join with our Lichting to act now, immediately. There is a place here for everyone with something to say.

Despite the paper shortages and the Kultuurkamer, despite the German government censors and the pressure exerted upon all cultural life, this is where the voices ring out from young, mostly unknown Dutch poets that want to be heard, free of political threats or ideological coercion.

In this first edition, Leo contributed three poems plus the first instalment of his own two-part translation of Jean-Paul Sartre's work 'The Wall' (the second part would appear in the second edition of *Lichting*). It made a considerable impression on another contributor, nineteen-year-old Gerrit Kouwenaar, writing under the pseudonym K. van Ritger: 'It's curious that it was in *Lichting* that I first came across the name of Sartre. It contained an extract from 'The Wall', and this left a huge impression on me. At the time I couldn't find the book itself anywhere'.

***

Yet another contributor to the magazine would be George Puchinger, the Utrecht student who had found homes in which Leo's father, sister and brother could hide and hopefully survive the war. Nico Frijda recalls that 'Leo knew George Puchinger because [...] he was the contact figure between Leo and the family since, of course, Leo didn't know where we were. So, if there was post for us, it came via George Puchinger'.

Puchinger was something of an oddity. Two years older than Leo, he had been brought up in one foster home, and then a second, after his unmarried mother died when he was just five. He was indoctrinated into a very strict, sober and rather joyless Protestantism that must have contrasted rather painfully with the warmth and good humour that would have greeted you in, say, the Boissevain household. One senses that whereas Jan and Mies Boissevain did what they did through love for their fellow man, Puchinger – as much as he was brave and decisively on the 'right side' – did what he did more out of obedience to his faith. 'Empathetic' would not be a particularly good description of Puchinger's character, although there may have been empathy lying deep and dormant within a man who over the years had not experienced a particularly warm family life and who always struggled with his sexuality. One aspect of Puchinger's brand of zealotry – a colleague would later describe him as a 'fiery Calvinist' - was the absolute certainty that on issues of faith and morality he was right. On one occasion that he met Professor Frijda in secret with the urgent purpose of helping the professor, Nico and Jetteke find safe hiding, they discussed the Bible and the Psalms. The Frijda family were not practising Jews, and it is hard to imagine that such subjects for conversation were instigated by Frijda, at such a time. 'They were strange conversations face to face between a student of scarcely twenty-two years of age and an eminent scholar and noble person', concedes Puchinger in his unfinished autobiography. He concludes, without any hint of irony or self-awareness: 'But I knew that it was I, and not he, who was right'. Puchinger took an immediate liking to Leo and Nico, describing both repeatedly as 'courageous'. He proclaimed Leo to be the 'only brilliant figure' from the *Lichting* group. He also found Nico to be a 'spontaneous, intelligent and sympathetic person'. Nico would live for some time in Puchinger's own family home under a false identity, with a feigned 'serious heart condition' that explained his non-attendance at school and inability to venture outdoors much at all. By contrast, Puchinger's memoirs refer to Jetteke Frijda just once in passing, and he gets her name wrong – 'Anneke'. Jetteke would face some difficult times during her years in hiding, moving addresses five times: 'For the last year I was in the home of a very religious family. I had to help a lot in the house and they tried to convert me'. Their situations were distressing for both Jetteke and Nico: Jetteke, under pressure to embrace a cold protestant faith, would later recall 'even worse things, about which almost nothing has been said to this day'; Nico, under pressure to give in to the unhealthy attentions of a six-year-older man, would later recall, only half-jokingly, that on his arrest by the Germans, his immediate wish was not to have to share a cell with Puchinger. Brother and sister both faced with the troubling dilemma that this man with a rather repellent side to his character happened to be the one who was saving their lives.

Puchinger might have recalled - although there is no mention of it in his autobiography - that like a schoolmaster he would sometimes assign homework to Jetteke. In itself, this was a considerate, constructive act. There are examples of resistance workers across the country that functioned like a secret mobile library, delivering piles of books to those in hiding whom they had taken under their wings. Boredom, constant fear, and the claustrophobia of incarceration were dangerous bedfellows that could threaten the sanity of anyone enduring month after month in hiding, and in turn endanger the lives of those who were providing the hiding places if they were to be discovered by, or anonymously reported to, the authorities. It was therefore very beneficial to all concerned to keep people's minds active and engaged. In this unfortunate case, however, Puchinger had come across Leo's verse 'Quatrain' in the first edition of Lichting, presented it to Jetteke, and instructed her to write a critical appraisal of those four short lines: a younger sister being asked, for the supposed purpose of improving her mind, to analyse the thoughts of her elder brother at a time when both were in danger of their lives. And then, as if that were not a wretched enough assignment, so lacking in human insight, Puchinger marked Jetteke's essay, and put schoolmasterly comments in the margin. Jetteke preserved that essay:

Quatrain

I will not toe the line,
Nor follow where they lead.
This life they choose to live,
Is not the same as mine.

At the heart of this poem is the poet's attitude to life; one can read the lines as a forthright confession. What is written is a deeply-felt truth.

It is perhaps not easy to do the exact opposite of what 'people say', and to shake off all conventionality, because in doing so you will confront many obstacles in dealing with the world around you. On the other hand, if life is pared back to the essentials (words that the poet uses elsewhere himself), this simplifies everything. Naturally, this could not be applied to the whole of society, otherwise everything would be in even greater turmoil than it already is. It is something that applies in respect of the individual. Furthermore, of course, people are generally too much accustomed and attached to their forms of social interaction, so it is impossible for most of them to shed their conventionality. The most stupid thing they can then do is to pass judgment on those who have broken free of this yoke, because those with the courage to do such a thing, who are able to find some inner strength to be able to express their views and defy the outside world, are in some sense to be valued. This is especially true if they are honest about their deeds and have the courage of their convictions, because otherwise, if their deeds become underhand and mean, then such a mentality ceases to have any value and it is then certainly appropriate to pass judgment over it. But this does not apply at all here.

Unfortunately, most people are not yet willing to accept someone into their circle whose philosophy is different from their own, and that is a huge mistake.

The poet says it clearly: 'that's what they do, so I will do the exact opposite'. And so long as this does not cross over into obstinacy, it is a philosophy that, whilst not shared by most people, is absolutely not to be condemned.

By no means can all of the deeds carried out according to this attitude be approved of. Nevertheless, we can be assured - once we have been given sufficient information - that the deeds were done with the best of intentions, since the person who carries out such deeds has nothing bad inside him. He is just a little different from the rest of us. And the fact that he always has the courage of his convictions is in itself very laudable.

For that reason one should think very carefully before commenting about others.

XVI

The cell structure of CS6

Reflecting on their wartime exploits in a letter to a friend, resistance fighter Paul Peters recalls: 'In fact, we were a pair of well-meaning adventurers who risked all sorts of daring exploits, partly – without doubt – for the great ideal (fighting the war, freedom, etc.), but also, and not insignificantly, as an ego trip'. Tina Strobos said about joining the resistance: 'It's just the right thing to do. I believe in heroism, and when you're young, you want to do dangerous things'. One might reflect here on the perhaps reckless things that Leo did in the first year of the occupation and that put the rest of his family – his father in particular - in fear for their safety.

Perhaps joining a resistance group like CS6 was to some young members akin to joining a student club. Student associations in Dutch universities had long traditions; they inspired loyalty amongst members proud of being invited to join. Leonard Frank, Leo's uncle, would explore these many generations of traditions in his short history of *Minerva*, the Leiden University student association of which he had been a member, published in 1927. By contrast, a student society at Amsterdam University - *MARNIX* – newly founded in November 1940, and whose members included Paul Peters, engaged from the word go in clandestine work against the occupying forces by providing help to Jewish people in hiding. During the years of wartime occupation, joining a group offered a sense of belonging, a common cause, a sense of being on the side of right, and not least – for some - the opportunity for adventure and heroics. Other, older resistance members may indeed have taken advantage of precisely these youthful enthusiasms – some might argue *cynical* advantage - to recruit younger members. But none of any age were ignorant of, or so naïve as to blithely disregard, the potential catastrophic consequences of involvement in clandestine activities. Even schoolchildren understood how fragile their liberty was. One schoolgirl aged just ten at the outbreak of war recalls: 'It was an anxious time, actually. This constant fear that something could happen to yourself or your family'. Nor did the official press do anything to hide the ruthlessness of the German occupying forces; on the contrary, notices of executions of resistance workers and agitators were invariably prominent on their front-pages. And, of course, had the *Jewish Weekly News* been widely read beyond its intended – and rapidly diminishing – target audience, Dutch people would have known by mid-1942 of the weekly deportations by train to the east: by the end of the year, around 40,000 Dutch Jews would already have been sent to the death camps. As Mien ten Dam-Pooters observed: 'You could play a big or small role in the resistance. Whether you were armed resistance, or distributed newsletters, it made no difference to the krauts. In either case you risked the death penalty, it was as simple as that. We all knew that.'

Whereas some were drawn towards CS6 though friendships and personal loyalties, others, like Marianne van Raamsdonk, seem to have fallen into the work: 'Sometimes it's argued that working for the resistance was a conscious choice. I am not so sure about that […]. Actually, in retrospect, I would say that I landed in it because of the exceptional times. The resistance was something that, as it were, *happened* to me'. And there were yet others who - once the group had been taken under the wing of the Military Contact (a group within the Dutch communist party tasked with sabotage activities) in the latter months of 1942 and early 1943 - would be recruited by older, more wily, leading figures. Figures like Dr Gerrit Kastein and Mik van Gilse, who had both played their small parts in the Spanish Civil War and who, like Sandor Baracs, believed that to defeat the Nazis it was necessary to *fight* them. The greater one's knowledge and experience of the depravities of European fascism, one could say, the more certain one felt that the only chance of defeating it was to fight it to the death.

Kastein had been a member of the NVM, a Dutch communist resistance group that had survived all of three months in the second half of 1942 before its leader, Samuel Dormits was captured and – remarkably ineptly - found in possession of a childishly simple-to-decode list of members, two hundred and twenty one of whom were quickly rounded up and interrogated. The two youngest on the list were aged 12 and 15. Whilst some were released, twenty-one were summarily executed; others transported to various concentration camps where 91 died. Another group leader, Henk Speksnijder, evaded capture and continued sabotage operations with a rump of surviving members until his own arrest in January 1943, when he tried, probably in some kind of pre-arranged pact with Kastein, to commit suicide by jumping, still bound to a chair, from the upstairs window of his interrogation room. And thus, for Kastein, a leader now lacking troops, CS6 was exactly the right group, ripe for picking at exactly the right time – an 'off the shelf' band of young, idealist men and women who would be the perfect recruits to his cause. Introduced to Hans Katan and Leo Frijda, for example, Kastein would later declare with a rather chilling glee: 'They are first rate. They're those genuine, baby-faced boys. They're the sort always willing to prove how really brave they are'. Mathieu Smedts, involved in the underground newspaper *Het Parool*, recalls that Kastein '... knew how to persuade others to put their scruples to one side.' Resistance worker Jan Bons also attests to the use of 'emotional and moral pressure' by older recruiters upon younger members like himself.

Some of those who were eventually recruited, however, understood the gravity of the decision and did not so eagerly jump at the chance. Tineke Guilonard, daughter of KLM director Piet Guilonard, recalls: 'I considered my answer very carefully. By saying yes, my life would hang in the balance, more than ever before'. By saying 'yes', she chose to progress from a defensive form of resistance activity to an offensive one: '...to attack, and to thereby do my bit for the struggle that would lead to the downfall of the Hitler regime'. Vic Roothaan, a student resistance worker from Nijmegen University, near the German border, also described the extent to which joining a resistance group was a turning point in his life: 'In retrospect I see this moment as the end of my childhood and the beginning of acceptance of the responsibilities of adulthood. It is possible that Leo Frijda went through a similar experience. It was a choice that only a small group of us made and it was a clear and deliberate choice.'

Sometimes, as the situation became ever more desperate, requiring a more effective response to the fully loaded trains leaving Amsterdam each Tuesday for the transit camp at Westerbork, the younger members of CS6 would take recruitment into their own hands. Through patient waiting and watching through the dead of night, resistance members could identify opportunities to act quickly and undetected to unload a person from a train carriage ready to pull out of the railway yard, bundle them into the back of a waiting car, and drive them to safety. However, the procedure was very time- and labour intensive, and required reinforcements. Harke Kylstra recounts a very injudicious attempt by Leo and Hans Katan to engage his brother in this kind of resistance work:

I had a brother one year my senior. He had schizophrenia, and was three times admitted to different mental hospitals. He was given electric shock treatment. He was registered as a student in the economics department of the University of Amsterdam. I took care of him. He was estranged from my parents. I checked on him one day and found him in a very strange and nervous state. It turned out that Leo and Hans had asked him to survey the railway yard in the Rietlanden in the east of Amsterdam. This he had done during the night. I did not know Leo and

Hans yet. This is a typical story for the CS6. It was NOT a professional organization. My brother, whose name was Rein, was very outspoken, but obviously not the right person for this task. So I took over and the rest is history. My brother Rein kept doing minor tasks for the CS6.

Joining a resistance group was one matter: membership forged a team spirit and close bonds of loyalty within a very short space of time. The actual undertaking of any form of illegal activity, however, was an entirely different matter. The first occasion for anyone, even assigned the purportedly least dangerous task of delivering messages from one group member to another, was nerve-racking. Henri Vleeschdrager, school friend of Leo, remembers being asked to deliver some papers to resistance workers at an address in Amsterdam:

At the end of the street I saw an unmarked SS car, which I recognised by its number plate (number plates were changed regularly to defeat resistance intelligence and avoid identification, but the resistance were tipped off regularly about new ones). Seeing the car, I could have turned round and gone back without completing the delivery, but I made a conscious decision to continue the task: I thought that if I backed out there and then, that would have been the end of my resistance activities – a kind of 'crossing the Rubicon' moment.

Whilst 'older brother' resistance fighters like Kastein and Van Gilse may have recruited younger, experienced members for armed resistance precisely because their youth and inexperience made them more susceptible to the emotional and moral pressure to join, it is also true that once these youngsters did become members, their elder patrons took efforts to disabuse them of any notion that the fight would involve anything other than lives lived in a state of constant fear and dread. It was precisely because Mik van Gilse, for example, had fought against the fascists in Spain that he could warn Marianne continually of the inherent dangers: 'Never underestimate the opponent. Always be alert'. And former medic Kastein, a specialist in the nervous system, had discovered during his short 'tour of duty' in northern Spain the methods by which information could be extracted from enemy combatants. Mathieu Smedts recalls a night-time conversation with Kastein in which the latter described at length how he had even applied such methods himself in Spain. Stories like this must have chilled his young audience, and one of Leo's comrades recalls Leo's particular terror at the thought of being pricked with needles during interrogation. It was generally accepted that, once caught, a resistance member could hold out for no more than twenty-four hours following arrest before surrendering the information demanded by his or her captors.

Kastein and others, notably Pam Pooters, could also be credited for attempting to change CS6 in a direction that was more militaristically efficient and that would also, if implemented properly, improve the chances of survival by increasing secrecy within the group itself. The organization was restructured within a cell system. Members ('militia') were placed in cells of – supposedly - no more than four men or women each, with the intention that they should have no knowledge of any member of any other team. Each cell was led by a group commandant; four group commandants served a section commandant; and four section commandants took orders from a brigade commandant. The brigade commandants together formed the general staff. Proposals for group operations would be put forward by the cells and the ultimate decision taken by vote within the 'top cell': Jan Verleun explains that 'the result of a vote was equivalent to an order; you couldn't then get out of it.' Although female members were not represented higher up the chain of command, it is nevertheless reckoned that they formed around one-third of CS6 members. There was little paperwork left behind by CS6 that survived the war, but a list of the nineteen group members executed on 1 October 1943, including Leo, indicates alongside each name their position within the chain of command. Two of those, Pam Pooters and Hans Katan, were of the highest rank – members of the general staff. Leo is designated as a section commandant, alongside three others, including Louis Boissevain, cousin of Jan Karel and Gideon.

Leaving aside the simple mathematics - such a structure would mean that each brigade would contain around seventy members (and there is no evidence that the membership of CS6 ever reached such high numbers) – there were three threats to the effectiveness of such a cell system. Firstly, many members were close friends who had committed themselves to 'the Boissevain group', then to CS6, before the system was imposed, meaning that it is unrealistic to suppose that one cell could be hermetically sealed off from another (an essential element of a clandestine cell structure). Secondly, even if members of one cell were ignorant of the names of members of another, there were direct links up the chain of command that meant that if a team member were to be arrested, they could reveal knowledge that would allow the Germans to follow that chain of command to the top. Thirdly, CS6 did not act alone: for example, some of its members worked alongside the *PBC*, an underground organization that specialised in the forging of ID cards for Jews and resistance fighters; others wrote for and distributed an underground student newspaper '*De Vrije Katheder*'; and others, as their reputation spread, gave their help to other resistance groups from towns and cities across the country. Indeed, you could be drawn in to the resistance by others without knowing who they were or the group they – and thus you - worked for. Tina Strobos recalls: 'One day a man came and announced he was a carpenter, sent by the underground to make a hiding place for us. My mother looked at me, 'Do you know this man?' I said, 'No, of course not, but if we can't trust him, who can we trust?' So she agreed: 'Okay, show him the attic.' That's how I found out I was part of a network. They didn't give you an official certificate. This carpenter built sort of an attic within our attic, almost inaccessible. In one or two of the raids the Gestapo went up there and knocked around, but they never discovered it.'

To some extent the cell system did nevertheless work: Marianne van Raamsdonk refers in interviews to specific senior members of CS6 and omits to mention others, precisely because she did not know of their involvement; there again, she lists six fellow members of her supposed four-member cell, three more than the approved quota. However, as further evidence that there was some measure of secrecy, another female member, Tineke Guilonard, describes the difficulty of producing hard concrete facts about CS6 'because within our section [...] there was an iron discipline as regards not saying anything to anyone else regarding your missions and tasks, and how you carried them out'. In fact, it was not until after the war that Tineke even learned that her small cell was part of a wider CS6 resistance group..

Female members were often recruited by male members. Around one third of CS6 members were women. Marianne and Tineke were recruited by Mik van Gilse and Jan van Mierlo, respectively, to be their couriers - or 'adjutants' in the group's quasi-military speak. Eva Keuls explains, with a certain sarcasm, that: '... I was only a humble message runner for the most part, following orders from higher up', and describes one occasion when she accused some male members of not taking the precautions she thought self-evidently necessary: 'I protested this dangerous practice as much as my humble position permitted'. Nor, according to Eva, was there much tolerance of any questioning of CS6's toeing, more or less, of the Soviet communist party line, and certainly not from a female in her lowly position: 'Bram Kuiper was my classmate at the Barlaeus Gymnasium, and an ardent communist. Like most Dutch communists, he did not come out against Nazism until after the German invasion of Russia. I remember discussing with him my opinion that the Soviets were just as bad as the Nazis, which resulted in a stream of communist propaganda from him'.

However, whilst there is no evidence that female members were promoted up the ranks of the organization, some would undoubtedly take on work every bit as dangerous as their male counterparts, with whom they would often pair up to give the impression of a courting couple whilst assigned, for example, to reconnaissance duties or, in time, to assassination missions. Mik taught Marianne, for example, how to fire a gun 'for self-defence purposes only'. And their male counterparts, in a display of some gallantry, instructed them on what to say to the Germans should they be caught together: Mik told Marianne that in the event of a night-time raid 'you are a whore spending the night with me. You know nothing, and you should feign ignorance. You must try everything to save your own life'. Sometimes, although frowned upon, such relationships were more than an act to deceive onlookers. Marianne spoke of an 'intimate relationship' with Mik; they even 'married' and took a short honeymoon in the south of the country, although for two people in hiding, both with false identities, any official form of marriage was impossible. Leo and Irma Seelig were recognised within the group as being 'an item' and appear to have been genuinely in love, or at any rate a considerable source of strength and comfort for each other. Similarly, Gideon Boissevain undertook resistance work alongside his girlfriend, Lucie Visser. Sometimes the appetite for 'total resistance' was stronger in the female than the male partner. Notwithstanding his commitment to the cause of building a 'new Europe', Guido van Suchtelen would seriously doubt the policy of targeted assassinations that his more fanatical and risk-taking girlfriend Reina Prinsen-Geerligs was willing to embrace for CS6, to the extent that this would put a strain on their relationship.

One might have thought that any women members of CS6 ensnared by the secret police and brought in for interrogation would be treated more leniently by their captors than the men. Indeed, Reina Prinsen-Geerligs would write to her parents from prison: 'Don't be afraid for me. The most I will get is a life sentence. It's much worse for the boys'. Her optimism would prove to be misplaced.

***

CS6 members would live in hiding at various safe addresses. Sometimes, in the immediate aftermath of resistance activities that intensified the efforts of the authorities to hunt them down, they might hide with families they could rely on to keep them safe for a night or two. A young Philo Bregstein recalls Leo one time hiding in their family home: 'I was a child then, but I remember very well that his personality struck me as very intense. I learned from my parents that he was a 'resistance hero' and my impressions were of course coloured by that knowledge. But I remember him as a very interiorised person, with an expressive face. The

151

way he played with great musical sensitivity on our piano impressed me very much. I was already then a classical music fan, so I could judge this better than my parents!' As for meeting places, different members had their own preferred venues to 'hang out' apart, of course, from the Boissevain family home that was headquarters to them all. Jan Eylders took pride in 'the strong anti-German sentiment' amongst the staff and clientele of his Café Eylders, a café frequented by students and the arts crowd, and a favoured haunt of Pam Pooters, who usually visited in the afternoons, and whom Eylders recalls undertaking 'frequent and dangerous work in the underground'. Similarly, it was at a big café called Amstelhoek where Jan van Mierlo usually arranged his meetings. And Leo was the frequent customer of an old-fashioned bar in the old centre of Amsterdam, a place that – according to CS6 member Hans van den Dries – 'played its role in our escape routes […] If I remember correctly it also had an exit near the toilets, so that you could shake off anyone tailing you'.

***

The reputation of CS6 would spread to other university towns in the Netherlands. In Nijmegen, Vic Roothaan was tasked by his student resistance group to come up with potential sabotage operations and develop contacts with other resistance groups in other parts of the country. That is how he met Leo and Hans Katan, although real names were not used: 'Katan called himself Bernhard, but I no longer recall the name used by Frijda'. The fact that CS6 had a strong communist identity by no means precluded cooperation with Vic's group, whose members were practising Catholics in a Catholic part of the country: 'Katan, Frijda and Pooters were Amsterdammers and devoted communists, I came from south of the 'big rivers' and our group was made up of devout Catholics. Nevertheless, we combined our resistance efforts against the Germans seamlessly, and in between exchanged our thoughts on ideological matters.' Vic further recalls:

I stayed myself several times in Amsterdam, the second time in an old house on the Nieuwe Herengracht where we hid weapons under a loose floorboard. It was the home of a woman known to Leo Frijda and Hans Katan - Mien Harmsen. I also attended a meeting of around 25 students from all over the country at the home of Reina Prinsen Geerligs. We discussed what ought to happen to the Netherlands after the war. As far as I remember, I went there with Hans and Leo. Pam Pooters was there too, as the only non-student. Afterwards a few 'slept' overnight, although in fact Pam spent half the night telling of his experiences as a communist activist in the years before the war.

152

CS6 not only operated within the Netherlands. It also sought connections with resistance workers in Belgium, firstly to help establish escape routes for Dutch Jews across the Dutch border into Belgium and then south through France and into Spain, or east into neutral Switzerland, and secondly to procure weapons. Because - however efficient the bomb-making factory below stairs at Corelli Street 6 - the group had a totally inadequate number of guns for their enterprise, and further supplies were extremely hard to come by on Dutch soil. Travelling across the border was no straightforward task. Resistance worker Henk van Randwijk observed that 'Anyone engaged in illegal work [...] needed to avoid train and tram journeys as much as possible'. A 9.15 morning train left Amsterdam for the small southern town of Bergen op Zoom, on which journey the tickets and – false – identity papers of Leo and others would be scrutinised. In front of the rail station in Bergen a few local buses dithered around, but it was necessary to make a dash for the bus headed for Putte, a village straddling the Dutch-Belgian border, to avoid a forty-five minute wait for the next bus. You then had to alight one stop before the border controls. 400 metres before reaching the border you had to take a left turn and then the first road to the right, as far as the barbed wire fence. Once scrambled through the barbed wire fence, on the Belgian side of the same village, you turned left and followed a short row of houses till you came to the fifth house, entered through an open door, and once inside tipped the farmer. Out of the back entrance you then crossed a drawbridge. Turning right you headed back to the main road, and a few hundred metres further brought you to a café where, if you went inside and bought something, they would tell you if there were any German patrols checking passengers at the adjacent tram stop. And then the onward journey to Antwerp, possibly further to Brussels, and the hope that potential contact addresses would prove to be worthwhile. There was always the prospect, inevitably, of having been sent on a dangerous wild-goose chase.

***

The fact that members of the resistance faced such uncertain futures – no military uniforms and Geneva Convention to help ensure their humane treatment if captured – meant that they lived their lives in a constant state of anxiety. Paul Peters may well have gently and self-deprecatingly bragged about 'well-meaning adventurers', but he also recalls the conditions under which he lived from day to day in occupied Netherlands. You never dropped your guard, day or night. Somehow you always learned to sleep with one ear pricked for any sound that threatened danger, and with the ever-vigilant mind required to be able to wake up and effect an escape in moments. One night Peters was sleeping above a

153

bakery. It was one of those rare times when he allowed exhaustion to completely overtake him, and he fell into a much deeper sleep than usual till he woke suddenly to the noise of clomping feet chasing up the front staircase. With no idea of how long or little he had slept, in panic and sensing an ambush, he made a barefoot dash for the back staircase, out through the back of the shop and into a side street, his boots left behind by the bed he had slept in. It was a day or two later before he dared return to the bakery only to discover that the footsteps had been those of the baker and his family beginning their normal activities at the start of the day; the baker's wife expressed surprise at the manner of his departure.

XVII

Two deaths close to Leo

On 9 October 1942 Anne Frank wrote in her diary of the deportations of Dutch Jews to the east: 'We assume that most will be murdered. They talk on the British radio of gassing, and perhaps that is the quickest way to die. I feel terribly upset'. Tina Strobos, an Amsterdam University medical student sharing with her mother a large house on one of the city's oldest canals, and who over the course of the war would provide temporary hiding places to more than one hundred Jews in the attic of their home, would also listen to the BBC broadcasts – despite the death penalty hanging over those caught in unlawful possession of a banned radio set:

'When Churchill, or the Queen of Holland would speak on the BBC, we had as many as thirty or forty people come to our house after dark to listen, mostly Jews in hiding who lived within walking distance. That's how many people we knew were in hiding. In Holland it's dark in the winter around 3 or 4 o'clock in the afternoon. The broadcasts were usually around 6 p.m. so they had time to go back home before curfew at 8 p.m.'

It seems plausible at least that news from London – reliable, albeit incomprehensibly awful, news - as to the fate awaiting those forced to board the waiting trains would have quickly spread by word of mouth around the anxious streets of Amsterdam.

The Germans have by now dispensed with the courtesy of written notices to Jewish families requiring them to report for work abroad. Instead, local police stations are given lists of nearby addresses that on scheduled round-ups they are instructed to empty first of their occupants, and then their contents. Vans with loud hailers patrol the Jewish quarter of Amsterdam, demanding that people leave their homes and come out onto the street. There are no waiting convoys of vehicles: there is no transport provided for those able to walk to their respective local police stations, and for the sick and elderly the Dutch police cars on standby will only turn up if specifically requested. Maurice Ferares recalls that 'The pogroms often continued till deep into the night. We scarcely slept at all, in order not to be caught out by unexpected events. Sometimes we took it in turns to sleep'. Meanwhile, in a matter of just two days, all the Jewish work camps in the

Netherlands are systematically emptied and their inmates sent to Westerbork transit camp: over 10,000 in one day. Within a month or so, trains would be pulling out of Westerbork heading not just to Auschwitz, but now to the more cutting-edge extermination camp of Sobibor.

***

There is hunger in the Netherlands. Not yet the deliberate starvation of the population that would kill around 22,000 men, women and children in the freezing cold winter of 1944/45, but hunger nonetheless. From the very start of the occupation the Germans had regarded the Netherlands as something of a land of milk and honey, thanks to its fertile soil, efficient agriculture and the quality of its dairy produce: the occupying forces immediately seized almost half of the 2.7 million dairy cows in the country, which over the next couple of years they slaughtered, butchered, and shipped to Germany, along with 52,000 tonnes of butter and 50,000 tonnes of cheese. In 1943 Dutch ration books allowed an adult per day: 250 grammes of bread of a gradually decreasing quality, 20 centilitres of milk, and just 20 grammes of meat. In an entire year they were allowed one egg. Children were instructed by their parents not to chew gum because 'chewing gum made you feel hungry, and there wasn't enough to eat'. Between 1940 and 1943 the incidence of infectious diseases increased as a large result of poor nutrition that in turn weakened immune systems: incidences of scarlet fever and tuberculosis doubled, whilst the mortality rates resulting from the staggering increase in cases of diphtheria amongst children and teenagers in particular were thirty times higher than they had been in the late 1930s.

Not only was rationing a problem, so was the cost of food: in the space of less than a year the average price of foodstuffs had risen by over 36%. Nor was there enough fuel – which was itself rationed - to cook such food as was available and affordable. Coal deliveries had virtually stopped: Jan Verleun describes an empty coal cellar at the family home with just a little coal dust remaining hidden in its dark corners. On 13 January 1943 the *NRC* newspaper suggested a way to save on rationed fuel supplies:

Save your rations with a haybox

Keeping food hot whilst using as little gas as possible is a real problem. In winter especially, you want to eat a nice, hot meal. However, we wouldn't be able to achieve this just on our gas ration were it not for something like a haybox. It offers a practical solution to these cooking difficulties, since you only need enough fuel to pre-cook food for 1/6 of its normal cooking time. You then put the food inside the haybox for at least two to three times its normal cooking time. If you don't have a haybox a pile of newspapers should do the trick.

For Jewish people stoically awaiting deportation, the *Jewish Weekly News* also chipped in with some suggestions for its 'female readers':

Soup from leftovers

It's always difficult to make a good soup when there's no meat, especially when there is not as much milk available as before, and when the elements of a water-based soup need to be nutritious. You can achieve something, however, with the following leftovers:

A few cooked potatoes – some leftover vegetables – 2 onions – a carrot – 2 teaspoons of butter - water – a dash of milk.

Fry the onion in the butter till slightly brown, then stir in the grated carrot and the starch from the cold potatoes. Dilute this mix with water and a dash of milk to the required consistency, and then simmer. Finely chop all the leftover vegetables and cut the potatoes into small dice. Put these into the soup at the last minute and let everything heat through. If the soup is too thin for your taste, you can of course thicken it with flour or other binding agent.

It was even harder for those in hiding to receive adequate quantities of food: those without false identity papers had no claim to ration books themselves and relied on the willingness of others to share what little they had. Help also came from resistance operations to steel ration books from distribution centres, forge ration books, and generally beg for contributions from anyone they could trust. Even with ration books, the procedure to obtain rationed foodstuffs was tedious and dispiriting: newspaper announcements informed you when you could use particular numbered ration stamps, at which shops and on what dates and times: by the time you got to the designated shops you were probably forced to join the end of what seemed like an endless line. Jews were only allowed to patronise non-Jewish shops between the hours of three and five in the afternoon, by which time there would presumably be little, if anything, left on the shelves. You also needed the money to pay for your purchases: without both money and the right ration coupons – no food. Mien ten Dam-Pooters found her own way to help those in hiding:

When I went to the grocers I would make a joke: 'Do you have anything for my naughty little children?' And although the grocer had no idea who I was, he nevertheless understood my joke and handed me a big bag full of groceries!'

There were also black marketeers. Simon Kalf was the twenty-two-year-old husband of the former maid of the Frijda family. Officially, he worked for the postal service, but on the side he sold chickens and eggs in Amsterdam. Black marketeering was a risk worth taking – a standard punishment was a trip to the police station, a stern reprimand, and a fine. But dealing with Jews was another matter entirely: 'If you dealt with a Jew, you went down with a Jew'. After Professor Frijda, Nico and Jetteke had gone into hiding, and Dora Frijda had escaped to Switzerland, Kalf stayed in touch with Leo. They came to an arrangement as to how to safely provide Leo with things he needed – just 'very ordinary things' such as, on one occasion, a bed sheet. Kalf would walk down a quiet street after dark, but before curfew, with a package under his arm. From out of the darkness – a literal thief in the night – Leo would run up to Kalf, grab the package, and disappear. That way, if anyone saw the event, it would appear that some person unknown had stolen property belonging to a forlorn Kalf. It was a tense little piece of theatre that happened on around five occasions, usually in the dark, quiet side streets behind the Palace on Dam Square.

***

CS6 could no longer forge ID cards as they had done in the early days at Corelli Street 6 – the Germans had made the process ever more complicated: the weight and colour of the paper, the print type, even the thickness of the lines. 'But as you know', Jan Verleun explained to his sister, 'the first thing people check is the stamp'. So they decided to steal official rubber stamps from a government building in The Hague that now served as offices for German administrative departments. Each day for a week a different member of the group cased the joint, focusing on the lunchtime activities of its staff. By joining the lines of those waiting to apply for ID cards they had the time to casually glance around them and study entrances and exits, office doors and the paraphernalia of desk tops. CS6 leader Pam Pooters, whose official job was to drive a van for the municipal food distribution centre, drove – as the unofficial chauffeur of CS6 – a number of his colleagues on the appointed day from Amsterdam to The Hague: 'He knew how to arrange things so that, without fail, he would be available day and night', recalls Verleun. Hans Katan and Leo had volunteered for the most dangerous task because, as Verleun explained, in common with the people for whom these official stamps had a value beyond price, they were both Jewish.

And so, out of the back of Pooters' van leapt Leo and Hans, in white overalls fastened at the waist by professional window-cleaners' belts from which shammy leathers and sponges dangled on hooks. The overalls of the one were too small and his trouser legs ended somewhere around his lower shins; those of the other were too big and his trouser legs had to be turned up twice. They might have been auditioning as a slapstick double act. They struggled to balance the extendable ladders across their shoulders, and buckets of water slopped everywhere. As they extended the ladders up to the first and second floor windows at the side of the building and climbed the rungs, they listened out for a third member on the path below who would whistle Figaro's Largo al Factotum in the event of any approaching danger. Through the window on the second floor one was able to enter an office, take a handful of rubber stamps, and slide them into his pockets. Mission accomplished, they returned to Amsterdam, drenched with water from the flailing buckets, in the back of Pooters' food distribution service van. Parking up outside a grocery shop near Corelli Street, they walked back to their CS6 headquarters at the Boissevain family home where a relieved Mies Boissevain expressed herself 'terribly glad that everything had gone well'. Leo was typically in a state of nervous exhaustion, lost in some troubled inner world that music – not people – could rescue him from: 'When we are tired', wrote Nietzsche, 'we are attacked by ideas we conquered long ago'. There was a gramophone player in the Boissevain household: Leo asked one of the Boissevain brothers if he would play a recording they possessed of Bach's Fugue in D minor. Music gave some kind of equilibrium to Leo's life. Perhaps it was through his poetry that he was able to confront the discord in his world, and in music where he found the harmony.

***

Irma Seelig, according to Jan Verleun, 'did the shopping and cooked for us. She always had the ration books and coupons in her bag in case she passed a shop where there was something to buy'. She was a great emotional support for Leo. They shared a bed, became intimate, and Irma became pregnant. It would have been impossible to keep the child - a Jewish child born in a country whose occupiers were well advanced in their ambition to wipe out the Jewish population - and equally impossible to legally terminate the pregnancy, since abortion had been a statutory crime in the Netherlands since 1911. A small item in the *Jewish Weekly News* of 2 July 1943 would inform pregnant mothers that the help of a midwife during labour could be requested from the Agency for Nursing Help between 3 and 4 pm each Wednesdays; but it left unsaid the stark reality that the long-term prospects for a Jewish mother and new-born baby were dismal. Alternative – pre-emptive – help came in the form of Ben Polak, who had almost completed his training as a general practitioner at the University of Amsterdam, and his 'oldest and best friend' Dr Kastein, eventual father figure of CS6; together they had been carrying out illegal abortions in the Netherlands for years before the outbreak of war. Polak acted as the duo's anaesthetist. The procedure was not without risks, but they performed their tasks much more safely than the many street-corner amateurs who, armed with darning needles and other crude and risky methods, became colloquially known as the 'angel makers'. Irma's pregnancy was thus terminated. Rita Klijzing, sister of CS6 member Ernst, explains that after the procedure 'My brother asked my mother if Irma could convalesce with us, which is what happened. She stayed in my room'.

Leo wrote to his sister Jetteke with the news in a manner that was provocatively repellent.

Dear Jet,

[...] what will interest you greatly is that a few days ago my girlfriend gave birth to a boy; he was mine. And although this worm was only into his third month, the intention was nevertheless good. His name is Erik, and he is currently preserved in excellent health in formaldehyde.

[...] I seem to remember you once asking me for a momento, a poem or some such thing. And since your cheerful optimism sincerely pleases me, I will begin in haste on a requiem.

Jetteke didn't believe him. She interpreted his words as the macho talk of a young male staking his claim to manhood. And whilst she was wrong not to believe about the aborted child, insofar as she refused to take this cruel and vicious streak in Leo's character at face value, her instincts were correct. Whilst one can only conjecture that the experience must have been painful – physically and psychologically – to Irma, the tremendous anguish that it caused Leo requires no conjecture: it is there to read in his creative writing. In poems contained in the first and second editions of literary magazine *Lichting*, Edgar Fossan – Leo – dredges the depths of this pain. In one of these poems he borrows from his literary hero Marsman the recurring theme of a journey from one existence to another as a journey by boat across water:

Strike Out

The song by which I used to fall to sleep
Grew into a great, wild melody:
a fantasy
a dream,
or the birth of a son,
a creation of my self-procreation?

160

'Stride onward to your grave, see
Where there is a track of light.
They have lied:
They spoke of darkness and of death.
Reach the ocean shore.
Step out from every shadow.
Be the driving force,
Let them sense your enmity.'

A second poem imbued with deep despair Leo published twice; first in Lichting, and then in a short collection of poems that were the result of a joint venture with his friend Theo Hondius, entitled 'A Fight to the Death':

What Remains

Wolves.
Linked arm in arm they moved
over the lead guttering of the roof
of the old house. Once or twice
they stopped still
and stared mirthless through a window;
they saw it all: the white bed
that was the cowardly grave,
that was the unripe fruit,
that was the illusion of a dead child.
The small cortege went on ahead,
and from where a heavy coping stone
juts out above our sea,
one of them plunged to the ground...
It is talked about no more.
He continued
to fight.

In the second version, Leo reworks the last lines:

[...]
The small cortege went on ahead,
and from where a heavy coping stone
juts out above our sea,
one of them plunged to the ground...
I have cut short this verse,
...but with him the world came down.

Jan Greshoff, journalist and poet, once observed: 'A loss is no loss, because we gain from it a farewell. A gain is no gain, because we lose by it a yearning'. In his sister Jetteke's poetry book Leo wrote down the aphorism in typically compacted form: 'A loss is no loss, because we gain from it a yearning'.

Meanwhile, as Leo write to Jetteke, his former work place as a medical analysit was currently being used for 'steriliastion purposes'.

***

Leonard Frank, Leo's uncle, might well have escaped to England with his wife Beatrix and their three young sons. Beatrix was British and she and the children theoretically enjoyed the protection afforded by a British passport. But although they had the prospect of refuge in Britain and it had crossed their minds numerous times to brave the increasingly perilous and arduous journey, they chose instead to remain in the Netherlands. Putting trust in his family's dual nationality, Leonard would continue his help to the destitute Jewish community through his pro bono work as a lawyer, and in his position on the board of the Jewish children's psychiatric hospital near the town of Apeldoorn. Secrecy was essential: Beatrix recalled that their sons 'had to learn to be silent, which is hard for children'. One day in December 1942 Leonard Frank set off for work and never returned home: he had been arrested in his office. Beatrix assumed that someone he had performed a service for had surrendered his name to the authorities, possibly during interrogation. Leonard, too, was tortured in a prison camp at Amersfoort where he was secretly visited by Beatrix, disguised as a man and on hands and knees as a cleaner to scrub the floors. They were able to exchange a few final words: despite torture Leonard had betrayed no one. His journey then took him to Camp Westerbork, and then on 18 January 1943 by train on the inexorable final journey to the death camps – the forty-fourth such journey made by Dutch Jews on that route. Bidding farewell to friends at Westerbork and reflecting that his non-Jewish friends had done all they could to plead for his life on the basis of all his good deeds, Leonard reflected that 'It has been an honour to have worked with my colleagues. I feel that they did everything possible in the matter'. The transport reached Auschwitz two days later on 20 January 1943; of the 748 deportees stumbling out of the cattle wagons just ten men and twenty-five women were singled out for work, led into the camp, and tattooed. The rest - 305 men and boys and 408 women and girls - were all systematically herded into the gas chambers and lay dead within the day. Leonard was amongst that number. Beatrix would later contrast her own character with that of her husband: whereas she didn't much socialise – didn't actually much like other people – Leonard was a 'wonderful man, a really good person: my husband loved his fellow creatures – I did not'. For their part, Beatrix and her three young sons – Leo's cousins - would experience, and survive, the horrors of Theresienstadt.

***

It was at the *Apeldoornse Bos,* the Jewish psychiatric institution restful in the forests near Apeldoorn, where Leo's beloved Irma had applied in vain to train as a nurse and instead worked for a short time as an ancillary worker; and it was at the *Paedagogium Achisomog,* the Jewish children's psychiatric hospital on the same site, where Leonard Frank - who on 20 November 1935 had been one of the welcoming party on a royal visit by Princess Juliana – served as a devoted board member. In 1939, the two institutions provided care in modern facilities for around 900 patients, including 94 children. The total evacuation of the hospital – patients and staff – for transportation to Auschwitz by an additional train especially arranged by Adolph Eichmann would be remembered as one of the most grotesque crimes of the holocaust perpetrated anywhere in occupied Europe. In 21 January 1943, in the middle of a bitterly cold night, lorries rolled up outside the hospital buildings; patients and staff alike were systematically dragged from their sleep, out of their beds, and into the waiting vehicles. Dr Presser quotes one eyewitness: 'I saw them place a row of patients, many of them older women, on mattresses at the bottom of one lorry, and then pile another layer of human bodies on top of them. So crammed were these lorries that the Germans had a hard job to put up the tailboards'. The loaded lorries then drove in convoy to Apeldoorn rail station to the waiting train. The stationmaster recalls: 'the loading itself was done without great violence. The ghastly thing was that when the wagons had to be closed, the patients refused to take their fingers away. They simply would not listen to us, and in the end the Germans lost patience. The result was a brutal and inhuman spectacle'. The nursing staff, promised that they would be allowed to return home after escorting their patients to their unknown destination, were herded into the back of the train, separate from their patients.

Rudolf Vrba, a prisoner who would later escape from Birkenau, vividly recalled the arrival of this particular transport:

'In some of the trucks nearly half the occupants were dead or dying, more than I have ever seen. Many obviously had been dead for several days, for the bodies were decomposing and the stench of disintegrating flesh gushed from the open doors. This, however, was no novelty to me. What appalled me was the state of the living. Some were drooling, imbecile, living people with dead minds. Some were raving, tearing at their neighbours, even at their own flesh. Some were naked, though the

cold was petrifying; and above everything, above the moans of the dying or the despairing, the cries of pain, of fear, the sound of wild, frightening, lunatic laughter rose and fell.

Yet amidst all this bedlam, there was one spark of splendid, unselfish sanity. Moving among the insane were nurses, young girls, their uniforms torn and grimy, but their faces calm and their hands never idle. Their medicine bags were still over their shoulders and they had to fight to keep their feet, but all the time they were working, soothing, bandaging, giving an injection here, an aspirin there.

[...]

One nurse walked slowly with an old, frail man, talking to him quietly, as if they were out in the hospital grounds. Another half-carried a screaming girl. They fought to bring order out of chaos, using medicines and blankets, gentleness and quiet heroism, instead of guns or sticks or snarling dogs.

[...]

Then suddenly it was all over. The last abject victims had been slung into one of the overloaded lorries. We stood there, panting in the chill January air.

The nurses were not allowed to return home, or to work in a modern mental hospital, because the SS doctor making the selection decided the nurses would share the same fate as their patients.

The nurses were loaded onto the lorries which roared off, swaying towards the gas chambers. Not a single nurse or patient survived.

XVIII

Poetic Synthesis

'...we regard art as one of the most essential expressions of life...'

Leo Frijda

The third edition of Lichting, dated January 1943, included a treatise by Leo on the role of poetry and the task of the poet, entitled 'Poetic Synthesis'. It begins with a quotation from Hendrik Marsman's 'The Temple and the Cross':

> *"...only through a blind*
> *and dark addiction*
> *to the fever*
> *of pleasure*
> *can the soul*
> *- released from blackness -*
> *breathe purity again ..."*

Gradually, over time, it has become abundantly clear to us that our laboriously woven attire, the garments of our sham values, have grown threadbare. We have been repeatedly struck by the complete insignificance of what we believe should have set us on fire. Are you taking about lighted matches or the Sexual Question? For God's sake, stop talking about these things, because the question of matches and sexual desire are making us truly sick. It would be better for you to take your place tomorrow in a mass grave, to be consumed by fire into a little white ash, than live as a pile of faded rags. Only the flames made us happy. Nothing matters! We need preserve nothing except the reckless pursuit of pleasure as a condition for life.

Given that we regard art as one of the most essential expressions of life, only art that serves the above aims can rightly be called art.

As to the method by which we will fulfil this, our lifetime's mission, we acknowledge that we would do well to work expeditiously, before it is too late, to tear down this wall of spirit and intellect that has gradually built up around us, freeing us in our search for the complete liberation of body and soul.

If we confine ourselves from the start to the soul, we must then as a necessary precondition completely eliminate the intellectual component from all forms of art. Under no circumstances should the artist - in our case the poet – become a philosopher or a thinker; the games of the intellect must be played out elsewhere. Art serves only to represent lifeblood and feelings; it has one goal only: to move the soul.

The various forms of art attempt to achieve all of this, each in their own specific way: music strives in this endeavour through melody, harmony and rhythm; poetry through content, image and sound. And although this specific emotion undoubtedly belongs within the domain of the arts, in no sense does it meet our highest aims. Submerged as we often are by the volume of music and verse that floods over us, once in a while we are confronted by a work that we can immediately say with confidence and certainty: 'That is it. That is art'. What struck us with such unimpeachable certainty was an emotion born not merely of beauty, but of a strange, far-away and inexpressible tone; or rather a scent, that gives us a sense of what happiness could be. And we recognise that in a situation like this we should dispense with any criticism or analysis; the only appropriate response is silence. In this context the adjectives 'good' and 'bad' make a mockery of everything that we call Art and anyone who ever felt such physical sensation will understand how absurd it would be to allude to the poems by Vestdijk in such a context.

These highest consequences are the same for all art forms. What music and poetry, as well as the visual arts, share to the highest degree possible is what I would call the absolute emotion; they express themselves in the same way, in a gratification that is often described in terms such as 'melancholy', 'seudah' [the biblical feast marking the end of time], and so on.

Where the artist is consciously able to strive for the specific, the beauty of the emotion in its absolute form, this leads to complete individuality. The emotion can therefore manifest itself in moments entirely bereft of beauty, and also beyond the control of the poet. We meet it within the rational framework of Marsman's The Temple and the Cross, as well as the soulful song 'A Winter by the Sea' by Roland Holst.

It is necessary, however, for there to be a total surrender of the soul by a powerful personality. No name can be put to the indefinable feeling flowing from the soul; it is a substance that is an absolute part of the soul, able to be woken by feelings. Through their surrender, such feelings are transformed into a substantive sensation.

The reader will experience this substantive transformation as a physical experience, and a new feeling will be created, entirely as a function of their own personality and circumstances, a feeling that can be of an entirely new nature.

In addition, this surrender of the soul creates a poetic mood that can give birth to entirely unconventional verse forms and which, surrendered in unaltered state, can be the medium for the aforesaid rarefied raptures of the soul.

Provided that the composer surrenders his soul to his composition, music is the art form that by its very nature satisfies these demands through the absence of all factors pertaining to the intellect, and in wishing to avoid the trumpeting of Rembrandt (cf. Vestdijk) we can say that other art forms - and in this case poetry itself - must, in order to call themselves art, aim to achieve the same.

In the same way that playing with sounds in music can achieve our goals, so should a poem play with words; in no sense on account of their sound, but purely in terms of the supra-individual associations that they are able to create.

This leads to the creation of a poem that, controlled by a feeling, perhaps the idea for a feeling, embodies this idea through associative wordplay or an associative reality.

***

At a meeting with George Puchinger to hand over letters to be forwarded to his father, brother and sister, Leo produced a copy of this third edition of Lichting, which Puchinger read there and then. And, just as Puchinger had entered into a lengthy debate with Leo's father on theological matters and concluded that his arguments were absolutely correct and the 'learned professor' was plain wrong, so he entered into a long debate with Leo about how his ideas on 'poetic synthesis' were woefully wrong-headed. It is questionable whether it was the cut and thrust of lively debate that Puchinger enjoyed, or rather that he relished any opportunity to let loose his 'fiery Calvinist' ways of putting other people right. Puchinger's own words surely justify the question and point towards the answer: he assures us in his memoirs – as though to pre-empt any suspicion to the contrary - that he engaged Leo in a long discussion 'not to lecture and admonish him, [...] although I did fiercely challenge him'. Not only in oral argument did Puchinger challenge Leo: his riposte to 'Poetic Synthesis' – entitled 'Poetic Synthesis or Nihilistic Revolution?' – was published in the next edition of Lichting. It was a harshly judgmental article, and one that Puchinger says he later left out of his 1982 collection of essays 'not because I no longer stood by it – on the contrary! – but because I would have thereby given a wrong impression of the noble Leo to many other people.' It says something about the 'humility' of Puchinger that he believed that Leo's reputation might have been dented by his attempted demolition of Leo's ideas.

Puchinger dedicates his said article 'To my friend E.G. Fossan' (Leo's pseudonym), and then cuttingly observes: 'His way of life is not mine, and neither of us will mourn that fact...at least not right now!' Did he foresee an opportunity to put yet another person right? Leo's provocative assertion that nothing is important in life beyond a reckless pursuit of (sexual) pleasure is labelled by Puchinger as a manifesto for a 'nihilistic revolution'. Puchinger argues that 'the poet should develop all his feelings, and thus all his thoughts, as a human being, and in such a way he should speak as a human being about what at a certain moment he holds dear, or what he hates'. He almost claims a moral standing on behalf of the poet, and then decries Leo's failure to live up to these high standards, claiming that Leo 'degrades everything to nothingness, reduces everything to sham values, and what one is then left with is raked together and called SYNTHESIS'. But Puchinger conflates - and perhaps even Leo himself conflates - Leo's apparent elevation of sexual gratification as the only thing that matters in life (which, if one is not to take the claim with a generous pinch of salt, one might well choose to characterise as 'nihilistic') with Leo's struggle as a poet to crystallize an 'absolute emotion' - *whatever that emotion* – an endeavour that cannot possibly be construed as *nihilism*, a belief in nothing. How can Leo be accused of nihilism in the face of his observation that 'Where the artist is consciously able to strive for the specific, the beauty of the emotion in its absolute form, this leads to complete individuality'? And lest his critics think that by 'emotion' Leo is still banging on only about sexual gratification, he cites as examples of this emotion collections of poems by Marsman and Roland Holst.

Puchinger might have more fairly, of course, given credit instead to Leo's concern for the individuality of the soul of the poet. Leo's thesis embraces the recurring theme within, even the rationale for creating, Lichting: the expression of the individual voice. Art has one goal only, claims Leo: 'to move the soul'. To reach the status of 'Art' the work should transcend the soul of the artist to enter the soul of its audience. The quality of a poem is as much about the individual, almost physical experience of the reader in response to the poem as it is about the individual soul of its author: a burning flame of individual emotion passing from one person directly to another. In this regard, Leo's treatise was, of course, totally anathema to both national socialist and communist doctrine alike, which held that individuality was a cancer in society that needed to be ruthlessly excised. It was the publication's joint editor De Jongh who recognised, in the December 1942 edition of Lichting, the need to engage in 'the battle between individualism and collectivism; between personality and a faceless crowd'. Leo was certainly no face lost in the crowd.

XIX

The Assassination of General Seyffardt

Let not anyone pacify his conscience by the delusion that he can do no harm if he takes no part, and forms no opinion. Bad men need nothing more to compass their ends than that good men should look on and do nothing. He is not a good man who, without a protest, allows wrong to be committed in his name, [...] with the means which he helps to supply, because he will not trouble himself to use his mind on the subject. It depends on the habit of attending to and looking into public transactions, and the degree of information and solid judgment respecting them that exists in the community, whether the conduct of a nation as a nation, both within itself and towards others, shall be selfish, corrupt, and tyrannical, or rational and enlightened, just and noble.

Address by John Stuart Mill, Rector, to the students of St Andrews University, Scotland, 1 February 1867.

In January 1943 Germany was losing its battle with the Soviets at Stalingrad, its wretched defeat just a few grindingly merciless weeks away. Such would be the scale of their disaster that this would be the first occasion on which the Nazi propaganda machine could no longer get away with spurting out endless proclamations of every minor military triumph. By the end of the month, as a musical curtain-raiser to the imminent report of surrender, German radio played what Bruckner had scored as a 'very solemn and very slow' Adagio to his seventh symphony, a fitting - if reluctant – dirge in tribute to the quarter of million dead on the Axis side, and the eighty thousand or so surviving prisoners-of-war who would never return to their homelands. Stalingrad was indeed a defeat on two fronts – the military, obviously, but also the propaganda – for here one saw also the limits of Goebbels's propaganda machine: they might be able to spin bad news, but it would prove impossible to blank out terrible news completely. Even the national socialist Dutch press such as the NRC hinted that things were not going so well: 'The only thing that one can say at this point about the developments in the Caucasus is that on this situation, as on everything else, the reports from the Soviet side must be taken with a huge pinch of salt'. And whilst the Allied invasion of Italy – the 'soft underbelly of Europe' – would not be launched for another six months, and the D-Day landings of June 1944 an even more distant, almost mythical hope of salvation dreamt by those throughout Nazi-occupied Europe facing the constant threat of deportation to the Polish death camps, nevertheless the USA *had* entered the war and the British and Soviets *were* unvanquished, so there was reason to believe that the Germans might finally be on the back foot. As President Roosevelt vowed in his State of the Union speech of 7 January 1943: 'Yes, the Nazis and Fascists have asked for it; and they are going to get it'.

The majority of the population, keeping their heads down until Allied forces could deliver them from the Nazi yolk, would achieve nothing through patience and prayer; theirs is a passive collaboration, with various attempts at justification offered. As Goffe Miedema wrote in his diary in June 1942: 'A lot is going on, but it all passes you by if it doesn't affect you personally.' And in December of that year, noticing how few Jews remained on the streets, he admits to sometimes imaging their suffering, although not for long because it would otherwise leave him feeling bad '...and anyway, am I my brother's keeper?' Whether unwittingly, or with brutally honest self-knowledge, he pleads the case of Cain, murderer of his brother Abel. It may appear strange that supposedly 'good' Christian men and women should wrap themselves up in an Old Testament world, as though Christ had never existed nor the parable of the Good Samaritan ever been told.

For those small numbers of resistance fighters in the Netherlands who, like Leo, want action to save the lives of Dutch Jews – their fellow countrymen - and to obstruct the relentlessly regular cattle-class rail service to the east, it is necessary to act *now*. In the words of CS6 member Harke Kylstra: 'Leo and his friends were frantic to do something. There was not a moment to lose. No time-consuming planning or lengthy discussion. There was urgency, and activities were carried out under the most stressful situations'.

As to *what* to do exactly, help had been handed to them when Hitler granted to the Dutch Nazi party leader Anton Mussert the grandiose title of 'Leader of the Dutch People' on 13 December 1942. Mussert would have no real power: that would remain in the iron grip of the fanatical Reichskommissar seated in The Hague - Seyss-Inquart. However, to dangle in front of him the slight hope of an eventual transfer of authority to a Dutch, civilian government, Mussert is now allowed to form a kind of 'shadow cabinet' of ministers. He begins making appointments in January 1943 so that his appointees are ready to assume formal duties on 1 February. In fact these 'ministers' are deputies with no greater task than to offer up obsequious advice to Seyss-Inquart in matters within their individual portfolios. Nevertheless these developments provoke an immediate reaction from London, which acts as yet further encouragement to the resistance. Prime Minister-in-exile Gerbrandy speaks to the nation that evening via *Radio Oranje*, urging all those in the civil service to undermine all measures 'aimed at feeding the German war machine with Dutch goods and Dutch manpower [...]. No Dutch citizen can remain in any doubt as to their duty. The Queen, Cabinet and Fatherland ask, indeed demand, your commitment in the fight to liberate our land'. But how far does the Prime Minister's push for more resolute Dutch resistance aim to go?

For Leo and CS6 the issue of whether the power distributed amongst Mussert's cabinet of deputies is actual or a mere sham is beside the point: these are persons who have actively sought to serve the Nazi occupying forces, to side with the Germans against their own people. They are persons in the public eye, and the rough justice to be meted out to them would likewise grab the public attention. After Mussert himself – who is given constant protection - there is another obvious candidate amongst the ranks of cabinet members deemed most deserving of a CS6 assassination: seventy-year-old Dutch General Hendrik Seyffardt.

Having retired in 1934 with a distinguished career behind him, Seyffardt rather blotted his copybook by venturing out of retirement to accept leadership of the Dutch Volunteer Legion in July 1941, an SS volunteer unit that would fight on the Eastern Front in the 'crusade against Bolshevism'. He rallied the troops with the words: 'It is a question of Europe, it is a question of the Netherlands, it is a question of you and your children. Forge ahead, Netherlands!' He has now also accepted appointment by Mussert as Deputy for Special Services. CS6 fear that this could signal the start of general conscription in the country; they would be jolted by Goebbels' speech in Berlin on 18 February 1943 in which he declared that it had now become necessary for the Germans to accept a total war – a war that would claim all resources and every effort from the entire population. The idea of 'total war' felt like an end game; now or never. And here in the Netherlands, young Dutch men are being encouraged more than ever before to join the volunteer SS legion. The *NRC* newspaper appeals to men between the ages of 17 and 40, of at least 1.65 metres in height, to volunteer for the Eastern Front to fight against 'Bolshevism and Judaism'. They have a choice of length of service - for the duration of the war, or for a period of two or four years - and insofar as those recruited are their families' breadwinners, their families would be provided for. Great pains are taken by the Nazi leadership to convince the volunteers they are joining a uniquely Dutch unit. Those who take the uniform are allowed to wear the Dutch tricolour on their sleeves and the *wolfsangel* (symbol of the Dutch national socialist party) on their collars in place of the traditional SS runes. It is reckoned that around 25,000 young Dutch men applied to join the Waffen SS; many do so because of the lessons drummed in to them at school that communism was about the worst crime imaginable. The Dutch Legion would suffer deplorable casualties. One volunteer, Paul Metz, described events on the Russian Front in his diary entry of 24 February 1942, one year previously:

'Yesterday we had our baptism of fire! And what a baptism it was! Sunday evening we had been ordered to relieve the 9th Company that held positions near a forest. At around 20.00 hours we arrived there. It was freezing terribly; an estimated minus 25 to 35 degrees. We had to lay down in the snow. This way we waited until 07.00 the next morning. Cold! You cannot imagine. I never thought a human being could live through this. We could not eat, since all bread was frozen solid, as was the coffee in our canteens. At 07.00 we had to try to attack and occupy the forest in front of us. I was one of the chosen ones. To sum it up, it was hell! We had hardly left our starting positions before we suffered our first casualties. The Russians were hiding in the forest. From the trees and from bushes; we were fired upon from everywhere. The worst thing was that we could not spot the Russians. We had to keep moving forward whilst bullets flew past us from every direction. How I managed to survive is still beyond me. Twice we attacked, a third attack was no longer possible. To cut things short, our company suffered at least 25 casualties with 12 killed in action. I do not understand how we can continue this way. Four of these attacks and the whole company will be wiped out. And the most pathetic thing is that we have hardly seen any Russians. There go Mussert's men!'

***

News of Seyffardt's appointment is announced in the Dutch press on 4 February 1943. The response of CS6, incited by their radical leader Dr Kastein, is swift and decisive. Through a virtually unanimous democratic vote by all CS6 cells as to which of them should carry out the first liquidation, the task falls to the top cell, of which Jan Verleun and Leo Frijda are members. The result of a vote is deemed equivalent to an order – it could not be avoided. The outcome 'didn't surprise me', Jan Verleun would explain to his sister sometime later: 'there were two marksmen in our cell'. What the marksmen lacked, however, were guns. Leo sought the help of Rita Klijzing, eighteen-year-old sister of his friend Ernst. Leo used to visit their home. 'He played the piano, like I did', recalls Rita. 'He could play Mozart's sonata K331 entirely from memory. He also played the violin and suggested that we played together. So I bought a Chopin nocturne with a violin part. I gave it him and practised the piece myself, but we never did perform it together'. Rita was fond of Leo, and eager to help. 'He wanted a pistol', she recalls: 'then he would feel safer, so he said. I found out from a friend's brother [...] that he knew a former policeman willing to sell a pistol for one hundred guilders. So I went to The Hague, met him in the Terminus bar near the Hollands Spoor rail station, and travelled back with the gun. I went for a walk with Leo along the Pieter Lastmankade. He asked: 'May I carry your bag?' The pistol was in the bag, and that was how he acquired the pistol.'

On the evening of Friday, 5 February Jan and Leo travel to The Hague and call at the home of General Seyffardt, whose address at Statenlaan 103 they find listed in the telephone directory. Seyffardt is alone at home: he is a recent widower and his housekeeper has been given the night off to attend a meeting of the young national socialists – the Jeugdstorm. Leo rings the doorbell. Seyffardt comes to the door. 'I had to shoot Seyffardt', explains Jan, 'and I found it terrible'. Leo would tell his friend Mien Harmsen; 'Oh, it was very simple. We rang the bell, he opened the door, and he was very friendly, because we said we had come to sign up for [...] the Russian front. Then we shot him.' Jan fired two shots, but not before standing to attention, saluting, and pronouncing a sentence of death on the elderly man standing there in warm slippers as though he had just got up from a cosy chair: 'General Seyffardt, I am here as a soldier to carry out an order. You have been sentenced to death under martial law for breaking your oath of allegiance to Queen and Country'. The retired general, in shadow and standing half behind the open door, is hit by both bullets, but would not die instantly. He manages to stagger to the phone to summon help. In the panic of their escape, Jan and Leo lose each other. Leo needs to offload their weapons in case he is apprehended on the return journey, but they are much too valuable to simply toss into some overgrown ditch. A fellow resistance fighter living nearby recalls that Leo turned up at his home that night and handed him – wrapped only in paper - 'the still smoking revolver and a second weapon' with the instruction to return the two firearms to Amsterdam: 'I don't recall how any more - perhaps on bike or by tram, I'm not sure – to the Hollands Spoor rail station and from there by train to Amsterdam'. He also recalls – indeed he wrote down the words immediately afterwards, since 'it is something, of course, that for the rest of your life you could never forget' - how Leo said of Seyffardt: 'He had such a beautiful voice'.

The illegal press would be divided in its views of the assassination. *Het Parool* jubilantly wrote of Seyffardt that 'the calcified shark had pocketed his earnings'. *Vrij Nederland*, however, was unsure whether such liquidations were 'political murder or political justice'. The Dutch government-in-exile in London, which had so recently demanded greater resistance from the Dutch people, held back from any comment, but the news received in London and published in even far-away Melbourne, Australia's *The Argus* newspaper on 10 February may hint at the attitude of the Allied powers to the manner of Seyffardt's demise: '[...] one of the most despised of Dutch Nazis, the only general openly working for the Germans, and regarded as the worst kind of traitor'. The German occupiers, however, give Seyffardt a majestically overblown state funeral. His coffin is placed on a dais erected in the courtyard of the mediaeval Binnenhof in The Hague, the political centre of an independent Netherlands since 1584. It is flanked by two cauldrons on top of square columns – the Nazis have a thing about fire – and the entire courtyard filled with massed ranks of military types in full dress uniform. After a solemn oration, all of the highest ranking German Nazis in the Netherlands, the German military and the Dutch own national-socialist hierarchy, followed by Nazi-supporting public, file past and honour the traitor with a Hitler salute. The coffin is then lifted on to a gun carriage and pulled at slow walking pace by six horses through the streets of The Hague, lined on each side with many onlookers. The entire production is artfully filmed from start to finish, to be played to cinema audiences throughout the country.

Was the assassination carried out in cold blood, as self-defence, or as an order obeyed? asked Jan Verleun's sister. 'A combination of the three', replied Jan. 'God will decide which carried most weight. I decided to do the task myself. I could have passed the order on to someone else; there is another sharpshooter in my cell. But what difference would that have made to my conscience? Because then the other guy would have been burdened with the deed, and I wouldn't have felt any better if I had been left to witness his suffering.' Matters of conscience to one side, however, Harke Kylstra confirms that 'We were convinced that such assassinations a) bolstered the resistance movement, and b) discouraged Dutch Nazi party members'.

It was Leo's first act of armed resistance. His friend, Mien Harmsen, observed from this that Leo had been brought thoroughly under the influence of Gerrit Kastein. 'Leo was NOT macho. In fact the opposite', as Harke Kylstra observed. 'The big question for CS6 and me was: To shoot, or not to shoot? Most people don't realise how devastating it is to be eye to eye in an execution. The reason I bring all this up is to stress the sacrifice that Leo and his friends made'. So when Bert Schierbeek would decades later remember Leo as 'fatalistically bloodthirsty' it just doesn't ring true; indeed in Schierbeek's own contemporaneously written book 'Terror Fought with Terror' the semi-biographical character closest to Leo is someone who must summon up every ounce of mental strength to carry out any act of resistance - whether or not involving physical violence - and in the aftermath, in a state of nervous exhaustion, be allowed the time and space to recover some semblance of normality. And this is exactly the determined but vulnerable character of Leo described by Jan Verleun to his sister. Kylstra sums him as follows: 'I found Leo the most 'normal' guy in the group. For me, that's a compliment'.

Had Schierbeek not made the observation, without providing evidence, that Leo was 'fatalistically bloodthirsty' but had suggested instead that he and his fellow CS6 members felt a compelling, instinctive desire for revenge, then he may have had a point. It is a perverse 'rule of law' that scorns natural justice and basic humanity to instead uphold and enforce through the police and judiciary every bludgeoning regulation imposed by an illegal occupying force upon those it subjugates; and in such a situation a 'kind of wild justice' – as Sir Francis Bacon berated the concept of 'revenge' - is perhaps better than *no* justice. Leo's brother, Nico, would decades later formulate the notion as follows: 'Power inequality is effectively diminished or annulled by revenge. One is no longer the inferior one, the one to whom things can be done. [...] Through revenge, one gets even in power.' And thus revenge restores self-esteem.

***

Revenge would also, of course, have consequences. Before he dies in a hospital bed the following day, Seyffardt has been able to identify his attackers as probable students. He has further expressed a wish that no hostages should be shot for his sake. Two days later, however, any hope for a measured response is abandoned when a second member of Mussert's 'shadow cabinet' – Herman Reydon – is shot in a second CS6 assassination attempt. Leader of the SS in the Netherlands, Hanns Rauter, reports immediately to Himmler for instructions and in consultation with Seyss-Inquart arrangements are made for the immediate round up and imprisonment of students from universities and technical colleges in the provinces of North Holland, South Holland, and Utrecht. It is a Saturday morning when the lorries arrive; there are no lectures and tutorials, many have gone home for the weekend, but there are still some assiduous students poring over books in musty university libraries or working on experiments in science labs, such as in the pharmacy lab of Utrecht University. Only 600 students are rounded up in this way – an unsatisfactory number - and female students are allowed to go home.

To increase the numbers, a new round up is organized for 9 February. In a letter responding to the crisis, Mussert observed that 'since so many of the working class have been sent to Germany, it is now time that a few thousand sons of plutocrats also be sent out'. Accordingly, a further twelve hundred young men aged between eighteen and twenty-five – students, and those Mussert describes as having 'little or nothing to occupy themselves' – are taken from their homes. From the cities of Amsterdam, Rotterdam, Utrecht and elsewhere the herded captives are eventually shuttled to rail stations and put aboard trains bound for a concentration camp newly opened in the south of the Netherlands: Camp Vught. The rumours that these young men would from there be sent to labour camps in Germany fills them and their families with another layer of dread. One anxious parent writes in a diary: 'Once more we are feeling this constant, intense strain. Throughout the country, the abduction of our boys just keeps on'.

The Utrecht contingent find that the concentration camp is totally unprepared for their arrival; in their barracks there are no blankets, in the canteen there is no food, and it is winter. The water supplied to the camp is contaminated and has to be boiled before it can be drunk. Those who have drunk water from the tap are sick for a week. Nevertheless, the matter is remedied within a month, when all pipes are rinsed through and connected to a fresh water supply, and overall this sectioned-off student camp is a less harsh regime than other parts of the camp: students are not required to shave their heads, they may wear their own clothes, and food parcels from home begin to arrive with a regularity that staves off the worst of their hunger pangs. They play a lot of sport, create hand-written newspapers and cartoons for their shared amusement, and gather in groups in the evenings to debate their ideas for the Netherlands and the world once the war is over. One of their hand-written satirical journals, called *Adam in Exile* – 'publication irregular, whilst stocks last' - borrows its title from a Biblical tragedy by seventeenth century Dutch playwright Joost van den Vondel. A cartoon depicts a communal latrine with the tag line 'Togetherness doesn't keep track of time'. Alongside is a recipe for a 'rabbit' dish that requires the chef to first catch two cats off the street ('not too thin'). The humour hints at privation. The youngsters are imprisoned, cold and hungry – missing their families and scared of what lies ahead – and for no reason other than that two persons unknown have assassinated a Dutch Nazi retired general.

***

On 13 March 1943 the German occupiers introduce a 'loyalty pledge' to be signed by all – approximately 14,600 - Dutch students. The pledge reads as follows:

I, *the undersigned...*
date of birth... place of birth...
current address...

hereby solemnly declare that I will comply in good conscience with all laws, regulations and other decrees applying in the occupied Dutch territory and will refrain from any act directed against the German Reich, the German army, or the Dutch authorities, as well as from any action or behaviour that could, given current circumstances, endanger public order in any place of higher education.

The students have until 10 April to sign; refusal will bar them from continuing their university education. The *Council of Nine*, the umbrella organization for student resistance in the Netherlands, publishes guidelines in an underground newspaper forbidding students to sign the pledge, and labels those who do sign as 'deserters'. On 7 April the government-in-exile's education minister, Gerrit Bolkestein, speaks from London via *Radio Oranje*. He not only instructs students not to sign the pledge, but forbids academic staff to induce students to sign through assurances that this will be to the benefit of their continued university education. By 10 April only fifteen percent have signed, but this increases to twenty-five percent when news of the arrests of some of their fellow *refuseniks* causes some to reconsider their principled stance. Of those who steadfastly refuse to sign, 3,500 are deported to German labour camps; the rest go into hiding. Those students already imprisoned in Camp Vught sign the declaration, convinced that the alternative of being sent to Germany would be a much worse fate.

There is a sense in which the Utrecht students feel their fate is being callously ignored by their teachers. The passivity of the university in resuming academic teaching in full compliance with the instructions of the occupying forces, and its seeming disregard of the 80% of its students who had refused to sign the loyalty pledge, causes genuine resentment. On 2 June 1943 a student representative body writes an open letter to the university's professors and lecturers that reminds them that 'students chose the difficult and dangerous path; most left their family homes and made themselves invisible to the grip of the occupying force'. By contrast, 'on several occasions your conduct in this period of persistent attacks on Dutch university life has disappointed us. [...] Our trust was again betrayed when none of you spontaneously resigned in response to the

177

demand that we report for deportation on 6 May, nor made any other sign of protest.' The students describe a 'gulf' between themselves and their teachers, and warn that this gulf will grow wider to form, even after the war, 'a huge obstacle to the rebuilding of university life, because virtually all trust in you, and all deference and respect towards you, will be lost. [...]We therefore urgently appeal to your sense of duty, your wisdom, and your courage'.

***

Within weeks of the assassination of Seyffardt it was possible to arrange a risky – and thus very rare – meeting between Leo and his sister Jetteke, who was in hiding in the small Dutch town of Zeist. Jetteke recalls: 'I met Leo outdoors, on the street, and we walked around for an hour or so, and then he said to me: 'I killed Seyffardt. I wanted someone within the family to know'. [...] And I asked: 'Do you know what the consequences will be?' Yes, he understood perfectly well. [...] I also remember that Leo told me that he didn't actually know what he would do once the war was over. It was something that I had asked him on that same day [...] Because, even having carried out such acts, you could still return later to a normal life. But that was something he strongly doubted'. This was the last time that Jetteke would ever see her elder brother.

XX

The decapitation of CS6

Laws fall silent
in the face of weapons and battle cries.
Necessity knows no law

Joost van den Vondel (1587 – 1679)

On 12 January 1943 the *NRC* newspaper announced the formation of an anti-sabotage security service. Volunteers are sought. They are to serve under the command of their local police forces (nota bene, the police forces that a few weeks later the Dutch government-in-exile would instruct to undermine – rather than assist - all measures 'aimed at feeding the German war machine'). These volunteers would not assume any police powers in their own right; they would be paid fifty cents per hour for each hour that they were actually on duty and, by joining, 'would perform a good deed in the interests of their fellow citizens and themselves'.

On 18 January 1943 the *NRC* reports that the Dutch police are seeking the whereabouts of a dangerous fugitive criminal, Karel Meijer, metalworker by profession. Aged 20, height 1.70 metres, slim build, dark-blond hair, high forehead. Shot at and almost certainly badly injured at an address in Rotterdam on the night of 11/12 January 1943, so that he would be in urgent need of medical assistance. Anyone providing information leading to the arrest of this fugitive would receive a reward of one thousand Dutch guilders. The newspaper report omits the fact of Meijer's membership of a communist resistance group – the NVM – probably on the safe assumption that the idea of shopping a brave patriot to the Germans, even for such a large reward, would be more repugnant to many readers than turning in a common criminal. The NVM is the group pretty much rolled up after a few months' operations in Rotterdam in late 1942, one of whose leaders, Henk Speksnijder, friend of Gerrit Kastein, would also remain at large till arrested at this time. There is no record of how Meijer is eventually caught, and whether anyone successfully claims the huge reward, but he and five compatriots, including Speksnijder, are executed in open heath land near Amersfoort on 14 July 1943, and buried in the pit where they fall.

The definition of 'sabotage' as applied by the laws of the occupying forces is not confined to deliberate acts of damage or destruction, such as the bombing of rail lines, let alone to the high-profile assassinations that CS6 is now undertaking. On 20 January 1943, as soon as the usual pantomime of pretend consideration, then summary dismissal, of any pleas for reprieve has been impatiently played out, two Dutchmen – 'saboteurs' - are executed. Their crimes were of having been communist party members of many years standing, and of having printed and distributed an illegal communist newspaper with the aim of endangering public order and safety in public life in the occupied Dutch territories. Partly in response to reports like this, and against the backdrop of the 'total war' threatened by the Germans and now beginning to unfold, there might well have been a growing sense amongst some of the disparate groups of the Dutch resistance that in determining the scope of their operations they might as well be hanged for a sheep as a lamb.

***

The day preceding the bombast of General Seyffardt's funeral, CS6 try to gain momentum in their mission to fight terror with terror by carrying out a second assassination. Neither Jan Verleun nor Leo, however, are sufficiently recovered from the psychological fallout of shooting Seyffardt to carry out another such operation, and therefore Gerrit Kastein determines to perform the deed himself, and single-handedly. His target will be a second nomination to Mussert's shadow cabinet and recent appointee as President of the Dutch *Kultuurkamer* - Herman Reydon. 'Our task', proclaimed Reydon in an interview in the Nazi press about his two new roles 'Is to open the eyes of our people to their future!' Members of CS6 may well have argued that the point of their resistance was to achieve the exact same effect. Jan Verleun said of their new target: 'This guy would have plagued our youth and indoctrinated our people. He would have become a second Goebbels. That's why he had to go the same way as Seyffardt'.

Kastein needs a firearm: the still smoking guns that had helped dispatch Seyffardt have not yet made their way back to the modest arsenal of CS6. A resistance comrade - Kees Dutilh – therefore introduces Kastein to a certain 'Anton de Wilde', a purported fellow member of the Dutch resistance, a man who could talk in detail – perhaps too much detail – about his time in London, and who could casually toss a packet of English cigarettes across a bar table to create the right effect. Kastein agrees to meet De Wilde. At this meeting Kastein volunteers a detailed account of his group's liquidation of Seyffardt, and insists that De Wilde should procure for him a gun for an imminent reprise. De Wilde is so shaken by the sheer menace in Kastein's demeanour - Kastein 'wouldn't take 'no' for an answer' - that he hands him his own revolver, there and then. But Kastein is falling into a trap. The name 'De Wilde' is one of a handful of aliases used by a Dutch traitor – Anton van der Waals - recruited by the head of the Gestapo's counter-espionage department in the Netherlands, Joseph Schreieder. Reporting back to Schreieder on the meeting, the colour has disappeared from Van der Waals's face as he warns his handler of Kastein: 'If that man thought there was slightest reason not to trust me, he'd bump me off without a moment's hesitation'.

Kastein's personality is an incongruous mix of types. On the one hand, he is careful, cold and calculating, immersed in Soviet spy craft. He is as willing to justify any and all of Stalin's maniacal excesses in Moscow as he is to put to the test the desire of his 'genuine, baby-faced boys' to prove their bravery on the streets of Amsterdam or The Hague. He takes a two-pronged professional, chillingly dispassionate interest – first as a medic whose specialist field is neurology, and second as a communist spy and resistance fighter – in modern torture methods and their effects. He also knows the need for caution: a master of disguise, he declares himself satisfied when a friend answering his ring at the door is unable to recognize him; on another occasion he impresses upon his young daughter Ina the need to ignore him as a total stranger should he ever pass by her on the street. On the other hand, there is ample tribute paid to his warm-hearted sociability. Leo and his contemporaries look up to him - perhaps ironically - as a paternalistic, protective figure, who refuses to coerce any of them into undertaking any enterprise they feel is beyond them. Others who welcome him as a discrete house guest in his unending race to remain one step ahead of his pursuers describe him as considerate and genial company. From some angles Kastein therefore appears a cold and calculating loner, from others a generous and warm-hearted friend and benefactor. But is he in any sense also dangerously hot-headed?

Schreieder confirms that Kastein's detailed description of the Seyffardt liquidation 'was exactly consistent with what we had discovered at the scene'. If so, that would suggest the likelihood of Kastein's confirmation that the two assassins were students, or of student age. Not a hugely significant disclosure, given that on his death bed Seyffardt had already imparted this evidence. But was there any need to go into any detail at all? Was this a risky exercise of 'bragging rights' otherwise without purpose? The sure effect would have been to confirm to Schreieder that this individual whom he did not yet know as Kastein was a big fish worth netting. And again, whilst Kastein drops absolutely no clues as to the person in line for assassination on 9 February 1943, he is nevertheless specific as to the date. But why? This detail would make it easier for the police and counter-espionage forces to look at any and all liquidations carried out on that day and check which, if any, could be linked with the gun that Van der Waals had surrendered to Kastein. But in the meantime, as Schreieder writes, 'We would have to wait till 9 February to see what would happen'.

This is what happens:

In the late afternoon Kastein, who has ridden by tram the short distance from The Hague to the nearby town of Voorschoten, approaches the corner house that is home to Herman Reydon. Having recce'd the area previously, he is aware of the German troops billeted across the road. Reydon is not at home, but his wife invites Kastein inside to wait for his return. There and then he shoots her dead. Later than expected, with a short winter's day drawing to a close, Reydon returns home and no sooner does he turn the key in the lock to his front door and enter the darkened house than Kastein fires three bullets into him from a firearm that he has wrapped in his hat to dampen the sound. Reydon will survive, only to die of his injuries several months later; one of the bullets has ripped through his spinal cord. Making his escape, Kastein still manages to alert colleagues in the vicinity of the urgent need for precaution: a ruthless round-up of possible culprits would inevitably follow. A friend and fellow medic, Dr Van der Stoel, decides to go immediately into hiding. Van der Stoel's wife is contemptuous of Kastein's deed: 'Don't mention that man's name to me. A doctor isn't someone who commits murder...'.

Alerted to this 'terrorist act', Schreieder attends the Reydons' home with a security service team. The spent cartridges picked up from the floor point to the shots having been fired with Van der Waals's revolver, and he logically concludes that the man who had so chilled the blood of Van der Waals is the man who has committed the deed.

The next day Kastein meets Van der Waals to return his gun and, in the same detail that he described the liquidation of Seyffardt, describes the attacks on Herman Reydon and his wife. Again, why? Van der Waals will use this detailed information in the future precisely to convince others that no one but he was the attacker and that he could therefore be trusted as a brave and loyal member of the Dutch resistance. In the meantime, Van der Waals is eager for the arrest of Kastein, not least because he fears his ruthlessness more than ever. Schreieder thinks otherwise, however, and instructs his double agent to maintain contact with Kastein and find out more about him, his activities and his relationship with Kees Dutilh.

***

On 19 February Kastein keeps his appointment to meet two underground contacts at The Crown café-restaurant in Delft, close by the railway station. His intention is to introduce his first contact – Pieter Wapperom, leader of the local communist party sabotage group for The Hague – to the second – the person he believes to be trusted resistance member De Wilde. The appointment is made for ten in the morning, but whilst Kastein arrives punctually at the appointed time, Wapperom has arrived early and De Wilde will turn up late. Had Kastein taken the precaution of reaching the meeting place sooner and watched from a discrete distance for the arrival of his two contacts, things might have not gone so badly for him; but maybe, because he is armed with no fewer than three guns, one of which is strapped to his inside leg, he feels sufficiently prepared for any difficulties.

What Kastein does not know – apart from not knowing that De Wilde/Van der Waals is a dangerous double agent - is that Wapperom had been arrested eight days previously and found with a diary note of the date and place of their meeting. His captors decide, following long days of interrogation, that Wapperom should keep that appointment and be used as bait. And so, at a quarter to ten that grey winter's morning a black BMW pulls up near the café on the corner of the street and Wapperom, semi-immobilized, is escorted by three SD (security service) men through the door: 'They had cut open my jacket through the pockets so that my hands could be bound together inside my jacket', recalls Wapperom. 'They also tied a long rod along my right leg, so that I couldn't move. They sat me down on a chair by a table in the window, and the three SD men took their places at other tables in the café'. This time in the morning the café is otherwise empty, the proprietor is busy cleaning the place, and chairs are still perched high on the other tables. One SD man closes the curtain across the window of the entrance door so that their stage set is hidden from outside. And then at ten, on cue, Kastein enters the café. He acknowledges Wapperom and approaches his table to sit down. It is a matter of seconds before the SD men are able to seize him, bind his hands, and make any escape impossible. They disarm him of two of his guns. Wapperom and Kastein are bundled into the BMW that had been lurking nearby and out of sight, Wapperom in the front, Kastein on the back seat. His captors, however, have overlooked the revolver that Kastein had taped to his inside leg. Even with bound hands, he is able to reach down and grab the gun from under his trouser leg, fire two shots, and then in the commotion jump out of the car. There is no great escape: catching him a second time is a matter of moments and the last of his armoury of the three guns is taken from him. They drive quickly but in silence the half-hour journey to The Hague, Kastein sitting alongside the SD man he has just shot and wounded, Dr Ernst Knorr, whose particular repertoire of torturing techniques the German secret service would summon up as needed by euphemistically calling for 'the doctor'. Beyond their shared car journey Knorr and Kastein would not meet again: the doctor is delivered to hospital and Kastein to the SD headquarters.

Meanwhile, Van der Waals/De Wilde arrives late at the café to be told of Kastein's arrest. The place is in uproar following the events of just minutes before. Shaken by the unexpected turn of events he immediately returns by train to The Hague. Back at HQ his handler, Schreieder, sarcastically wonders why Kastein hadn't yet shot him dead. Van der Waals is angry, confused and in fear simply for what might have played out: 'If I hadn't arrived a bit late it could easily have been curtains for me. He would have straight away assumed that it was me who had betrayed him'. To Schreieder, the stressed-out Van der Waals seems to be losing the plot. But Schreieder, too, is disconcerted by a train of events that didn't go as planned: it was as unexpected to him as to his double agent. He phones around the various departments of the secret service and Gestapo, clearly jealously protective of their own spheres of activity and sources of information. He discovers that the head of a certain department IV A, in concert with the head of the Gestapo in Rotterdam, had agreed that the first man they had arrested – Wapperom - should keep his appointment at The Crown café, and in this way help engineer their arrest of Kastein, a valuable catch in a deadly cat and mouse game whom Schreieder had wanted to toy with for a while longer. Of worse news to Schreieder, but a source of immense relief to Van der Waals, is that a captured Kastein will not be disclosing any more information about the Dutch resistance. Underground newspaper *De Waarheid* reports the story:

He was brought to a room on the second floor of the Binnenhof. There were four men there sitting waiting for him. With all the vigour that was part of his being, he took control of the interrogation and instigated a heated political debate. Later, two Gestapo men left the room to get coffees and a third to use the toilet. Gerrit seized his opportunity. It is not known if at that moment he was still tied up. In any event, he struck the one remaining Gestapo man, smashed a window and jumped.

Kastein fell to his death. He had once told his friend Mathieu Smedts: 'If the Nazis ever catch you, they will force you to talk. Be under no illusions, you'll talk. [...] I hope that I will be able to end my own life, but I will take a German down with me'.

***

A leader is expected to lead his troops, and Dr Gerrit Kastein did so, but no one anticipates that their leader should be the first to fall. And so their shock, and sense of loss and indebtedness is great when CS6 members learn of his sacrificial leap from the second-floor window of the Binnenhof interrogation room. Verleun murmurs despairingly 'I don't know how we can continue now he's gone', and indeed one might imagine that without their assumed leader, CS6 must now feel disorientated, panicked and dysfunctional. The truth is more nuanced. The 'father figure' whose death Jan Verleun sincerely laments was aged just thirty-three – in age, more like a big brother than a father to most CS6 members through all its quasi-military ranks, Leo included. Nor could the ruthless change in tactics urged by Kastein that encouraged Leo and others to carry out political assassinations be described as the act of a 'father', whose paternal instinct is surely to protect his children from danger, and not – with the certain degree of relish that chilled those who heard his words – to lay them open to it. Furthermore, there were others in the group of a similar age to Kastein, including Jan van Mierlo and Pam Pooters, who were also looked up to and leaned on for support and encouragement by the younger members of CS6. Indeed Pooters, distrusted by the Dutch communist party elite for championing the Trotskyite cause, reveals a calm and quiet defiance in separating his faith in a communist utopia from his utter rejection of Stalinist dystopia in a way that a blindly obedient communist party member like Kastein could not or would not. Kastein's intervention in the history of CS6 was of critical importance, certainly, and maybe even catastrophic in its eventual legacy, but his tenure was short-lived: he arrived on the scene late and left early. The spiritual home of CS6 was 6 Corelli Street, the Boissevain family home, where above the basement munitions factory light flooded the home through big windows; a home that was warm and comforting and alive with music on the gramophone; in whose garden Mies Boissevain – 'Mammie' – bred rabbits (thirty-six of them at the time of her arrest) so there would always be something extra, tasty and nutritious to feed her wildly extended family, scattered through a warren of hiding places throughout Amsterdam.

For Leo, Kastein's death is a portent of things to come. Later that month, on the birthday of his friend Mien Harmsen, whose brother's identity he has borrowed, he writes in red ink in a book he has bought her as a gift, using his literary pseudonym Edgar Fossan:

> Blackness moves like a gas. Will someone grasp
> What has been lost? A pile of bodies
> Barricade the door, and only –

185

via many steps – can the muddy ditch be reached.
And she, who played, came a final time
Upon the son who, lying slain,
Uttered...'water, give me water, please'.

XXI

A new style in riposte to the New Order

Only this is what we can tell you today:
that which we are <u>not</u>; that which we do not want.

Eugenio Montale (1896 – 1981), from his poem 'Ossi di Seppia'

In January 1943, alongside their continuing work on the more ambitious literary project *Lichting*, Leo and Theo Hondius produce a short collection of poems entitled *'A Fight to the Death'* under their respective pen names Edgar Fossan and Theo Haag. The collection is divided into two short parts; the first comprising four poems written by Hondius under the heading 'Life' and the second four poems by Leo under the heading 'Death'. The back page colophon informs the reader as follows:

A FIGHT TO THE DEATH, a collection maximum and minimum (optimistic – pessimistic, positive-negative) poetry for our time by Theo Haag and Edgar Fossan, typed in the Erika font on first-rate trashy grey paper.
Produced in 40 copies of which copies numbered I to II are not commercially available, nor are copies III to XL.
The typographical work was contracted out.
January 1943.
This is copy no. **

Each of the four poems written by Leo appears also in Lichting. There are others of his poems, however, that he keeps entirely to himself:

Death's Solace

He has finally bowed down to his fate
and understood that he has lost,
once time had extinguished all his fire,
and on his lips death's kiss placed,
and he did not learn the reason for his birth.

Yearning that is born from sobs
and sadness that is killed by lust,
in the lurching between the sun and moon

did not turn back,
and died.

But just once their wounds will open up!
They will gasp and sink upon the graves
and with the crosses at the heavens strike;
proving what was never understood...
and drunk once more upon their blood.

***

In 1941, eighteen-year-old student Gerrit Kouwenaar, a student quietly watchful of the social ease with which his journalist father mixed in artistic circles, had self-published a collection of poems entitled 'An Early Spring Day'. He had cast a wide net for inspiration, enthralled by American modernists, the 'Auden group' and Dylan Thomas - poets who gave him the support and confidence to realise that 'all the things you were vaguely and hesitantly searching for here had already established a sound basis abroad'. A year later he would be recruited by Hans Engelman, a friend he shared with Gerrit Jan De Jongh, co-editor of Lichting, to donate poems to their new journal. From contributing to the Cobra group of artists in the late 1940s to membership of the 'Fifties' movement of young Dutch poets to emerge from the shadow of the war, it would not be until his split from this movement in the 1960s that he would begin to absorb a style that had flourished in Italy during the inter-war years and since: *hermetic poetry.* The precise aim of the hermetic movement was to create obscure and difficult poetry – the intentional antithesis of any 'understandable' poetry – a condensing of subjective language and imagery to briefly-delivered essentials. Italian poet and Nobel laureate Eugenio Montale would describe in an essay his wish '[...] to wring the neck of the eloquence of our old courtly language, even at the risk of a counter-eloquence'. Some Dutch poets and critics would decry this development in Kouwenaar's eventually-adopted style as 'cold and impersonal', but Kouwenaar's response was unapologetic: 'If you are in search [of comfort] then I think you should go to the church and speak with a priest, not search out a poet'.

Juxtaposed with Kouwenaar's more obviously orthodox work in a second edition of *Lichting* dated December 1942, Leo presented something audaciously new in Dutch poetry: a 'hermetic' poem with ideas brutally compacted into five lines, the first and fifth which are brooding, wordless spaces:

Dark of Dawn

. . . . . .
On this there can be no doubt.
Let the water clear the tables:
Words are never misconstrued.
?

This edition of their literary project begins with a rather long editorial and the crystallization of the *Lichting* poets' sense of their mission: 'Since the start of this war, we - or those of us who are sentient human beings - have fundamentally changed, or, expressed differently: this change, happening by the day, happening *to* us, and created *by* us, changes everything that is of a human-temporal nature, not least in our literature'.

The *Lichting* contingent could hardly have been aware of Italian hermetic poets such as Ungaretti and Gatto – the one an open supporter of, the other a communist activist at one time imprisoned by, Italian dictator Mussolini; poets whose lives and work serve as evidence that fascist Italy did not force the artist adopt the shrill, emasculated voice of the state propagandist parroted by those anxious to survive the bullets and bonfires of censorship in Nazi Europe or Stalin's USSR. Indeed, in a 1923 speech Mussolini had declared: 'Art falls within the sphere of the individual. The state has only one obligation: not to undermine it, to provide humane conditions for artists.' It is true that by 1938 there was considerable censorship of the arts in Italy, demanded by the fascist party and the Roman Catholic Church alike, and that by March 1942 – even absent any specific legislation that prohibited Jews from publishing books - some 800 such works were listed as banned. Nevertheless the situation in Italy makes it clear: it was not a necessary precondition for the survival and success of totalitarianism that the individuality of the artistic spirit be so totally crushed. Nazi and Stalinist dogma that condemned the expression of individuality in any form as a danger to the regime, and that furthermore rejoiced in the crushing of this spirit, was a display of chilling paranoia.

There is certainly no mention of either the hermetic movement or its leading poets in any contemporaneous documents pertaining to *Lichting*, or indeed in any later recollections of any of its contributors. Nevertheless, some of Leo's *Lichting* poems, and especially the ideas expressed in his essay *Poetic Synthesis*, come extremely close to espousing the complex style of these Italian poets. It is true that there may also be an apparent divergence in ideas since, whilst Leo pleads for the exclusion of the poet's *intellect* to thereby create some kind of emotional purity – 'the

189

games of the intellect must be played out elsewhere' – the Italian hermeticists would never have dismissed the role of the poet's intellect in this way. But even this distinction may have to be blurred at the edges because, whatever Leo argues in favour of eliminating the intellect in poetry, his essay and his own later poems are abundant evidence of his search for a new language to communicate intense feelings, *a search that is necessarily guided by a keen intellect*, and he can't have it both ways.

Whilst the *Lichting* poets form much too broad a church – intentionally so – to be identifiable as even a loose, prototype artistic movement, some of them have nevertheless clearly abandoned the calls of their hero Hendrik Marsman to speak with a 'crystal clear voice' and are advancing in the opposite direction – towards what one might call obscurism or hermeticism. This is especially true of Leo. So it is perhaps a pity that Gerrit Kouwenaar – who would become recognized as one of the Netherlands' greatest twentieth-century poets and a renowned translator of work by politically engaged writers including Brecht and Sartre - would indeed acknowledge Leo's translation of 'The Wall' as a compelling introduction to the name and work of Sartre, whilst offering up no credit to Leo or to *Lichting* as any early inspiration for his decades-later adoption of a hermetic style of verse. It is hard to imagine, however, that Kouwenaar could have read Leo's poem 'Morning Dark' - published alongside a number of his own more conventionally drawn lines - and not felt just a little intrigued by this new, unexplored and somewhat extreme path.

As the *Lichting* editorial makes plain, each of this hidden generation of young writers is struggling for an individual voice that serves as a fitting response to the war raging around them – not to a traditional war fought on the battlefield with its time-honoured, if dubious, chivalric codes, but to a total war; a war fought on the streets right outside their homes, in their public places, in the press, via radio broadcasts from Hilversum and on cinema newsreels; a war that seeks to exterminate millions, destroy cultures, and eradicate the individual spirit. A war that puts their lives in danger merely for the 'sabotage' of expressing their feelings in lines of verse and prose. As Kouwenaar would later observe: 'I sensed that the reality of the war (which I experienced rather intensely, in common with most of those of my age) was in direct conflict with the way in which poetry had been penned at that time. So I was searching for something new. In simple terms I was searching for the unusual, the extreme. It was, after all, an unusual and extreme time'. In his farewell letter to his family, Leo would refer to a struggle throughout his life, expressed *in word and deed*, which perhaps mirrors Kouwenaar's search in poetry for the 'extreme'. Leo writes: 'I have unconsciously struggled towards the *absolute*'.

XXII

The last of Lichting

The sixth and final edition of Lichting appeared in April 1943. Theo Hondius wrote not its obituary, but an announcement of a break in its publication:

With this sixth and final edition of Lichting in this first half-year subscription, we bring to a close a period of fruitful collaboration and growing activity. We have grown to learn the work and aspirations, as well as doubts and uncertainties, of the Young Turks of our literature, and we have discovered - through the many and varied influences of older generations – new paths and renewed hope.

Hondius stressed that there was no lack of interest in the project, nor lack of contributions. But it was becoming increasingly difficult to maintain the secretive contacts between the Amsterdam and Utrecht editors and their respective groups of contributors, and these difficulties were compounded by the increasingly impossible task of obtaining enough paper: 'Unfortunately, due to the limited space available we have been forced again to decline many contributions'. These, then, were two of the three reasons why *Lichting* would never appear again:

It is a source of pride that despite the difficulties of contact and organization and the limitations arising from lack of materials, we were able to publish a number of prose works that undoubtedly demonstrated promise for the future. Because it was exactly with regard to this kind of work that we fell unavoidably short: many fine contributions had to be rejected due to their length or for other typographical hitches. Furthermore, many colleagues were forced to end their involvement for purely personal reasons: but they joined the crusade [...] in the firm conviction that a New Lichting would follow.

Despite Leo being consumed in the maelstrom of intensified CS6 operations he was nevertheless able to contribute a substantial prose work such as that described above by Theo. Given its length, however, only fragments of the work that Leo entitled *Arrow* were published in *Lichting*. In a letter, Leo explains his concept:

'Arrow' is a kind of surreal prose poem based on concrete feelings - in other words, normal feelings such as can be experienced by any of us... grief, joy,

rejection, etc., - sung in the way in which I used to fantasize at the piano, except that now I use words instead of notes, chosen in part for their sound, and in part for the way they create an atmosphere that (for me) is at the core of my emotions. 'Word music' is the best way of describing it, so long as you don't take the words literally.

These ideas connect with those that Leo explored in his treatise 'Poetic Synthesis':

> *'Art serves only to represent lifeblood and feelings; it has one goal only: to move the soul. The various forms of art attempt to achieve all of this, each in their own specific way: music strives in this endeavour through melody, harmony and rhythm; poetry through content, image and sound'.*

Leo's prose poem *Arrow* appeared in numbered collage-like sections, with perhaps a nod to Eliot's 'The Waste Land', published nearly a quarter-century earlier. The final section could be described as Leo's valedictory verse:

> *Gratitude for this distant view?*
> *I know well*
> *this gaze upon an early death*
> *from whence it came.*
> *The Arrow by which I sail*
> *points that way too.*
> *Indeed, we shall soon all*
> *succumb.*

***

The third and most immediately compelling reason for calling time on *Lichting* was the attention various contributors were receiving from the Germans. Mien Harmsen, who helped arrange the stenciled sheets in page order, recalled an early episode: 'I know, for example, of one occasion when we were raided – by that I mean that a German came to poke around – and I was sitting there working on *Lichting* [...] and even though the copy was spread all around it didn't seem to interest him one bit. He was otherwise very friendly and simply left, even though there was a cello case standing there, in which we stored a few weapons.' On a later occasion, on 1 Apri 1943, at the same time as his father was being arrested by the Germans just metres away, Theo Joekes was ensconced in an outbuilding on the family's land, typing up the sixth edition of *Lichting*.

Discussing the matter later with Theo Hondius, Joekes expressed the view that 'It had probably all become a bit too risky'.

***

By way of postscript, late in the evening of 11 May 1943 the rooms that Gerrit Kouwenaar shared with his brother David in Amsterdam were raided by three Dutch members of the secret police: the thorough search uncovered various copies of *Lichting*, together with a number of poems laced with anti-German sentiment. 'The search involved a lot of roaring and intimidation', recalled Kouwenaar. 'When they found the incriminating material in my part of the digs I was promptly knocked to the ground. I wasn't allowed to get up, and had to lie where I had fallen. I had only recently stained the wooden floorboards and I could now see from very close quarters how the woodstain had collected somewhat in the joints between the boards.'

Kouwenaar was taken to the cells on Amsterdam's Euterpestraaat. The secret police headquarters had been a girls' secondary school before the war; the cells had once been the bicycle sheds where he had often waited outside to meet a female companion. He remembered reading an article published before the war about the German concentration camp at Oranienburg where the intimidation of prisoners extended to locking them in a 'stone coffin'. As he entered his dank basement cell he thought to himself 'Dear God, it really exists, this is the stone coffin'. The next day Hans Engelman was arrested, and a few days later Gerrit Jan de Jongh. Then Theo van der Wal. All by virtue of their involvement with *Lichting*. They were all interrogated 'in an anything but a mild manner'. In the cell next to Kouwenaar was Johan Benders, a thirty-six-year-old resistance fighter, who had been a teacher of history and Dutch at the Amsterdam Lyceum where Leo had sat his last year of school. Benders had helped find many addresses for Jews going into hiding and therefore had valuable information he could impart to his interrogators: to avoid the inevitable betrayals elicited through torture he tried twice during the night of 5/6 April to take his own life. At a third attempt, by leaping from a third-floor prison balcony, he succeeded. In July 1943 Kouwenaar and the others were transported by train to prison in Utrecht. At the end of their trials Gerrit Kouwenaar and Hans Engelman were sentenced to six months; Gerrit Jan de Jongh to eight. The sentences included the months in detention awaiting trial, which meant that Kouwenaar and Engelman were released the same afternoon. Kouwenaar went into hiding rather than surrender to membership of the *Kultuurkamer*.

***

After the war Theo Hondius would observe: 'Even in retrospect, *Lichting* [in English, 'generation' or 'draft'] was not such a crazy name. After liberation by the Allied Forces I and all those of my age group were declared to belong to the so-called 'forgotten generation' that was excused the call-up for military service. We'd already done our fair share.'

***

Six editions of *Lichting*. A total of eighty pages in folio format. A not insubstantial body of work. Theo Hondius wrote in the last edition of the magazine their joint hope and intention - 'after the war' – to publish a selection of the best work from Lichting in book form: 'Our literature will without doubt go through a difficult period, and we will consider our efforts amply rewarded if our magazine proves to have forged a bond that retains its worth in the midst of conflicting ideas'.

XXIII

Leo's War is Over

'A soldier is victor enough if all he wins is time'

Joost van den Vondel (1587 – 1679)

If Nico wanted to know how he felt, wrote elder brother Leo, he could find the answer in the character of Chen in Malraux's novel 'Man's Fate'. In this depiction of a failed communist insurrection in Shanghai in 1927, a work that CS6 members revered almost as their Bible, Chen puts to death a sleeping man in an act of supposed revolutionary zeal. What motivates the assassin? What does this act do to him? asks Malraux. Being brought so close to death, to be the instrument that turns a living human being into a lifeless corpse, Chen is overtaken by fatalism and a desire to kill again, to thereby fulfil his destiny as a terrorist, a destiny that controls his life. The assassination he commits should at least have bonded him with the revolutionary group that he fights alongside. Instead, he comes away from the deed with an unutterable feeling of solitude and the knowledge that what he has done has separated him from the rest of mankind. In a short space of time he becomes so haunted by death and his powerlessness over his fate that he yearns for his own death as an end to his torment. In the meantime, as time ebbs away, continued terrorist activity gives some kind of meaning to his tortured solitude.

Leo, who as a young boy had loved writing playful letters home, full of childlike energy, has grown ever more introverted and reluctant to share his news and much darker preoccupations even with sister Jetteke, to whom he writes:

I am sure you will have begun to think that I have something against you, given my long silence. Nothing could be further from the truth. However, apart from the news that I am in good health and work hard – you know the kind of work I mean – there is nothing interesting to report. [...] Amsterdam is growing quiet. There is now obviously much less of the blindingly-bright yellow colour around. [...] Perhaps I can soon visit again and talk with you, which you know I always very much enjoy. But this would be beyond the realms of possibility, and so I will

confine myself to sending you my greetings in this letter to guard against
anything worse happening.
Yours,
Leo

Parts of Amsterdam are indeed becoming menacingly 'quiet' and Jews labelled with the yellow star of David are emptying from the city's ghetto, as Leo reports. For the German occupiers, this marks a transitional period: SS-General Rauter announces that from 1 May 1943 all remaining Jews are to be 'removed' from the Netherlands: in previous weeks German orders have forbidden Jews from living anywhere in the Netherlands outside Amsterdam, thus corralling the nation's remaining Jewish population into one small ghetto. With the scheduled deportations eastwards by train to the panic-strewn unloading ramps of Auschwitz and Sobibor a mission therefore almost accomplished, Rauter and the rest can now turn their relentless attention to smoking out the suspected thousands of Jews in hiding in Amsterdam and in villages, towns and cities across the country.

CS6 members work tirelessly; their efforts are not in vain, and what they achieve relative to their numbers is remarkable. Bert Schierbeek reports on 16 April 1943, for example, that Ernst Klijzing is to be found 'at home' – wherever that may be at any given time - only an hour a day: 'He is now entirely preoccupied with the underworld. [...] An extraordinary effort in all areas of the conflict, working with paper and with the bullet. Feverish intensity, always at boiling point, and always at the point of being torpedoed by the Gestapo.' The sister of group members Bram and Sape Kuiper reports to a friend that Bram 'works from early morning to late at night on just one document for the organization.' CS6 has done much to find hiding places for many Jews, and its 'couriers' continue the dangerous task of distributing painstakingly forged ration cards so that those risking their own lives to provide these hiding places and those they hide can all get enough to eat. The group has also worked tirelessly to provide false identities both to those choosing to venture forth along the complex and perilous escape lines to Switzerland or Spain, including Leo's mother, and to those choosing to hide 'in plain sight' in their home country – to Jews, like Leo's father, sister and brother, to the working-age men evading conscription to the German labour camps, and to fellow resistance fighters. The thousands of nameless faces on portraits preserved on the surviving one hundred and sixty rolls of film commissioned by CS6 stand testament to the extent of these endeavours.

Meanwhile the Germans rely on their own repository of photographs as a rather vile visual aid in the capture of Jews hiding in their midst. When Tina Strobos is arrested for providing a hiding place to a Jew she responds to her interrogator 'But he has blue eyes and blond hair. How could he be a Jew?' The Gestapo officer explains the 'science' behind his detection work: 'Some Jews are like violets in the woods. They hide by having blue eyes and blond hair [...] I will show you pictures'. And, as Tina explains, he does exactly that: 'He showed me pictures of eye corners. That's right. There were about sixteen pictures of the corners of eyes. 'That's what we're looking for in the streets,' he said. They did, too. They arrested Jews and half-Jews in the street, even though they didn't look Jewish. A half-Jew they could recognize. To me these people didn't look Jewish at all'. Rauter has no shortage of willing assistance from two sources: the Dutch police officers of the Bureau for Jewish Affairs, and the *Henneicke Column* comprising fifty-three Dutch Nazi collaborators tasked with ferreting out and arresting Jews in hiding. Ignoring impassioned instructions via radio broadcasts from London to obstruct the execution of German policy, these two groups inspire each other to greater efforts on behalf of the occupying forces. Together they would deliver up to nine thousand Jews to the Nazi authorities, at a not inconsiderable bounty of seven and a half guilders per Jew, double that amount if the individual caught was on a wanted list for 'criminal' activity.

In response to Allied successes in North Africa, German defeat at Stalingrad, and a sustained four-month aerial bombardment of the German industrial heartland of the Ruhr, Seyss-Inquart and Rauter fear – with justification - a growing confidence amongst Dutch resistance groups. Closer to home, on 19 April 1943, partisans in Belgium attack a railway convoy transporting Belgian Jews to Auschwitz: two hundred and thirty-six Jews escape in this the most successful of such attacks anywhere in Europe. This victory cannot have escaped the attention of CS6, and one of the few surviving documents written by, and for, CS6 members is a list of instructions for blowing up railway lines. The instructions stress the need for sound reconnaissance work. A scout would be sent out to discover if the theoretical location was suitable. How is the line protected? Are there any enemy objects in the neighbourhood? The scout should draw a clear sketch of the location, provide a detailed description of any available retreat route for the quick and safe return of CS6 militia, and identify an absolutely reliable nearby address to which a package could be delivered and kept for a couple of weeks. In a no-nonsense attempt to thwart this growing confidence that the Third Reich could well be defeated, the Dutch newspapers of 20 April 1943 announce a staggeringly bold order by General Christiansen, commander of the German armed forces in the

Netherlands, for the internment of almost 300,000 members of the surrendered Dutch army in German prison camps as prisoners of war. Christiansen intends this move to benefit the German workforce, and to remove trained men from potential membership of the Dutch resistance. He neither intended nor anticipated that this should result in the six-day general strike, protests and demonstrations throughout the country that became known as the 'April-May Strike'. However, it was a strike that left Amsterdam largely unmoved, its residents filled with fearful recollections of the brutal response to their protests of February 1941. Furthermore, railway workers would not come out on strike - a cause for despondency amongst strike supporters, who had hoped for a more clearly nationwide protest. The rest of the country would indeed experience what Amsterdam feared: Rauter imposed emergency measures under which strikers the length and breadth of the country – almost two hundred in total - were arbitrarily arrested and executed without trial, or simply mowed down by bullets in the street. 'Wherever he went', reported communist newspaper *De Waarheid* on Rauter's trial after the war, 'gallows and firing squads came too'.

***

As membership of the resistance grows, so does the necessity to trust new volunteers: CS6 has long since expanded beyond the tightly-bonded core of youngsters who had attended the same classes at the same few Amsterdam schools when war broke out. A surviving 'internal order' from CS6, dated June 1943, stresses the need for secrecy given that the tasks they undertake are a matter of life and death. Item no. 2 of the order continues: 'Especially never forget that, as militia, members of CS6 are subject to martial law and that any betrayal of our military objectives is punishable by DEATH BY FIRING SQUAD'. The tone of this missive feels like a legacy of CS6 having handed its leadership to an unquestioning, ruthlessly loyal communist party member such as Dr Gerrit Kastein, whom some might have argued was as prepared to fight to the death to defeat one maniac's reign of terror, as he was to fight to the death to defend another's. But the language may have been mere bluster: there is no evidence that any such threats were ever carried out. Nor did the underlying dogma go unchallenged. Bram Kuiper's angry torrent of communist propaganda in response to Eva Keuls's opinion that the Soviets were every bit as bad as the Nazis left Eva entirely unperturbed. Harke Kylstra had to balance his loyalty to Leo and his belief in the rightfulness of CS6 operations on the one hand, with his intense dislike of the extreme-left politicization of the group on the other: 'I hated the CS6. I was offered a military rank but I scoffed at the idea. To me the name was wrong. Nobody knew what it meant except the Gestapo and the KGB.'

Daniel Blom is a former member of the communist youth movement, and someone who helps make false identity cards for the resistance. Dismissed as a Jew from his civil service job, he then sets himself up as a seller of women's cosmetics. With a cabaret group called 'The Blue Lantern' he puts on benefit shows for the resistance. Daniel feels 'safe' to be with. Not just 'safe': a twenty-seven-year old family man, Daniel is great fun to be with – outgoing, charismatic and charmingly flirtatious. He brightens the days of those he visits, women especially: Mien Pooters recalls him as 'a darling young man, very handsome, who would sometimes drop by to tell you the latest jokes'. He would also visit a neighbour's home to listen to the BBC and Radio Oranje on their illegal wireless set. However, Daniel is an agent for the secret police. He has been seen entering and leaving the secret police headquarters on Euterpestraat with impunity, something which no Jew would possibly contemplate without some assurance of German protection. Blom's easy charm hides a disturbing indifference to those around him, even his own family. He has no qualms in engineering the arrests – and thus the deaths - of his own sister and brother-in-law. He may have betrayed up to forty-five individuals. It is decided within the leadership of CS6 that Leo and Hans Katan should eliminate this dangerous traitor as soon as possible. Neither has met him, so Nel, sister of Mien and 'Pam' Pooters, assists them in the enterprise. It is arranged that she should follow some distance behind Blom to help Leo and Hans identify their target. Daniel is shot on the street where he lives, on his walk back home, and dies in hospital of his injuries some time later. There are many traitors like Daniel, but with his death there is one less.

Leo is acquiring a reputation beyond CS6 as a 'go to' person for the elimination of dangerous traitors. Via a common acquaintance he has agreed to a meeting requested by Paul Peters. Paul is surprised by Leo's appearance: he looks so young for his age; so short and slender that he could still pass for a schoolboy - scarcely the physical embodiment of a cold assassin that Paul had imagined. Paul explains to Leo that he has discovered his uncle, John Mair, to be a traitor and agent provocateur in the service of the Germans. Uncle John is the black sheep of the family; he has never made anything of his life; a difficult childhood is attributed to a fall from a roof causing concussion from which he has never properly recovered. In May 1942, Uncle John had undertaken to help several family members including Paul's sister Els – the Jewish side of the family – escape to Switzerland. Another uncle – James – had paid money up front for

John's help. But Uncle John is an anti-Semite: he would later write that the war had made him '100% anti-Semite. No: 1,000%'. He is also, according to later psychiatric reports obtained for his trial, 'an amoral psychopath with hysterical tendencies'. On the train journey from Hilversum to Maastricht the three hopeful escapees were arrested in a manner that seemed pre-arranged, removed from the train and taken to prison in The Hague. They would eventually be killed in Poland. Els is saved, but Uncle John reminds her whom she should thank for that. Satisfied that there is no innocent explanation of John's actions, Leo and Paul agree that he must be got out of the way. But CS6 are short of weapons – it seems to be a chronic shortage that the group never seems able to make good; Paul records that at that time CS6 had no more than five pistols in total. There have been rumours circulating, however, that the Belgian resistance – the White Brigade – has been amassing weapons dropped by the British over Belgium. Accordingly, Leo and Paul agree that Paul will travel to Brussels to ask whether they could spare a number of small firearms. On his return they would then deal with Uncle John.

***

Leo now feels like a solitary, hunted animal. He writes to George Puchinger: 'With regard to the decision I have taken, there is now nothing more to do except wait. [...] Now that I stay out of the light, I only see the city by night and in the current warm weather I take long bicycle rides. Tonight the air has been very restless'. But he is not by far the only member of CS6 to feel that time is running out. Together the group decides to resume its plan for 'high-profile' assassinations in their determination to answer terror with terror. The task has been made more difficult since the assassinations of Herman Reydon and his wife in their own home by Kastein: Mussert's team of shadow ministers have now been assigned bodyguards. Harke Kysltra recalls discussions within the group:

'All of us – Leo, Hans Katan, Bram and Sape Kuiper and the Boissevain brothers, decided from that moment on not to kill anyone indoors, to make some excuse to be allowed through the front door, like a domestic murder, but to make the assassination more spectacular, or more 'sportsmanlike'. Leo was especially in favour of this approach. I travelled with a female colleague to the Achterhoek where minister Posthuma lived on a farm. When we got there it appeared, having spoken with the farm manager, that the bodyguard had gone home because he was feeling bored to death in a backwater such as this. Even though, having heard this news, I decided not to shoot Posthuma because it would no longer be 'sportsmanlike' without the bodyguard being there, I nevertheless took time for a chat with him. Here was this senile old man, sat in front of the hearth. All the more reason not to

shoot him dead. Leo agreed with me, but apparently not everyone else did. Jan Verleun, so it was reported, did kill him off.'

Harke has the chance to travel with Leo on a 20-hour journey by roundabout means to the Veluwe for what would prove to be a failed attack upon a train. This time together gives each of them long enough to open up a little to the other. Leo talks about his father, his father's opposition to the Jewish Council, and their strained relationship. Harke in turn confides in Leo that his father had angrily accused him of having a death wish: Harke is from a Quaker family and his father could not accept Harke's belief that killing traitors was ever justified.

At the end of June 1943 Police Inspector Peter Kaay, a 'Jew hunter', is identified as a deserving target for assassination, having been closely involved in the arrests of twelve resistance members involved in the burning down of the Amsterdam Civil Registry three months earlier. He will die on 3 July, the day after the execution of the twelve prisoners, including artist, writer and vehement opponent of the Kultuurkamer, Willem Arondeus. The preparations are meticulous. A couple of weeks previously, Mik van Gilse had asked Marianne van Raamsdonk, members of the same CS6 cell, whether she would spend a week in Enschede and keep a careful watch on Kaay: 'Check out precisely where, when, and at what times he can be regularly found at specific places. Take detailed notes, because a lot rides on it'. It is no easy task – travelling alone as a young woman from east to west across the country, finding a local bed and breakfast for a week's board, and obtaining vantage points for spying on Kaay for long hours each day without being watched herself. With her nerve-racking task done, it is now a question of appointing the executioner. 'As for shooting someone dead, that's a different matter', recalls Marianne. 'But Lou Boissevain could do it. Whilst he was an extremely tall, blond and striking man, and therefore less suited for such an extremely dangerous assignment, on the other hand he was extremely cold-blooded. Mammie dyed his hair black and Lou travelled to Enschede. He carried out the deed'. Louis was accompanied by Reina Prinsen Geerligs, so that they could pose more innocently together as a young couple. At around 7.50 on a sunny Saturday morning Kaay came out of his home, mounted his bicycle and set off in the direction of the town's police station. 'Lou' – Louis - Boissevain, cousin of Gideon and Jan Karel, followed by bike and, catching up with his prey, fired a bullet into his chest before racing off. Marianne heard the news on the radio that same morning, via a German broadcast. She also heard a very precise – and accurate - description of the 'terrorist' that the Germans were looking for.

***

Leo is asked by Vic Roothaan, student resistance fighter in Nijmegen, to help in an armed operation:

'In Nijmegen we had no experience with weapons. Through contact with reliable police officers we heard that they weren't prepared to work with the resistance unless we first succeeded in removing the particularly 'German-loving' police commissioner. After the necessary discussions within our group and one of us having even consulted an expert on ethics, we decided that this had to be attempted. For such purpose I got in contact with Katan and Frijda. They could help me get weapons as well as sabotage materials and were even prepared to take part in the assault. Katan was the first to visit Nijmegen, but that attempt misfired. Katan and later also Pooters and Frijda lodged each time in my home. I can't remember the purpose of Pooters' visit to Nijmegen. Then Frijda travelled here to have a go. He and I went together into the centre to a street where it was suspected the commissioner would travel down. Leo arrived there on the back of my bike. I was to stay some distance behind to provide cover if that were needed. But the commissioner failed to appear and we cycled back home in the dark. There were British planes overhead to drop bombs on the Germans. The Germans were trying to trap them in the searchlights. Suddenly, in the sky about 15 to 20 kilometres away from us one of the planes was spotted by a searchlight and immediately three or four other searchlights fixed on it and the anti-aircraft guns went into action. In Nijmegen we had witnessed this before, but for an Amsterdammer it was something new. The plane was hit and burst into flames and came down close to us. Leo was completely overcome. At such a moment the war is suddenly close at hand. To begin with, we in Nijmegen had had the impression that these Amsterdam communists were the real tough guys, but clearly this wasn't the case.'

Leo is so deeply immersed in the organization of a rapid sequence of liquidations and attempted liquidations of Dutch traitors – there would be a total of 24 such liquidations carried out in 1943 to be laid at the door of CS6 by its historians and biographers – that he omits to send greetings to his father on his 22 July birthday. This is the same day on which CS6 members Sape Kuiper and Henri Geul (a sprinter who had represented his country at the 1936 Berlin Olympic Games) would conduct one more of these liquidations. Waiting for the last patient to leave the dental practice of 'half-Jewish' dentist Dr H.E.B. de Jonge-Cohen (in 1940 awarded honorary membership of the Academy of Science of Madagascar) they enter the eminent dentist's home and shoot him dead – retaliation for his treachery in supplying the Nazi secret police with the names and whereabouts of Jewish patients who had gone in hiding. Leo's 'slight' is most certainly felt by his father who, writing as 'Uncle Jan' in a letter dated 7 August, adopts a somewhat injured and accusatory tone:

Dear Leo,

If I had a suspicious mind, then I would think that you would prefer not to receive any letter from me and that is why you do not write to me. But I am not the suspicious kind and put it down to your hard work for the exams that you did not get in touch even on 22 July.

Here everything is satisfactory. At the moment there is the to and fro of all kinds of holiday makers now returning to their own firesides before Monday. I haven't gone on holiday myself yet. I am staying quietly here until the special measures have been lifted, so that I can then go on holiday myself.

I hear good reports from the children. Nico appears to be enjoying the open air and writes of the delicious apples and fine melon he is given to eat. He is to be envied, even if it is for only a couple of weeks whilst he is on his excursion.

How was your birthday? Did you receive my letter in time and have you found something to buy with the money I enclosed?

Now, son, let's hear from you soon. Remember that we are still something of a family and that you can't ignore your family completely.

All the best, as always,

Uncle Jan

It is hard to know, given the date on which it was written and having regard to the cautiously roundabout manner in which it would have been delivered, whether Leo ever received this letter. What is for certain is that when Paul Peters returns to Amsterdam from Belgium without the hoped-for weapons - the contact addresses in Antwerp revealing themselves as blind alleys - Leo is no longer around. Leo has been arrested and taken for interrogation on Euterpestraat. And Leo's arrest was not the first, nor the last. The rolling up of CS6 by the Gestapo is well underway.

XXIV

The Cell

It takes years to mould someone into a decent human being. A couple of months in prison are enough to totally crush him.

Edward Veterman

'You always knew when it was the Gestapo coming to visit', recalls Tina Strobos. 'They rang the bell hard and banged on the door. All at once, they opened the door wide and jumped in, men in mufti, civilian clothes, with hidden guns. They wouldn't say their business until they had closed the door behind them'.

They banged on the door of Corelli Street 6. On the morning of 2 August 1943 the Gestapo woke the occupants of the Boissevain family home - the address to which CS6 owes its name. Father of the family John Boissevain is already imprisoned in concentration camp Vught following his second arrest in March. A niece, Theodora, is staying in the house at the time: 'At around half seven in the morning a number of men walked into my bedroom. I had just got up and wanted to wash. I asked them to leave the room so I could get dressed. After a minute they returned and marched me downstairs with a gun pushed into my back.' Other occupants of the house had already been shepherded together, including Mies ('Mammie') Boissevain, 24-year-old CS6 member Dio Remiens, and two of Mies's three sons, Jan Karel and Frans. The third son, Gideon, is arrested later the same day on the street in front of a bank as he waits for his girlfriend and fellow CS6 member Lucie Visser to join him: a Gestapo agent notices from a passing car a 'young man with a blanched complexion pacing back and forth. We stopped and searched him. He was carrying a firearm, a 7.65 caliber pistol.' Mies would recall that after their arrest 'there was someone posted in our home for the next three weeks and various people who called by were arrested in this way'. Frans believes that over seventy individuals were thereby detained and questioned. An Amsterdam police agent working for the Gestapo, Wouter Mollis – an 'extremely dangerous' collaborator with a glass eye – tells Mies: 'You'd be surprised how much we already know.' Mies had been renting out neighbouring houses including number 16 – forcibly vacated by their Jewish occupants - to

Gestapo officers such as Emil Rühl and charging them rent, no doubt with the belief that the closer an eye you kept on your enemies the safer you would be. But there was an alternative viewpoint expressed by resistance fighter Edward Veterman that highlighted the risk: 'An *illegal* house must not only be sure of its occupants, but also of its neighbours – to the left and right, at the front and back'.

On 15 August they bang on the door of Mien Harmsen. Having arrested her and searched her belongings they find an address in her handbag. It is the address of Ed Hoornik, journalist and author of the Kristallnacht-inspired poem 'Pogrom' the last line of which had warned darkly of the rail line heading east. So, in the very early hours of 19 August they raid the home of Hoornik and his wife at Stadionstraat, who are celebrating their wedding anniversary with a small circle of friends. Ed Hoornik will survive imprisonment in Dachau concentration camp. Amongst their number is a CS6 leader Hans Katan who, as Hoornik's wife later claimed, was then hiding undercover in their home. Katan is at the top level of the CS6 hierarchy and his arrest is one more disaster for the group, which is fast becoming leaderless and thus rudderless.

The blood sport in which CS6 and the Dutch Nazi administration participate as both hunters and hunted continues apace for as long as there are any leading CS6 members of the group still at large. In the police stations and Gestapo headquarters there are files and lists of names and photographs of known and suspected resistance workers. The net is tightening. In turn, the Dutch resistance produces lists of the most dangerous collaborators in an underground publication called Contra Signal – their names, aliases, and last-known home addresses. There is even a London edition of this directory of traitors, containing one hundred and fifty or so of the most dangerous amongst them, with the promise of more extensive lists to come.

The day following Katan's arrest, Louis Boissevain and Truus van Lier travel – as a courting couple - to the small town of Bussum to execute a Dutch police officer E.J. Woerts who, like Kaay, has acted on the principle that hunting down Jews was more important than performing tasks more commonly associated with his job description. Ninety per cent of the Dutch police, it was claimed in a trial after the war, had assisted in the arrest of the Jews. The liquidation is a carbon copy of that of Kaay: on the appointed day and hour, preceded by days of careful observation and note-taking, Louis follows Woerts at a distance on his bicycle ride to work, races to catch up with him at an appropriate point on the route, fires two bullets into him and races away.

***

'The summer of 1943', recalls Harke Kylstra, 'was the final epiosde in the Jewish persecution. Most Jews made their own way to the assembly points before the onward journey to the concentration camps'. There were also final, frenzied round-ups of those Jews more reluctant to surrender. One of those assembly points for a 20 June pogrom was the Olympiaplein, the large recreation area created for the 1928 Amsterdam Olympic Games. 'The weather was beautiful that day', writes Abel Hereberg, 'and people were playing tennis on the nearby courts. The waiting Jews could hear the balls bouncing off the court and the players calling out the scores. They weren't Dutch Nazis, they were just there to play. They weren't our resistance fighters. They were the majority of the Dutch population. It was just something they had all got used to!' But the Dutch underground newspaper – *Vrij Nederland* – leaves no doubt as to the fate awaiting the over 100,000 Dutch Jews sent east. On 10 June 1943 it wrote:

Our Jewish compatriots are being exterminated like animals. […] Here and in Poland they are being killed in cold blood, sometimes a hundred at a time, in a manner that has no parallel in history. Others are being tortured, or succumb to death on the journey, or under forced labour. And yet again others who are subjected to the most grotesque mutilation of body and soul imaginable - sterilization.

The *Jewish Weekly News* of 28 September 1943 has almost no readership left; the days of even its writers and editors are now numbered. Its editorial looks forward to the approaching Jewish new year – Rosh Hashanah. 'What the future shall bring is uncertain. But we should keep our focus on one thing: let us view the difficulties and burdens of today as a trial that we must endure, battling with ourselves, without yielding, until such time as we have won the prize of a strong and beautiful faith in God.'

***

The stresses are taking their toll on all ranks of CS6 members. 'There were different moods according to the situation,' wrote Harke Kylstra: 'Making plans - depression. Immediately before – positive. Afterwards – panic. At the end: prison, contemplating execution and – judging from some farewell letters – greater calm than one would have imagined'. For some, the constant need to stay one step ahead would eventually induce a punch-drunk desire for the chase to end: not a literal surrender – a laying down of weapons - but an emotional surrender to exhaustion, and to what was beginning to feel like an inevitable conclusion. Tineke Wibaut-Guilonard had tried to remain free by dying her hair blond, sporting a pair of glasses, and adopting a false identity under the name of Thea Beerens; but when she was nevertheless identified and arrested she gave in to some small sense of relief. Pam Pooters, the always affable, always reliable 'elder brother' of CS6 - with 'a smile so irresistible that you couldn't refuse him anything' - became a sad, subdued and nervy shadow of his former self, inflicting a responsibility upon himself for the fate of those younger members of CS6 already rounded up. 'Today or tomorrow they'll pick me up too' he told Jan Eylders, a friend whose café he frequented almost every lunchtime. When Pooters is warned by his wife and Jan not to attend a meeting with a stranger that they fear may be a trap, he chooses to take the risk. It was indeed a trap, as he had perhaps – subconsciously - hoped. Guns are fired, Pooters is shot in the leg, arrested, and dragged into the back of a lurking car.

Leo is arrested, likewise his girlfriend Irma. Leo's obituary as published in his former scout troop magazine *De Spil* describes the manner of his arrest. Its unnamed author, someone who had met up with Leo often during these last days and months, recalls: 'When you ran away from your last attack, people called out 'catch the thief, don't let that bicycle thief go' and thanks to this well-meaning idiocy you were captured. Then it was easy to make the connection with your underground work'. There is perhaps a hint of fate's sardonic laughter in Leo's capture, such as Leo had caught in his translation of Sartre's *The Wall*.

***

'The first impression that a cell makes upon you is a feeling of improbability. You simply don't believe it. The idea that someone would lock you behind a door – and what a lock! - and that there's no way you can get out; it seems ridiculous and incredible.' So wrote Eduard Veterman.

For the first night following her arrest, Marianne van Raamsdonk was thrown not so much into a cell as into a 'sort of cupboard' where she could only sleep standing up. The following day – transferred to the city's women's prison – she was put in a cell four metres square already occupied by ten other women. The only sanitation was a barrel in the corner, and in the incessant heat the place stank. In cell A1-10 in the prison on the Weteringschans Jan Verleun was tied down by his hands and feet, day and night, for all except the briefest times when permitted to eat. Although the women are generally treated less inhumanely than the men, all suffer torture. After three months in her cell Marianne was interrogated for the first time. She was surprised to see her pet dog by the side of her interrogators, one of whom – 'revolting Mollis, with his pig-like head' and the appearance of a bouncer - barked at her: 'This dog is a mongrel and so are you'. He took his revolver and shot the dog in front of her eyes. It frightened Marianne half to death as Mollis ended their appointment with a few thwacks around her head: 'Now you understand what will happen to you. Go back to your cell.' It was at this point, recalled Marianne, that 'hell opened up'. Throughout each of around ten consecutive nights the light in her cell would be switched on and off every three minutes. It made sleep impossible, and with each sleepless night Marianne became weaker; her food ration was halved, she became depressed, and suffered a throat infection and fever. In his prison, Jan was interrogated from 'early in the morning to late at night'. They beat him up: 'They've broken my back. They take such pride in their work'. During Mien Harmsen's interrogation it became clear to her that it was all over: 'I saw that the net was so tight around these boys, that there was nothing more that could be done, that they would never get free'.

'No one is watertight', observed Bert Schierbeek: 'When they tighten the thumbscrews, the greatest of heroes can talk'. Nevertheless, the young men and women of the Dutch resistance tried, and often succeeded, in surrendering little information of much value. It was essential to play for time. Tina Strobos, for example, claimed she could understand no German. The few precious seconds in which she heard the questions fired at her first in German, and then translated into Dutch, gave her a little extra thinking time before she answered. By figuring out what the Germans already knew they could confirm this knowledge without furnishing additional information. The Boissevain brothers, Gidoen and Jan Karel, managed to smuggle messages to their comrades outside the prison walls by a sympathetic Dutch prison guard; messages that they wrote in blood with broken finger nails on pieces of lavatory paper: 'Slow down the process, play for time... chin up!'. They could tap out messages in code on pipes that passed from one cell to another. They scratched messages and words of comfort and inspiration, as well as words of warning, on their cell walls.

Leo knew that his capture was a death sentence. Nevertheless, perhaps imprisonment in a cell on the Euterpestraat offered a small ray of hope that a train journey to the concentration camps and their gas chambers did not. The first thing Leo asked Gestapo officer Herbert Oelschlagel was whether his beloved Irma could be saved. Only, Oelschlagel replied, if she was willing to work for the Gestapo. Soon after her own arrest, Irma realised how much the Germans knew about her already: that she and Leo were a couple, and that she was Jewish. 'I was living through those days in a sort of feverish angst. I didn't know what to do and I was being threatened from two sides, by the Germans and by the resistance.' Oelschlagel then intimated to Irma that she in turn could save Leo if she cooperated. And Oelschlagel, whom women prisoners had warned each other had such a hypnotically persuasive manner on the female sex that they should avoid looking him in the eye, worked his tricks on Irma. It was agreed: Irma would be released from prison under very close watch, to make contact with those of her comrades still at liberty and so betray them. It was a familiar ruse adopted by the Germans. Nevertheless, other female prisoners faced with the same stark choice, including Truus van Lier, had refused to cooperate. 'Irma sometimes went to a chemist's shop, sometimes for a walk, but never without being followed by a man who was certainly armed', noted Jan Verleun before his own arrest. 'They were hoping, of course, that someone would approach her or that she herself would recognise someone.' Irma would indeed betray others - including Jan van Mierlo in an elaborate sting - but there were other 'betrayals' of greater or lesser significance. Dio Remiens had quickly revealed the secrets of the basement at Corelli Street 6, whilst the arrest of Sape Kuiper, CS6 member along with his brother Bram, was an eventuality dreaded by his comrades who assumed he was a certain bet to talk during interrogation: Sape was extremely frightened of physical violence such as the extraction of fingernails. In any event, as the Germans had boasted to Mies Boissevain at the time of her arrest, they already had surprisingly large files of information about CS6 even absent these betrayals.

Tineke was alerted to Irma's treachery by a stark warning on a cell wall: 'Irma is banged up and blabbing'. To warn the others, Tineke wrote messages on strips of cotton, at first using watered-down jam and later a smuggled pencil, which she carefully threaded inside the seams of a hand towel sent home for her mother in a small bundle of laundry. Tineke's own sense of betrayal ran deep. After the war she said in an interview: 'Naturally I hope that we never go through another war. But if we do, watch out for women who will go to bed with anyone. Because then you have to ask yourself what they would be prepared to do for their next squeeze'.

***

The trial of nineteen members of CS6 was, in keeping with the governance of the Netherlands by the German SS and their willing Dutch lackeys, a travesty of even primitive notions of justice. Within a police court system instigated by SS leader Rauter the normal protections afforded to the defendants had been torn up: even their defence was conducted by the German SS. Nevertheless, such a trial at least brought closure; the bestial torture was over; and those about to die were brought out of their dark cells to the daylight of a makeshift Amsterdam courthouse to be reunited. As Fritz Dekking wrote about the trial of those tried for setting fire to the Amsterdam Civil Registry: 'There was a sense of togetherness, and a shared sense of pride that there was not one amongst all these people whom you had reason to feel ashamed of. It was from this perspective, and not from any nervous reaction, that you acted cheerfully; it was entirely natural, and it continually perplexed the krauts.' Between those awaiting sentence, Dekking described an 'atmosphere of homoeroticism that affected us all, an immense mutual admiration and feelings almost of tenderness towards each other.'

The trial lasted around ten hours. A short report of the trial was published in the Nazi newspaper *Volk en Vaderland*:

Here sat the co-murderer of Lieutenant-General Seyffardt – the 20-year-old medical student Frijda (the communist Dr Kastein, who fired the shot that killed the general, had since committed suicide to avoid his proper punishment [...].
They were all just students! The brigade commander of a large-scale secret organization for murder and sabotage was just a young biology student; 24-year-old Hans Katan and his group and section commandants were each and every one of them kids aged 19, 20 and 21.

Leo, by claiming it was Kastein who had fired the shot at Seyffardt, had tried to save the life of Jan Verleun. This quick-wittedness did not go unnoticed. The author of Leo's obituary in *De Spil* wrote: 'You were one of the first to take part in the active resistance. The above article from the kraut press shows clearly how you acted like a hero. That you stood firm till your last moments on earth to save someone or other from his doom is the greatest proof of this'.

All nineteen defendants were duly sentenced to death.

In an almost sadistically flippant observance of Dutch law under which convicted female criminals could not be sentenced to death, the Germans transported three female CS6 members – Truus van Lier, Reina Prinsen Geerligs and Nel Hissink - to Ravensbruck concentration camp in Germany, a nation with fewer such compunctions. On 24 November 1943 all three were shot dead at the camp, and thence trundled to the camp's crematorium.

***

Jewish resistance fighter Maurice Ferares wrote: 'Even if those in hiding and those in the resistance – and this applies only to those of them

211

who survived the struggle – did not endure hell itself, they nevertheless lived at the gates of hell.' These deep psychological traumas would remain with them for the rest of their lives. A doctoral thesis in medicine by Jan Bastiaans dated 1957 on the subject 'Psychosomatic consequence of oppression and resistance' identified long-term psychological problems in almost 50% of 3,000 ex-members of the resistance – men and women – who formed the study group. Perhaps offering slight comfort by way of contrast, many of those who did not survive – those arrested and about to die – seemed to find, as Harke Kylstra observed, some equanimity in their final hours. They sang in their cells to keep their spirits up. They sang hymns and they sang the Dutch national anthem. 'I shared a cell with Johan Verbrugge, aged around 28', wrote Kylstra: 'He had a young wife and a small child with hydrocephalus. He was expecting the death penalty because he had provided a Jew with shelter and operated a radio set by which he kept in contact with England. He could sing beautifully in the cell. He could have sung on the radio'.

These young people were not the untamed, trigger happy and naive communist ideologues afforded little more than a begrudging footnote in the history of the Dutch resistance. They are not the awkward exception to the oddly boastful assertion of Dr Lou de Jong – chronicler of his country's fortunes in World War Two - that the Dutch resistance was characterised by its 'moderation' – as though fighting tooth and nail against genocide was somehow a bit vulgar and 'un-Dutch'. These youngsters should be accorded the dignity of their individuality and respected for their deep-rooted motivations: Harke Kylstra was from a Quaker family, the Boissevains were Mennonites, and Jan Verleun had been a Catholic altar boy. Leo Frijda and Hans Katan were from liberal, educated, non-practising Jewish families. Christian, Jewish, or humanist they acted partly out of faith and idealism, partly out of an instinctive, justified rage against evil. The great, overriding commitment of CS6 had been to save lives, not to take them. Bram Kuiper's arrest, for example, occurred in Brussels on his journey home from leading for a second time a group of Jewish escapees to safety in Switzerland. What motivated them is sometimes hinted at in the final messages they were allowed to write home. On the eve of his execution, Jan Verleun wrote: 'My desire was to serve God and my Fatherland to the best of my ability'. Hans Katan wrote to his parents: 'So far I remain calm. I wish the best for your future and for that of the Netherlands and of the World. I am certain that those who have really known me will not condemn me. So you should also take courage'.

On the eve of execution on 1 October 1943, two months following his twentieth birthday, Leo Frijda wrote a farewell letter that he trusted would eventually be passed on to his family. With each of his parents, brother and sister separated and in hiding, isolated one from the other, Leo wrote as though all had found a safe haven in neutral Switzerland in order that their hiding places in the Netherlands not be tracked down. He knew, in any event, that the first they would hear about his death would be the reports in the press, and not from his own pen:

Dear Mrs. Van Diemen,
Now that all my family are in Switzerland, I would like to send you a short greeting as an old friend of the family. Within a very short time I shall be executed. It will be reported in the press. It is not beyond possibility that in the future you will once more meet Father, Mother, Jetteke and Nico. There is not much I am able to write. Tell them that I shall die without fear. Nico will still know the poem Goya 1941. I will write it down. I have felt good about life. I haven't sacrificed myself for any political ideal or suchlike. I have striven for myself alone and I meet death in the same way. I have unconsciously struggled towards the absolute. Work has made me isolated. I wanted that isolation. Thank Father and Mother for my life: it has given me so much. My life has not been for nothing. Thank my little Irma too. She has been my dearest support over these last few months.
My best regards to you, Mrs. Van Diemen and, in due course, my best wishes also to Father, Mother, Jetteke and Nico. Do not stay sad for long.
Goodbye.
Leo

Frans, younger brother of Gideon and Jan Karel Boissevain, was summoned from his cell. Gestapo officer Rühl infomed him: 'Your brothers will be shot tomorrow. You can now say your farewells'. The corridor was full of the German police. 'Gideon looked in a terrible state and totally shaken. Jan Karel was holding up well', recalls Frans, who was allowed five minutes with his brothers. Jan Karel told Frans: 'Till now you were the youngest son, now you are the eldest. Look after Mum'. Early the next morning Frans heard the rattle of keys, the engine of a lorry, a creaking open of a heavy door, and the lorry driving into the distance. On board were his two brothers and seventeen of their comrades.

When Leo faced his executioners he wore no blindfold.

Leo had for a long time been fixated with Goya's revolutionary depiction of the horrors of a firing squad, the victim, without blindfold, staring wild eyed into the regimented row of assassins' rifles. Harke Kylstra had for a long time contemplated such a similar fate: 'As a 13-year-old boy I kept a large photo in my bedroom of the execution of a man during the First World War: he was wearing no blindfold. The report of Leo's execution thus became something of an obsession for me.'

In his fictionalised account of CS6 Bert Schierbeek describes the execution of 'Matthieu' the character closest in description to Leo: '[...] *released from himself, into a world that he had always desired: his soul set free from the tyranny of the body.'*

Epilogue

My husband, who found himself in Rotterdam during the bombardment, described how the startling heat that this generated caused the chestnut trees to suddenly burst into leaf, then flower, and then turn a charred black. And whenever he told that story, it made me think of Leo. Such an explosive burst of life in such a short space of time, with death a virtually inevitable end.

Mien Harmsen, in conversation with Dr Piet Calis

'All three of us have known the wonderful person hidden beneath that apparently gruff and indifferent exterior', wrote Leo's father, Professor Herman Frijda, to Jetteke and Nico on 4 October, once the bare facts of Leo's arrest and execution had been published in the Nazi-controlled newspapers: 'And perhaps it was because he was the most difficult of the three of you, and caused me the most concern, that I always reserved a special place for my dear, dear Leo.' A year later, Herman Frijda would perish in the gas chambers of Auschwitz. Leo's mother, a refugee in Switzerland, would have read the Press Department News Sheets 35 and 36 from the Dutch Legation published in Bern, October 1943, which offered her some crumbs of comfort: '*To judge from the reports, all victims displayed incredible courage for the greater good; for the sake of our people they pushed themselves to the limits, choosing the only way that the usurpers left open to them: they took the lives of those who threatened our very existence...*'. Months after the war's end, on 9 October 1945, Dora Frijda-Frank wrote (in English) from Lausanne, Switzerland to Professor Sir Dennis Holmes Robertson in England:

For months I had the intention of writing to you to ask how you came through these awful years and to inquire after you [...]
I was very touched when I got your Red Cross note in spring 1941 and I hope you got my answer [...]
Prof. Frijda was hidden since summer 1942, found out in 1944 and deported to Poland. He died in Auschwitz, I am not quite sure when.
My eldest boy was shot by the Germans in 1943. He belonged to a group of students-resistants. They were arrested and executed. He has been very brave. He was only 20 years old; it is very hard to bear.
This is about all the news in a nutshell. Not so very bright as a whole. My brother is dead too – deported. My sister lost a son trying to escape from Holland (the son). All in all I lost 15 relatives either on my side or on Prof. Frijda's.

215

The children are very big now, and though we are great friends in correspondence (we didn't hear from each other for nearly three years) life together would not be an easy matter.
[...]
With kindest regards,
Yours truly,
Dora F. Frank

In January 1948 Irma Seelig, with whom Gestapo officer Oelschlagel had fallen in love and spirited out of the Netherlands at the end of the war to be cared for by his own parents in Germany, was taken prisoner by the British and returned to the Netherlands to face charges as a collaborator. On 21st June 1948, whilst awaiting trial, she wrote to Dora Frijda-Frank:

What must you think of me, dear Mrs Frijda? I know that I have done a terrible thing and I don't know how I can ever put this right. But you were so kind and so motherly towards me and you gave me back a little courage.
My poor Leo was so courageous and I must therefore also try to accept the punishment I have been handed. I think back with so much love to that difficult, but also wonderful, time that I was able to share with Leo. I was willing to do anything for him and tried to be everything for him and as far as that goes, I think I have nothing to reproach myself for.
Probably you have heard things about Leo and me from Mien. I really did love Leo and it is a terrible thing that fate has been so cruel to us both.

The manner of Irma's trial signified a restoration of the rule of law to the Netherlands: she was convicted as charged, but prior to sentencing the court commissioned a psychiatric report. 'In the relative protection of a good marriage she would have made an inconspicuous, somewhat neurotic housewife', argued Rabbi Konig in support of a reduced sentence: 'Once she is influenced by somebody, she becomes, in my opinion, blindly obedient'. Irma is sentenced to eight years imprisonment and upon her release in 1955 nothing further is ever heard of her.

***

Jetteke Frijda remembered the feelings that stayed with her long after liberation: 'The darkness of those years, the way in which you defied your fears, alienation, insecurities, humiliations, and grief – all this lay wrapped around you like a lead sheet.' In 2000, Jetteke assisted in the making of a programme for Dutch television that told the stories of three different resistance fighters. It began with the story of her brother Leo. On the evening of its broadcast she sat down at home alone to watch the programme unfold, and in the following days would put her thoughts in writing.

The Film

I sit in front of the TV and press the 'on' button. It is ten-thirty five. I have arranged myself on the sofa, glass of wine by my side.

She is sitting there, to the left of the picture. Entirely alone in her own living room. She sits quietly in her chair and looks at me. Not just at me, but at all the other people watching in their homes. I know her very well, but on the screen she seems like a stranger. She looks well turned out. Even her usually chaotically placed wig has had the attention of a hairdresser. She sits alongside a table laid with photographs and open books. Soon she will say something about these, I think. There is a shoulder-high cupboard behind her chair. There are a few sculptures on display. I recognise them. One is an alabaster model of a mother and child. She copied it from a Chinese image sculpted in ice that she had seen in Groningen. It is very moving. There are a few other statues. The audience is given a glimpse of a domestic, cosy atmosphere.

The invisible interviewer asks a question. The woman answers, and reads a poem:

> *Do not speak.*
> *Just as they did not speak.*
> *Perhaps just a name, quietly brought to mind.*
> *When they in cold blood were slain*
> *Five coffins laid in wait.*
> *Soon*
> *A silence, accompanied by music.*
> *Another shame to last eternity.*
>
> *Do not speak.*
> *....*
> *Let us now leave*
> *It is what I promised them this night.*
> *We are an illusion,*
> *a long-vanished*
> *vision.*

The first line is the title of the film. It is about her brother, who died aged 20 as a member of the resistance. She reveals something about his activities, and the last time that she spoke to him. It was in Zeist, where she had gone into hiding and he wanted to meet her. As they walked together he told her about his most recent acts of resistance. He had put bombs along rail lines and shot General Seyffardt dead.

217

He talked about it as anyone else might talk about a walk in the countryside or a visit to an exhibition. There was no particular emotion, pride or arrogance in the way he told his story. Only the facts, the circumstances…. and, left unsaid, the possible consequences.

I watch and listen attentively. This quiet person seems miles apart from me. Her voice sounds a little affected, although clear enough. I can understand her perfectly. What she says, I could have said myself: the same voice, the same intonation.

I begin to feel a little more connected to the person sitting opposite me on the TV screen. The image of the walk near the bus station of Zeist on that spring evening in April 1943 will never again disappear from my retina. Other thoughts and feelings rise to the surface. I push them away. For now I want to focus all attention on the stories of those others who follow her on the screen.

[…]

The film closes with the endless procession of people who visit the war graves during the May 4 commemorations, movingly framed by the music of the Ave Maria.

I turn off the TV, dry my eyes and open a folder containing the photos shown in the programme, and many more besides. Then I surrender to the memories, to the emotions, and to the remembrance of my brother, who was shot dead in the sand dunes near Overveen on 1 October 1943 and who now lies in the war cemetery surrounded by friends, colleagues and others.

I have opened this folder so often. I have told various people what I still remember of him. I have read them the short letters that he wrote to his parents as a small child, and showed them the childhood photos and school reports. I have shown them his stories and poems, most of which they already knew. There are people so interested in his personality, his qualities, his deeds, his writings, that they have written articles and books about him – or plan to do so. If I ask why, they answer from different perspectives. I answer all questions as best as I can, because of course I am rather proud of my brother, whom I knew for just seventeen years. But what does it mean 'to know'? A while ago I received a letter from 'an old girlfriend' of his, who 'was crazy about him' and told me things about him that I had never known.

I close the file and put it away. I look at the portrait that hangs in my room.

Then I open my diary. Tomorrow is another day.

8 April 2000

Jetteke Frijda (1 December 1925 – 7 December 2016)

***

A First World War general of the British Army described the loss of a generation on the battlefields of Belgium and France: 'They were so young, these lads. The mark of the school bag was scarcely off their shoulder'. Leo was not yet seventeen when Germany invaded the Netherlands on 10 May 1940. Most members of CS6, men and women, were of similar age: still at school at the start of the war, many of the friendships they forged there would form the backbone of their resistance group. Jan Verleun describes a scene played out in spring 1943 in which, with a planned attack on an Amsterdam labour exchange in the offing, Leo and a CS6 colleague go on a reconnaissance mission and deploy diversionary tactics:

A tram halted in front of the theatre. Two boys, apparently secondary school pupils, jumped out. They were both dressed in shorts, long sports socks and hockey shirts, and carried hockey sticks. They had tied their jumpers around their waists to camouflage the fact that they had outgrown their shorts.
The smaller of the two - Leo - suggested they look for pebbles to see who could throw them the furthest over the ornamental pond. The other liked the idea but declined to help in the search for the pebbles through fear that his shorts would burst apart if he bent down.
They started play fighting to draw the attention of a policeman whose daily routine they have been keeping an eye on. They wrestled on the grassy slope by the water's edge. The policeman, pulled to the scene as intended, asked Leo why he sprung at his friend's neck in the way he did: that kind of thing could be dangerous. 'Dangerous?' asks Leo: 'Is it dangerous if a flea jumps on the shoulder of an ox? Have you ever fought with someone twice your weight? My height and weight force me to use such tactics. Not that I am proud of them, but...'

***

Leo Frijda lies buried in a cemetery amongst rolling sand dunes between Haarlem and the North Sea, nestling protectively in the folds of the dunes, out of sight of the road and slightly uphill. A winding path takes you there on foot, giving you the vague feeling that this short walk is also a journey from the modern world to times as misty now in the memory as the sea mists at dawn that blindfold the eyes. A pilgrimage too. And as you walk, the sea-salt wind billows through the trees and long grass sweeping around you with a sound like waves tumbling onto a beach. You walk through a gatehouse beneath a small bell tower. The cemetery is formal and rectangular in shape, surrounded by a low slate wall and a few steps lower than the surrounding ground, nestling into the folds of the protective dunes. The headstones are all the same, neatly set into flower beds. But the scale is intimate and the natural materials are sculptured seamlessly into the surrounding landscape, so that the cold regimentation of these lines of headstones is softened by the abstract, weathered shapes of nature. Here lies his headstone, and you recognise the names of those who fought, and now lie, alongside him. There is a line from his own poem on his headstone.

You do not stay long. To have done so would somehow have interrupted the tranquillity of a place that is strangely beautiful, even in the cold, grey daylight of a February afternoon, and so you walk back down the path towards the car parked by the road, sad only with the reflection that this place lies so very close to the embrace of the sea, so close to the beginning of a dangerous, exhilarating voyage by boat to a freedom that Leo sought twice and twice failed to reach. For it is here instead, in this peaceful burial ground, where he finally found his freedom.

***

Laugh and Dance

Laugh and dance,
Laugh and dance
But remember that when a final chance
Of laughing extirpation comes,
It comes through self-renewal,
And self-renewal is less painful,
Though more deadly, than the poison
Of eternal rest.

Were we froth,
Were we flakes of rusting tin,
Our parting could not be as light as this.
If we must die, then fine,
But remember this,
The primal source: body – ground – pleasure.

Leo Frijda

RESEARCH MATERIALS

PRIVATE CORRESPONDENCE

Jan Bons, Philo Bregstein, Jurjen Brinkman, Dr Piet Calis, Marius Flothuis, Carel Frank, Giselle Friedlander, Jetteke Frijda, Prof. Nico Frijda, Govert A. Gezelle Meerburg, Eva Keuls, Harke Kylstra, Paul Peters, Vic Roothaan, Ruth Rosenthaal, Daniel Teeboom, Mien Ten Dam-Pooters, Dr. Henri Vleeschdraager, Rita Walthuis-Klijzing, Milly Weisglas-Kaufman.

ARCHIVES

The Amsterdam Lyceum
Amsterdam Municipal Archive
Digitale Bibliotheek voor de Nederlandse Letteren
Dutch Resistance Museum, Amsterdam
Frysk Histoarysk en Letterkundich Sintrum
Institute for War, Holocaust and Genocide Studies, Amsterdam
Jewish Cultural Quarter – Kenniscentrum – Amsterdam
Leiden University Library
Resistance Museum, Amsterdam
Swiss Federal Archives
Trinity College Library, Cambridge, UK

BOOKS

S. Bakker et al., Bert Schierbeek en het onbegrensde, De Bezige Bij, 1980
J. Beishuize / E. Werkman, De Magere Jaren: Nederland in de crisistijd 1929-1939, A.W. Stijhoff, 1980
M. v.d. Berg / S.W. de Groot, Met het verleden bezig, A'dam, 2001
J.J. Boolen. / J.C. v.d. Does, Nederlands Verzet, David, 1946
F.W. Boterman, Duitse daders: De Jodenvervolging…., A'dam 2015
P.J. Bouwman, De april-mei stakingen van 1943, Martinus Nijhoff, 1950
B. Braber, This Cannot Happen Here, A'dam Uni. Press, 2013
P. Bregstein / S. Bloemgarten, Herinnering aan Joods Amsterdam, De Bezige Bij, 1994
P. Bregstein, Gesprekken met Jacques Presser , Baarn, 1972
K. Broersma, Buigen onder de storm – levensschets van Philip Mechanicus, Van Gennep B.V., 1993
J. Buitenkamp, Geschiedenis van het Verzet, Fibula, 1990
K. Clark, Looking at Pictures, Beacon Press, 1968
K. Evers, De andere stemmen – Portret van Bert Schierbeek, De Bezige Bij, 1993
J. Eylders, Eylders: het leven van een tegendraadse Amsterdammer, A.W. Bruna & Zoon, 1971
M. Ferares, Violist in het Verzet: Herinneringen van Maurice Ferares, De Bataafsche Leeuw, 1971
J. Gans, Het Vege Lijf, Peter van der Velden, 1981
S.H.M. van Goozen et al., Emotions: Essays on Emotion Theory, L. Erlbaum Associates, 1994
G. Goudriaan, Verzetsman Gerrit Kastein 1910 – 1943, De Nieuwe Vaart, 2010
B. de Graaf, Dood van een Dubbelspion, SDU, The Hague, 1997
M.J.G. de Jong, Een perron maar drie treinen, Sijthoff, 1970

L. de Jong, Lecture given Sept. 1958: Anti-Nazi Resistance in the Netherlands, Pergamon Press, 1960

J. v.d.Kar, Joods Verzet, Amsterdam, 1984

G. Kastein, Het Rassenvraagstuk, Pegasus, 1938

A. Kok, De Verrader, De Bezige Bij, 2013

A. Kraaij, 75 Jaar Cindu Bedrijven, 1997

L. Lee, A Moment of War, Penguin, London, 1992

T.G. v.d. Linden, Joods Zandvoort, Een pioniersgeschiedenis (1880-1943), Boekencentrum

G. Maas, Kroniek van de Februari-Staking 1941, Pegasus, 1961

A. Malraux, Man's Fate, Hamilton, 1968 (London)

A Martens, The Silent War, Hodder and Stoughton, 1961

M. Mayer, They Thought They Were Free, Chicago University Press, 1955

P. Mechanicus, Russische Reisschetsen, Alg. Handelsblad N.V., 1932

I. Meijer, De Interviewer en de Schrijver, Prometheus, 2003

E. Montale, The Second Life of Art, Ecco, 1982

B. Moore, Refugees from Nazi Germany in the Netherlands, Martinus Nijhoff, 1986

A.D. Morse, While Six Million Died, Random House, 1968

J.W. Mulder, Kunst in crisis en besetting, Het Spectrum, 1978

H. Olink, Vrouwen van Vught, Bas Lubberhuizen, 1995

R. van Olm, Recht al barste de wereld, Conserve, 1998

J. Paardekooper et al., Aen de Rivier, Deventer, 1985

H. Piek, Zwart en Wit uit het Roode Rusland, Scheltens & Giltay, 1930

J. Presser, Ashes in the Wind, Detroit, 1988

G. Puchinger, Jonge Jaren 1921-1945, Aspekt, 2001

H.M. van Randwijk, In de schaduw van gisteren, Bert Bakker, A'dam 1975

J-P Sartre, The Wall, 1939

J. Scott, Behind the Urals: An American Worker in Russia's City of Steel, Indiana University Press, 1989

M.G. Schenk / J.B. Th. Spaan, De Koningin sprak, Amsterdam, 1945

B. Sijes, De Februari-staking, Nijhoff, 1954

M. Smedts, Waarheid en leugen in het verzet, Corrie Zelen, 1978

Z. Steiner, The Triumph of the Dark, Oxford University Press, 2011

A. Venema, Kleine Oorlog, A'dam, 1990

A. Venema, Schrijvers, uitgevers en hun collaboratie, (1988-1992)

E. Veterman, Keizersgracht 763, A'dam, 1946

S. v.d. Zee, Voor Führer, Volk en Vaderland, Just Publishers, 2017

ACADEMIC PAPERS / ARTICLES

L. Baas, 'Mussert moet dood' – Anti-fascistische actie in NL in 1933, University of Utrecht, 2016

J. Bastiaans, Psychosomatische gevolgen van onderdrukking en verzet, N.V. Noord-Hollandsche, 1957

P. Calis, Het ondergrondse verwachten, Meulenhoff, 1989

P. Calis, De korte, onstuimige bloei van Leo Frijda, De Gids, 1988

A. Dessing, De Grote Oversteek, 7e Jaarboek RIOD

M. de Keizer, Verzetsblad in Oorlogstijd, NIOD

H. Monkel, Kinderen in de Onderduik, Biografie Bulletin, Jaargang 19, 2009

A. Savin, The 1929 Emigration of Mennonites from the USSR, Academy of Sciences, Novosibirsk

M. Schwegman, Het stille verzet, Socialistische Uitgeverij, 1980

L. Winkel, De Ondergrondse Pers 1940-1945, NIOD, 1989

PRINTED MEDIA

WHF-Verzamelkrant 12, Interview met Guido van Suchtelen, August 1994

Nederlands Dagblad: 1943: Kameraden in de knel (W. Bouwman), 16 August 2000

Het Parool: Interview with Prof. Nico Frijda, 24 July 1993

Trouw: Het Apeldoornse Bos (by M. van der Kaaij), 21 January 2013

The Washington Post: Obituary for Dr Tina Strobos (by Emily Langer), 29 February 2012

Het Parool / De Waarheid/ Rotterdamsch Nieuwsblad / Algemeen Handelsblad: archive articles

WEBSITES

www.emotionresearcher.com:
   Nico Frijda: War, Love and Emotions as States of Action readiness

www.harpers.org/archive:
   John Roberts Tunis: The Olympic Games

www.historischnieuwsblad.nl:
   Bas Kromhout: 1935: Mussert of Moskou?

http://statelessprog.blogspot.com:
   Mattern, J.: A short history of 'Dutch statelessness'

www.castrumperegrini.org:
   Stichting Castrum Peregrini

www.ajr.org.uk:
   Association of Jewish Refugees in Great Britain

www.annefrank.org:
   Anne Frank Stichting

www.cityeconomist.blogspot.com/2015/01/active-resistance-to-nazis-jan-canada.html:
   The City Economist blog (Boissevain family)

www.weggum.com:
   Willem Mugge / Suzanne Biallot-Siebert

www.ingramcontent.com/pod-product-compliance
Lightning Source LLC
LaVergne TN
LVHW011224080426
835509LV00005B/297